The Last Inch

THE LAST INCH

A MIDDLE EAST ODYSSEY

CLAUD MORRIS

KEGAN PAUL INTERNATIONAL
London and New York

First published in 1996 by
Kegan Paul International
UK: P.O. Box 256, London WC1B 3SW, England
Tel: (0171) 580 5511 Fax: (0171) 436 0899
E-mail: books@keganpau.demon.co.uk
Internet: http://www.demon.co.uk/keganpaul/
USA: 562 West 113th Street, New York, NY 10025, USA
Tel: (212) 666 1000 Fax: (212) 316 3100

Distributed by
John Wiley & Sons Ltd
Southern Cross Trading Estate
1 Oldlands Way, Bognor Regis
West Sussex, PO22 9SA, England
Tel: (01243) 819 121 Fax: (01243) 820 250

Columbia University Press
562 West 113th Street
New York, NY 10025, USA
Tel: (212) 666 1000 Fax: (212) 316 3100

© Claud Morris 1996

Phototypeset in 11 on 13pt Baskerville
by Intype London Ltd

Printed in Great Britain by TJ Press, Padstow, Cornwall

All rights reserved. No part of this book may be reprinted
or reproduced or utilized in any form or by any electronic,
mechanical or other means, now known or hereafter invented,
including photocopying and recording, or in any information
storage or retrieval system, without permission in writing
from the publishers.

ISBN 0–7103–0552–4

British Library Cataloguing in Publication Data

Morris, Claud
  The last inch : a Middle Eastern odyssey
  1. Morris, Claud 2. Conflict management – Middle East
  3. Mediation, International 4. Arab countries – Politics and
  government – 1945– 5. Arab countries – History – 20th century
  I.Title
  956'.04'092

ISBN 0710305524

Library of Congress Cataloging-in-Publication Data

Morris, Claud.
    The last inch : a Middle Eastern odyssey / Claud Morris.
    240pp.21cm.
    Includes index.
    ISBN 0–7103–0552–4 (alk, paper)
    1. Morris, Claud. 2. Journalists—Great Britain—Biography.
3. Arabists—Great Britain—Biography. 4. Arab countries—Politics
and government—1945–   I. Title.
PN5123.M69A3   1996
070.92—dc21
  [B]   96–15455
                                                          CIP

TO PATRICIA, WILLIAM, ANN
AND MARGARET MORRIS

'Now listen to the rule of the last inch. The realm of the last inch. The job is almost finished, the goal almost attained, everything possible seems to have been achieved, every difficulty overcome – and yet the quality is just not there. The work needs more finish, perhaps further research. In that moment of weariness and self-satisfaction, the temptation is greatest to give up, not to strive for the peak of quality. That's the realm of the last inch – here the work is very, very complex, but it's also particularly valuable because it's done with the most perfect means. The rule of the last inch is simply this – not to leave it undone. And not to put it off – because otherwise your mind loses touch with that realm. And not to mind how much time you spend on it, because the aim is not to finish the job quickly but to reach perfection.'

Alexander Solzhenitsyn, *The First Circle*[1]

CONTENTS

ACKNOWLEDGEMENTS xiii

Part One

1 The right to be heard   3
2 Fire in the valley   16
3 No end to a nightmare   21
4 Death of a newspaper   25
5 The conspirators   33
6 Unforgettable friends   38
7 The hornets' nest   43
8 Abandoned   49
9 The crash   54

Part Two

10 The great King of Arabia   67
11 The young man in Gordon's palace   78
12 With G at Benghazi barracks   92
13 Envoys extraordinary   102
14 CIA: Mission impossible?   107
15 Roman holiday   114
16 Hard lines   121

Part Three

17 With Zayed at Al Ain   131
18 The donkey's journey   135
19 Retreat from Tripoli   143

CONTENTS

Part Four

20 Shaping the news   153
21 The strange case of Margaret McKay   160

Part Five

22 The Bhutto disinformation game   169
23 'We're all Palestinians now'   180
24 Unexpected gremlins and moles   186
25 Darkness before dawn?   192
26 The box of tricks   198
27 Darkness in my eyes   205
28 Was my journey really necessary?   210

Epilogue

29 The two cousins approach   217
30 More haste less speed   224

ABBREVIATIONS   228
NOTES   229
REFERENCES AND SOURCES   233
INDEX   235

Illustrations

between pages 82 and 83

1. Claud Morris, the author
2. HH Sir Sultan Ali Abdul Karim of Lahej
3. The author when he was Chairman of the South Wales Newspaper Proprietors' Association
4. The Welsh press that dared, a constant unending initiative. The *South Wales Voice*
5. The Lord Christopher Mayhew of Wimbledon
6. Mrs Elizabeth Collard
7. Examining the disaster after the fire at the *South Wales Voice* press
8. Lord Lyons of Brighton
9. Dr Ali Khushaim
10. General Numeiri showing the author 'his dream'
11. The author at a Sudanese Cabinet meeting
12. Ali Shummo examining *Voice* distribution lists in Wales
13. The author at the *South Wales Voice* with a group of Sudanese visitors
14. President Numeiri and Claud Morris
15. Gaddafi and Numeiri
16. Gaddafi in the desert near Sert
17. King Faisal of Saudi Arabia shortly before his assassination
18. The author with HH Sheikh Zayed bin Sultan Al-Nahyan
19. HE Sheikh Ahmed bin Hamed al Qubaisi
20. In Tunisia. The author sitting next to HE Abdul Aziz Rowas
21. Adnan Omran talking to the author
22. Sa'dun Al Jasim
23. HE Sheikh Saud Nasir Al-Sabah
24. HM Sultan Qaboos bin Said

ILLUSTRATIONS

25 HH Sayyid Fahad bin Mahmood Al-Said of Oman
26 The author with Abdul Karim Al Mudaris
27 The campaign to save Bhutto's life
28 The author speaking to the international press conference he organised to discuss the Arab image in Western mass media
29 Ibrahim Al-Abed
30 Lord Caradon (Hugh Foot)
31 Three-day International Press Seminar in 1984
32 The author's son, William
33 Sir Frank Rogers. *Photograph by Snowdon*
34 Jaweed Al-Ghussein
35 His Grace the Duke of Devonshire. *Photograph Bill Burlington*
36 The author and his wife Pat

ACKNOWLEDGEMENTS

As life moves along I become more and more aware of the kindness and tolerance of my friends, both in the Arab world and the West. This book has taken many years to bring to publication, and although many of my Arab friends are recorded here, there are many who are not. Their contribution to my odyssey has been great and I owe them much. I wish to record here my sincere thanks to:

Sheikh Ahmed bin Hamed Al-Qubaisi and his family for their great hospitality and kindness to my wife and to myself;

HE Sheikh Saud Al-Sabah, Minister of Information, Kuwait who from the time we met in 1972 has been such a resolute and resilient friend;

HH Sayyid Fahad bin Mahmood Al-Said, Deputy Prime Minister for Council Affairs, Oman, with whom I have spent many memorable hours over the years on my frequent visits to that beautiful Sultanate;

HE Dr Issa Ghanim Al-Kawari, the right-hand man of HH Sheikh Khalifa Al-Thani, former ruler of Qatar, for his unfailing courtesy and support;

HE Abdul Aziz Rowas, Minister of Information, Oman, and HE Hassan Said Mohamed, Secretary-General of the Office of the Deputy PM for Council Affairs, Oman, whose kindness and help will always be remembered;

Two faithful friends who have served as ambassadors at the Embassy of Saudi Arabia, London, HE Sheikh Nasser Al-Manquor and the wonderfully talented poet, HE Dr Ghazi Algosaibi;

Acknowledgements

Dr Ali Fahmi Khushaim, a true friend through all the storms;

Michael Rice, Peter Mansfield, William Conner, Don Loeman and Dorothy Stoddart for taking the time to read and advise;

Peter Hopkins, my publisher, for his infinite patience;

Ibrahim Al Abed, Christine Fernandes, Jacqueline Gulliford, Jennifer Jones, Kay Dunlop, Sylvia Lloyd and Mike Winniberg who have over the years researched and assisted me in every possible way.

And finally my family – William, my son and companion through many of my travels, who sweated agony in his efforts to rescue our publishing house from disaster and succeeded; my daughter, Ann, who has become editor par excellence of *Voice of the Arab World* and Daniel Donovan her husband who has managed to convince me of the miracles of the technological age; my youngest daughter Margaret, whose quiet confidence has been an inspiration to us all; and above all my wife, Pat, who puts in a full day's work before most people have opened their eyes and works all the hours that God knows.

Grateful acknowledgements are made to the trustees of The Weinstock and Rayne Foundations, The Bouverie Trust (Lord Goodman), The Reader's Digest Trust (Russell Twisk), The Harold Hyam Wingate Foundation (Roger Wingate), HM Sultan Qaboos, HH The Emir of Qatar, HH Sheikh Mohamed bin Rashid Al-Maktoum, The Duke of Devonshire, Sir David Alliance, Lord Mishcon, Andrew Stone, Zein Mayassi, Jaweed Al-Ghussein and other major donors to the Next Century Foundation who prefer to remain anonymous.

My gratitude is great. If a new Middle East is to emerge it will be through them. All that I have experienced has convinced me that we are at last on the right course for the twenty-first century.

Claud Morris
London, December 1996

PART ONE

– 1 –

THE RIGHT TO BE HEARD

– 1 –

I looked up from the street at the chandelier glittering behind the windows of the Mayfair house where I was to have dinner on that August evening of 1969. I didn't know where my few steps across the road would lead. If I had, I would have turned around and walked far and fast.

I strolled across the street, pressed the doorbell and was politely shown inside. In the reception room were about fifteen people, chatting and drinking. The six-foot crystal chandelier dominated the ceiling which was inlaid with gold leaf. I circulated until my eye caught a handsome Arab of about forty in an immaculately cut Saville Row suit. The Arab stood with his back to a magnificent Adams fireplace. The person next to the Arab was my host and friend Bill Conner, a quiet kind Ulsterman, and ex-'Desert Rat' whom I had known for thirty years. Bill held the occasional dinner party for people interested in building better relationships between the Arabs and the West. He now fluttered a casual hand. 'Oh, let me introduce you. His Highness Sir Sultan Ali Abdul Karim.' The Sultan held out his hand and bowed, almost imperceptibly.

'How do you do?'

I took in the brown, polished-pine film-star looks, regal nose, piercing eyes, proud nostrils and generous mouth. Sultan Ali's face held a calm, imperturbable expression. The man stood out in that dinner party like a fine Newmarket runner – four or five generations of breeding. When we sat down to dinner I found myself next to him.

'Where's your home?' I asked.

'Aden – the state of Lahej,' Sultan Ali replied, adding with a smile, 'but I've been deposed by the English. It's not mine any longer.'

'What happened?'

'I joined the South Arabian League. They backed land reform. The British didn't like it. In those days the governor regularly had me to tea at Government House. I suppose he spotted what I was up to. So one day while he had me in there stuck in one of his tea parties, he occupied my palace with the Argyll and Sutherlanders. Sent me packing up the Red Sea in a destroyer.' He told the story with the bland expression of a poker player but anger lay near the surface.

'You must be bitter?' I asked.

The Sultan raised his hands expressively. 'I'm afraid I told him so.'

I later learned that Sultan Ali's parting words to Sir Kennedy Trevaskis, the governor were: 'You British always betray your friends. You've done it everywhere.'

After dinner I turned to the Sultan. I liked his courage. 'Look,' I said, 'I've been interested in publishing an international newspaper with the aim of building understanding between people. It could start by putting the Arab point of view. Let's get together on that.'

For some years I'd been interested in international publishing with the aim of creating better understanding between nations. I wanted to see more accuracy and fair play in the media. I had a motto for my staff: 'Press freedom is real when you give someone space for his point of view, especially when it's not your own.' Perhaps because of this our small family publishing company always had trouble keeping its head above water. We had a printing works based in Wales and in our halcyon days, offices in John Street EC4 where Thomsons had partnered us in our industrial magazine projects. It was when we broke with Thomsons that the international scene began to beckon.

Now I sniffed the possibility of a wider scene so I repeated my invitation to the Sultan. He thanked me and added, 'I'm at North Row, off Park Lane – the flat of my aide, Ali Assem.' He gave the telephone number.

Two days later I made some appointments with MP friends to take Sultan Ali down to the House of Commons. The visit was a dismal failure. 'Aden – oh, God,' said my friends. Only one man, Gwynfor Evans, the Welsh Nationalist who lived over the Black Mountain not far from my newspaper plant in Wales, and who then represented Carmarthen in Parliament, offered any sympathy for what was clearly a minority case. Most MPs seemed interested in ruling Arabs rather than in ex-Sultans down on their luck. Everything might have stopped right there, except for an odd coincidence.

– 2 –

The doorbell rang at my Westminster home. Since the days of the Thomson partnership our family had kept a home in London as well as Wales, yo-yoing between the two. Our three children had enjoyed a half-Welsh half-English education and their loyalties bridged Offa's Dike, sometimes resting on one side more heavily than the other. My wife, Pat, managed the dexterous job of keeping both houses going, encouraging the three now nearly adult children and acting as a sounding board for new projects and old projects which both enthused and plagued me.

The doorbell rang again, this time more urgently. Outside on the road was a familiar old Ford estate car. At the door was a jet-haired woman, bright eyes, jutting jaw, an old pullover over a denim skirt. It was Manuela Sykes, at the time a Labour candidate for Parliament and Councillor at Westminster City Council, a proponent in her own way of individualistic Christian action, the kind of uncomfortable woman who provides the fuel for semi-lost causes.

I asked Manuela in for coffee.

'There's a paper run by some friends of mine that's in trouble. They can't get it printed because of pressures,' she said. 'Bill Conner sent me along to see you.'

'What's its name?'

'*Free Palestine*.'

The coincidence crossed my mind. There was I thinking of the paper discussed with Sultan Ali, and a few days later Manuela appears talking about a paper for Palestinians. Surely, Palestinians were an example of the sort of thing I had in mind when talking with the Sultan – a bedevilled, embittered minority without a voice in the press. I put down my coffee. 'OK. Let's see these Palestinians.'

Manuela's wheezing Ford spluttered across Vauxhall Bridge Road, down Warwick Way, past a row of dingy little hotels and rooming houses, into the heart of Pimlico. We drew up outside a nondescript private house in Cambridge Street. Manuela rang the bell. An emaciated, suspicious-looking Arab face appeared and beckoned us in. He showed us down a few steps to a narrow entrance hall and into a room on the left. Sitting there was a slender brunette of around 35, with skin like melba toast and eyes like cinnamon. They were slightly hooded, sleepy eyes and appeared rather contemptuous of her Western visitors.

'This,' proclaimed Manuela, 'is Thelma Elgindi.' Accompanying Thelma was a fashionable redhead with the film-star name of Vanda Dawdrey.

Thelma sat behind a tatty desk, surrounded on all sides by wall posters of young men throwing bombs and bayoneting dummy targets. She talked, gesticulating, arms signalling at the slightest provocation, tongue running fast as though she could not catch up with her thoughts.

'We'll manage the bill, cash monthly, if you take us on,' Thelma said. 'Of course, you might get into trouble if you print us. The last printer had union people who refused to handle our stuff. They got telephone threats too.'

I laughed. It seemed absurd.

She looked at me curiously, then shrugged her shoulders. 'What's your price?'

I scribbled figures on the back of an envelope. They were low. I wanted the work to fill what printers call 'down time' on a new and expensive web offset press. Profit didn't come into it. The cinnamon eyes sparkled. 'We're in business,' she said.

I thought my agreement to be with dispossessed Palestinian nationalists. It was to be much later when we began printing *Free Palestine* that I discovered my meeting had been with the PLO and that 'Mr Big' behind the paper in distant Beirut was Yasser Arafat.

My next date that afternoon was with Dennis Lyons[1] at his flat at Falconer's House in a slightly musty Victorian red brick pile called St James' Court, near Buckingham Palace. Dennis was a public relations man extraordinary; a Falstaffian figure of nineteen stone with wide, semi-hunched shoulders, twinkling brown eyes and Edwardian sideburns like half-moons. What that other brilliant Jew, Arnold Goodman[2] was to Harold Wilson on the legal side, Dennis was on the PR and press side. He was continually in and out of 10 Downing Street where Harold reigned as Prime Minister at the time. Dennis was in his middle-fifties. In his third-floor flat, Dennis sat sprawled out in a leather armchair, hands akimbo. He had been a friend for thirty years.

'What have you been doing?' Dennis asked.

'I landed myself this morning into printing a paper for the Palestinians,' I said.

Dennis laughed. 'You would! I know they may have some case, but these Palestinians are bloody paranoiac. They're worse than the bloody Zionists. I don't think many of your friends will peel a banana with you if they hear you're printing for Arabs on the side.'

– 3 –

The next day I went down to Wales, to our printing plant based at Ystalyfera in the Swansea valley. I carried a little bundle of copy for the first issue of *Free Palestine*. It was all on rough scraps. The English was appalling.

From the top of the Darren mountain which hovered over Ystalyfera like a brooding eagle, the floor of the valley seemed dominated by the *Voice* building. In Welsh they called it *Y Llais*. Here stood the unlikely headquarters of our independent family press.

Mine was a varied and original business that had taken half a lifetime to create and sustain. It was, in its own way, the fruit of some mad inspiration to build my own 'fringe' publications and print for minorities which would not otherwise find a 'voice'.

As Hazlitt said: 'Some idea takes possession of the brain, and however ridiculous, however distressing, however ruinous, haunts us through life.'

From this base we had tried to help Dom Mintoff set up *Voice of Malta* when his Maltese socialists were an abused minority, long before Dom, in turn, abused yesterday's majority. Men from the *Ashanti Pioneer* in Ghana and the *Pilot* in Nigeria, friends of my old friend Joe Appiah, the Ghanaian lawyer/politician, had come here to discuss how they could fight attempts to suppress the African press.

Here we printed for local Labour parties across Britain. Here, too, was the home of Gwynfor Evans's Nationalist paper, *Welsh Nation*, whose editors sometimes arrived out of the fastnesses of Carmarthenshire to write rebellious words against the English establishment, their voices hoarse from protest at courts of justice where the perfidious English refused to grant them trial in their own language. And here, too, was the headquarters of *South Wales Voice*, or *Llais Llafur* (*Voice of Labour*), my valley's own local weekly, as well as *South Wales Magazine* (edited by Pat, my wife) and half a dozen other publications.

We had our own tradition. In the reporters' room hung a printed phrase I had culled from Wilbur Storey, one-time editor of the *Chicago Times*: 'It is a newspaper's duty to print the news and raise hell.'

I went into the *Voice* works and up to my office. The Hepplewhite-style chairs in the room had been a gift from Roy Thomson's Managing Director, James Coltart. Before he joined the Thomson juggernaut, he had been a director of my *South Wales Voice*. The chairs had come out of the boardroom of the Kemsley press when Thomson bought it. My office wall held an impish David Low cartoon of a former employer, Lord Beaverbrook. There was a paperweight given me by my friend Tony Berry,[3] Kemsley's son and one-time Managing Director of the *Western Mail*. I turned this slowly over in my hand.

Did Palestinians really have a right to print? The copy in my hands was violent and crudely written, but the answer was clear. Both sides should have every opportunity of dialogue.

I walked down the creaky stairs to the deserted press room with its sweet, pervasive smell of printer's ink and newsprint. I leaned on the large stone, the lead metal table on which the newspaper pages were assembled in the old hot-metal days and the place where I traditionally held my works meeting. This press had been through many battles. We'd relinquished support from the nationalised Coal Board when we attacked wasteful pit policies. Local council advertising was severed when we attacked Labour Party Council corruption. The battles had been endless. I had left the chairmanship of the Welsh Newspaper Proprietors Association when I decided to support the workers' side in an unpopular strike. I'd lost the good opinion of over half of Fleet Street when I decided to rally the *Guardian* and the *Observer* into battle against my friend and one-time partner Lord Thomson when Roy tried to buy *The Times*. Why, now, bother with Arabs? Why be Don Quixote again?

My Number Two at the Swansea valley works was Vernon Morley Thomas, a stocky, bustling young man, sporting a moustache that would twitch for business streets away. Vernon was one of three or four key men, some from the shop floor, some from management, who had put a great deal into our independent press over the years. I appreciated him as a first-class salesman, but he was even more concerned than I when he saw the *Free Palestine* copy.

We printed the paper for a few months, laboriously cleaning up the copy, shaping it into something that looked modestly professional. But it was hard work and no one, from the faithful Vernon to the men on the floor, was happy with its, to us, self-defeating and strident tone.

Then one morning I had a brain-wave and called Vernon into my office.

'I've studied this Palestine paper,' I said.

'Good,' said Vernon. 'You're going to stop it.'

'No. What I'm about to do is to start another paper. Offer a platform to Arabs or pro-Arabs who realise that they'll never convert anybody unless they put their case in a better way. A paper dealing with the Arab world as a whole, trying to improve relationships with the West and find an answer to this Palestinian problem. There must be an answer. We could give moderate Arab opinion a chance to be listened to.'

'How do we finance it?' asked Vernon. 'Could we get advertising?'

'No – not at the start. But there's been a paragraph in today's *Times*.' I pulled out the paper and thrust it under his nose. 'It says Christopher Mayhew MP[4] has received a gift from HH Sheikh Zayed President of The United Arab Emirates to set up some sort of foundation. The aim's to improve Arab-Western understanding. That sounds like small beer but he's planning a couple of scholarships for Arabs to Oxford. I'll suggest a paper in which his foundation cooperates.'

– 4 –

Christopher Mayhew and I met for lunch in London on 1 June 1970, for me – had I but known it – a fateful day which would hitch the Arab cause to my own wagon for the rest of my days. A tall, lanky man, well over six feet, handsomely chiselled face, glasses, conservatively dressed in a dark blue suit, he was courteous and careful. He had an air of guarded friendliness and listened intently.

Mayhew had been an intelligence officer concerned with the French Resistance during the Second World War. Elected to Parliament for South Norfolk, he had held government jobs as Under-Secretary of State for Foreign Affairs, then as Minister of Defence (Navy). Harold Wilson once called him 'the only Arab in the Labour Party'. Sir Maurice Oldfield of MI6, whom I once met when I was PA to Manny Shinwell, called Mayhew one of the heads of the tribe of 'White Arabs' whom he insisted, with some amusement, camped out in the corridors of the Foreign Office. This was precisely the reason I was anxious to rope Mayhew in.

I had gathered in the vaguest terms from Hector McNeil, another Under-Secretary at the Foreign Office and an ex-journalist colleague of mine on the *Daily Express*, that Mayhew had at one time played an undefined role in a rather mysterious 'Psycho-Ops' department. It was aimed at defeating or de-stabilising fellow-travellers at home and putting a patriotic 'spin' on official and other news printed abroad. Charles Foley, one-time *Express* foreign editor, had mentioned that the whole thing had been temporarily 'blown' when Hector had mistakenly introduced Guy Burgess to Mayhew. Burgess became Mayhew's assistant and then betrayed his boss by trading propaganda secrets and lists of British information agents behind the Iron Curtain to the KGB.

Almost everyone in the Labour Party (except the left wing) regarded the crisply efficient Christopher Mayhew as one of the White Knights of some undercover, anti-Communist campaign. As for me, I imagined he had long since put his intelligence days behind him, but of course in this I was undoubtedly mistaken. I have learned since that once an intelligence man, always an intelligence man. At the time the knowledge that he'd been involved did not bother me. My only calculated concern was that he was clearly pro-Arab and therefore must have some influence in Arab circles. I was hard-up for printing to feed my hungry presses.

As he toyed with his food, I explained my proposals for a new magazine.

'This foundation of yours sponsored by Sheikh Zayed might provide some seed money?' I asked.

He was tentative. 'I'd have to ask the other trustees.' He did not say who the other trustees were, but I gathered from various references he made that one was Sir Harold Beeley, now a retired diplomat but formerly British Ambassador in Cairo and highly knowledgeable about intelligence affairs throughout the Middle East.

'Send me a bit of paper,' said Mayhew and we parted with my promise that I would send him a prospectus.

When I spoke to Dennis Lyons about the Mayhew meeting he weighed in with advice. 'Don't hold the majority share in any company you might form with Mayhew's crowd. Avoid control. You might be blamed for the actions these people take.'

It was the one time that Dennis gave me what proved to be a bad steer. But I took his advice and avoided the control I could easily have taken when terms for the magazine were being set. Previously I had always heeded the words of my old sparring partner, Roy Thomson: 'I take 51 per cent. I like to sleep at nights.' Mayhew, as I was soon to find, was a far shrewder man than I had guessed. Educated up to the eye teeth, he was not a man to go duck shooting with. He had once been mooted as a leader of the Labour Party.

The next meeting with Christopher Mayhew was at his home adjoining Wimbledon Golf Course. His wife, Cecily, kindly gave us tea. Mayhew was suddenly enthusiastic, so I suggested a scheme, based on Dennis's cautionary words. We would have four shareholders. I would take 40 per cent of the shares and nominate someone else as a friend on my side to hold another 10. This would give 50 per cent under my control. Mayhew would also take 40 per cent of the shares and nominate a friend of his to hold a 10 per cent slice, making 50 on his side. Thus control would be balanced. It was based on a certain trust. He said he felt he could get the trustees of his new Zayed-backed foundation to subscribe for copies, 'but of course they'd want some veto on policy.' The words slid by me at the time. I hardly noticed them in my new enthusiasm.

My scheme was that the paper would eventually be financed by appealing to Arab governments to subscribe for copies to be sent to their embassies, to universities or to organisations of their choice. The governments were to pay in advance. I would extend credit on printing and publishing facilities. I needed Christopher Mayhew's reputation as a pro-Arab parliamentarian to attract the Arab subscription support. It seemed a fair division of responsibilities.

Mayhew next proposed that I meet a man described as his 'right hand' in whose views he 'placed a lot of confidence.' The new arrival on the scene was John Reddaway, bespectacled and in his middle 50s, neatly assembled in a pin-stripe suit, sporting a walrus moustache. He was director of the Council for the Advancement of Arab-British Understanding (CAABU). Mayhew proposed that Reddaway should hold 10 per cent of the shares on the Mayhew side. Reddaway had been chief administrative secretary on Cyprus during the conflict there, working under a Cornish friend of mine, Hugh Foot,[5] who had been governor before becoming British representative at the UN. Reddaway was clearly a fervent anti-Zionist. Following his Cyprus stint, he had spent years administrating the UN relief among Palestinian refugees. The experience had embittered him. He hated the Israelis with a deep passion.

From our first meeting, John Reddaway said little and clearly played life by a cautious code. So far as the meetings regarding the new paper were concerned, he butted into conversations only at polite moments when he could carefully review arguments and, I suspected, was used to getting his point of view accepted. He also preferred to make suggestions through Mayhew rather than directly.

It was on a visit to Tremanton Castle, Hugh Caradon's home in my own county of Cornwall, that Hugh's wife Sylvia described Reddaway as a 'brilliant manoeuvrer' but quietly 'a bit of a bully'. She said that he had opposed Hugh's peace and meet-the-people policies on Cyprus. The normally affable Hugh joined in, shaking his head wearily. 'He was the only enemy I ever made during all my years in the diplomatic service,' he said. 'He was a bitter foe.'

The opposing differences between the two men were sincerely felt on either side. John Reddaway was a hard-liner, seeing conflict on the islands. Hugh was for reconciliation.

Within a couple of days of Reddaway's appointment as director, Mayhew came along with Reddaway's proposal that I should incorporate another publisher, Elizabeth Collard of *Middle East Economic Digest*.

It was Manuela Sykes who updated me on Elizabeth Collard. Elizabeth Collard's first husband had been D.N. Pritt, MP, QC, the most noted Marxist of his day. Her second marriage was to the son of Edgar Wallace, the author, and when he died, she eventually married Collard, a leading member in his day of the British Communist Party. With Collard she had started *Middle East Economic Digest*. A lady of independent mind and fiery courage, she was known in parliamentary circles as having been largely instrumental in getting together an early pro-Arab lobby in Britain, and was co-founder of the organisation known as CAABU, the Council for the Advancement of Arab-British Understanding, of which John Reddaway had been appointed director.

Whatever the background, it didn't matter too much to me. It just seemed senseless to share our work with another publisher, and I said so. But I didn't know then how determined John Reddaway could be once he had a plan. He was a man who operated by the back-door. Get a foot in, then let his friends in.

It was difficult for me to nominate someone of Middle East experience to hold the 10 per cent that made up my 50 per cent 'balance' of shares. I didn't know any pro-Arabs personally, so in the end I invited Anthony Nutting, Minister of State for Foreign Affairs in the Conservative government between 1954 and 1956. Nutting had resigned following the Suez crisis and was subsequently shunned by sections of the Conservative Party and regarded warily by the Foreign Office. He was a bony, fit-looking Scot, heavily tanned. We met for afternoon tea in the garden of his Kensington home and I persuaded him to join the board. He tried to warn me against Mayhew. 'Why do you want that fellow on the board?' he said. 'I have a group that meets in the House of Commons. You could come along and address them.' Mayhew had said the same thing about him.

I made the new company a painless operation for the directors. Each was committed to a small investment. They were to get expenses. There was only £100 capital. No actual money, beyond a few pounds, would be required in the scheme I worked out. I would be financing the early set-up costs through my own company and utilising my own publishing facilities on a credit basis. The new journal was christened *Middle East International.*

Christopher Mayhew and John Reddaway suggested the appointment of Tom Little as editor. Tom was a gentle, witty, gregarious Geordie who had worked with distinction in Aden, Cairo and Beirut as founder of the Arab News Agency, later taken over by Reuters. It would be some time before I learned that Tom had also been a key figure in Middle East intelligence in his day and as a result had been awarded an OBE. I was hemmed in by these ex-intelligence men, or intelligence men. Looking back, I was as blind as the proverbial bat, as naive and innocent as a babe.

Plenty of people seemed to have a peculiar interest in the new magazine. One evening I was sitting at home in London reading. It was around 10.00 p.m. The phone rang. I picked it up. 'Hullo?'

A voice said, 'I have a message for you Mr Arab-lover. Your new magazine. You'll never live to see it out.' There was a buzz of disconnection. I imagined it could be some enthusiastic pro-Zionist. I was getting the first fruits of my link-up with Mayhew and Reddaway.

On other occasions I would be talking on the line when there would be a soft click, then silence. In the years to come my family became so used to the odd sounds on our phones that they made jokes about them. Our policy was that we had nothing to hide, so why worry.

– 5 –

Within days of the agreement to set up *Middle East International*, I was told by my secretary that the bank had called.

'We would like to see you at your early convenience,' was the message left by my bank manager.

I walked through the revolving doors into the big banking hall of the central London branch where we had banked happily for years. The roof of the hall was held up by four pompous marble pillars. The accounting machines clattered away in a mechanical chorus behind high plate-glass walls. A uniformed attendant occupied a little cubicle near the manager's office. The attendant led me past the sign 'Stocks and Securities', selected a Chubb key from a ring in his pocket, and snapped back the lock. I entered the manager's room. A pin-stripe trousered figure rose, with the non-committal smile of the professional money man.

'Hullo, how are you? How's Wales?' My bank manager produced a bulky file and began fingering the pages, the hundreds of letters that represented my firm's banking history over the years.

'You've been running near the limit for a bit.' The voice was cautionary. Behind him his window looked out on the street where, during my occasional days of affluence, I had lunched at fashionable restaurants with my bank managers.

'Under present circumstances we might look for a little more security on your overdraft,' he said.

'You think so?'

'Yes,' he continued, apologetically. 'Head Office are leaning on me. They don't seem awfully happy about you at the moment. That Palestine paper you're printing. Then your plans for this venture with Mr Mayhew. That Palestine journal has been criticised in the press. The *Jewish Chronicle* and *The Times* have mentioned your activities. Of course, you know best.' He seemed pretty well informed.

I shook my head. The board I had assembled had no private resources, at least for publishing. However, before signing a personal guarantee for a larger overdraft, I rang Louis Heymann, the merchant banker of Leopold Joseph and Sons Ltd, who sometimes advised my firm.

'I shouldn't sign anything,' advised Louis. 'Don't.'

I paused after Louis was off the phone. Not to sign meant to stop the printing of *Free Palestine* and cease plans to publish the new Middle

East magazine. It would be a blow to those I had encouraged. 'Sign,' said that inner voice that so often got one into trouble. 'Commit yourself.' I decided it was the only way to start the Middle East paper and keep other projects rattling along. I signed and walked home.

It was a bleak, indeterminate kind of day. Depressing. I walked through St James's Park and stood on the concrete bridge that spanned the lake. Staring at the ducklings chasing each other in murky water four feet below, I thought, Good Lord, I've done a bloody stupid thing. I've given the bank control over all my personal assets in order to continue this dubious pro-Arab publishing programme. I was now firmly locked in.

– 2 –
FIRE IN THE VALLEY

– 1 –

It was on a warm day early in April 1970 that Vernon Thomas came into my office to say, to my surprise, that some traders in Swansea were beginning to ask questions about our publishing policy. 'What's it to do with them?' I asked Vernon.

'I don't know. But there's gossip about it. Somebody said there's even been a mention in the Jewish press.'

'They are extraordinarily well informed.'

'I've had one or two come up, quite deliberately, and say they don't think you know what you're doing. They don't like it. Some customers may stop advertising.'

'Tell them it's just another printing job,' I told Vernon sharply. 'Besides, I don't like the idea of Swansea traders telling us what we do or don't print.'

Vernon raised a doubtful eyebrow. 'OK. If you say so.'

– 2 –

Forty-one days after my meeting with Mayhew, at 8.00 a.m. on a Sunday morning, the phone rang in our London home. It was Vernon from Swansea.

'I should have called earlier. We've been up all night,' he said. 'We've had a hell of a fire. The rotary went. The police think it was arson.'

My heart turned over. 'How much damage?' I asked.

'The insurance assessors are coming this morning. The press is gone. All the newsprint has been burnt out. Half a dozen titles of magazines stacked for despatch are ruined. God knows how much is up in smoke.'

Pat and I boarded the first possible train from Paddington. We arrived at Neath station, disconsolate and worried. The rain lashed down in torrents as only valley rain can. We clambered into the car we usually left in the station courtyard in our seemingly endless commute between Wales and London and wheeled up towards the mountains, towards Ystalyfera, half mist-hidden in the late afternoon.

At the *Voice* works, the front building was intact but all that remained of the rear which had housed the rotary press was a steaming, smoking ruin. The heat had been so intense that the building had imploded rather than exploded. Five-hundredweight drums of printing ink were thrown into corners. Tons of smouldering newsprint lay in reels on top of one another. The charred press itself was blackened, wooden catwalk burnt through, rods bent, wires bare, twisted, hanging. The heat had eaten deep into the concrete. It was a chaos of burned paper and charred metal. It was a fine old rotary press built in 1898 that had come from Kemsley Newspapers in Gray's Inn and had been a gift from Lord Kemsley to a struggling Welsh newspaper proprietor, my predecessor Ebenezer Rees. It was the icing on the cake when I bought the press. It could turn out 20,000 copies an hour and I loved it. I felt sick.

We drove to our Swansea valley home. A riot of red roses lay on one side of my study window. Through the window I could see the enormous bulk of 'Y Darren' mountain. The rain had eased off. Dusk was falling. A myriad of lights came on over the shadowy shape of Ystalyfera.

I turned my mind back. I had not only started to print the Palestine paper and planned *Middle East International*, I had put in hand a whole programme of Middle East and Third World books. Was it possible that some enthusiastic anti-Arab had tried to put a halt to the new business by setting light to our press? Christopher Mayhew came on the phone. 'I hope you have not taken on too heavy a burden by championing us,' he said.

– 3 –

On Monday I went to the office. The CID arrived, two plain-clothes men and one uniformed officer. As one questioned me the others watched quietly.

'You know,' the CID man said, raising a quizzical eyebrow, 'this might have been a job by agents from somewhere, what with the sort of printing you do. Had you thought of that?'

He went laboriously through details in his notebook. Just after midnight a policeman on the beat had seen two figures come out of the works. They had gone off in a Morris car. Another witness had seen the two men go into the works earlier. Shortly after they left, flames were seen. Three fire services were called. By the time they got there the building was pretty far gone.

His recitation was enormously depressing. When they finally left I tried to get down to work. In the panic I had not seen my mail. Doreen, my secretary, had brought in some personal letters which had been waiting my arrival from London. On top was a buff envelope. I thumbed it open. The contents were unexpected.

'Ask Mr Thomas to come in.' I waved the letter as Vernon entered. 'Look. *Free Palestine* have written to say that they are removing their printing contract.' It seemed the ultimate irony after my visit to the bank to negotiate continued support in order to go on printing it.

'My God!' said Vernon. 'We print their paper. Our press is blown up. And these Palestinians say goodbye.'

At that moment Alan Hitchens came in. A bespectacled wiry cockney whose hobby was long-distance running, Alan had been on the London *Sunday People* as features editor and writer of the 'Man of the People' column, before making the disastrous choice of joining my band-wagon to look after the editorial side of our papers. Alan had performed a miracle in transforming *Free Palestine* into something resembling a professional production.

'Shalom and Napalm!' exclaimed Alan with a grin. 'They've kicked us in the ass!'

I telephoned Thelma Elgindi of *Free Palestine*. 'I got your letter,' I said when she came on the phone. 'I was amazed that you took the printing away from us.' There was a pause. Then I told her the news of the fire. 'We've been through hell here,' I finished.

There was another long pause at the other end of the telephone. 'I warned you that you might get into difficulties if you printed for us,' she said at last. 'Some Arab offices in New York had a petrol bomb thrown through the window a week ago. Rabbi Meir Kahane,[1] the American Zionist, is suspected.'

I felt that sickening feeling again.

'I'm sorry for your trouble,' Thelma went on. 'But we're governed by circumstances and pressures. We had to remove our printing.'

'But,' I said, 'how were you forewarned? Your letter taking your printing away coincided with the fire.'

She went on to talk about costs and make excuses, but I couldn't understand her.

The phone clicked off. A passionate Thelma in her warm Pimlico front room was no match for the icy wind of self-concern blowing in Ystalyfera that morning.

– 4 –

I returned to London to try to repair our severely damaged business. Tom Little came around. He was not only editor of the new *Middle East International* but also London Correspondent for *Al Ahram*, the famous Egyptian daily. He wanted to write a story for *Al Ahram*.

I told him about our rebuff from Thelma Elgindi, the fury it had raised in our Welsh works after the insurmountable losses from the fire. I ended my tirade with, 'I cannot understand them . . . the Palestinians.'

Tom laughed. 'They don't always understand themselves. It's a paradox. Of course there are many factions. Sometimes they speak one thing and do another. Cutting you out could have been a decision by someone in London trying to be smart, or it could have been some intelligence agent on *Free Palestine*. Most of the Palestinian movements are infiltrated by agents of one sort or another. There are Zionist agents – Palestinians – who are constantly being detected around Arafat, then kicked out or shot. Others oppose anything backed by Arafat – and *Free Palestine* is a case in point. The last thing any of these characters want is to encourage a moderate publisher who might in the end clean up the Palestinian case and present it as justified.' He sighed disconsolately. 'It could be that they didn't like you starting *Middle East International*. The Zionists probably thought you had been joined by too many former anti-Zionist Foreign Office top brass like Mayhew, Reddaway and Nutting!'

Tom paused and sucked his ever-present briar. 'These people feed low-grade political gossip about one another. Some are dead against Mayhew. Others think you might get too big for your boots. And I imagine the Israelis would want to scare you off.'

It was all a mystery to me. Sometime later the newly appointed editor of *Free Palestine*, Louis Eakes, said in an interview in the *Beirut Star* that he had never understood why, having found a safe haven with a responsible and sympathetic publisher, they had given that publisher the push.

I went back down to Wales, this time by car instead of by train. Driving like a madman through Abergavenny and Brecon, turning sharp left at the Cray Reservoir, I went down through green Forestry Commission country until I throttled back above Ystradgynlais, Ystalyfera's neighbouring village.

I swung into the drive of our house and hoisted myself out of the car. Pat was at the door.

'I've bad news,' she said. 'Bob Owen's had a stroke.'

Our works foreman, Bob was the man who after the fire had humped the reels of smouldering newsprint about. He had trained our son William in the beautiful art of type. He was also a fine gardener who had gone to the Chelsea Flower Show with us every year. Bob had now fallen victim to overstrain, tension and pressure.

I suddenly felt cold. The adrenalin pumping through my system since the fire disappeared. What for God's sake was happening to us all? What would be the final price exerted by the mysterious fire in the valley and by my stubbornness in not retreating before obvious pressures?

'Are you going to carry on?' Pat asked.

'Yes,' I shouted as though ready to damn the devil. 'We've committed ourselves. I've told the *Middle East International* people we'll publish them. Anyway, I've got to prove that in the long run pressure doesn't pay. We've had the fire. The price of our independence has been met. But I'm damned if it means we've been stopped.'

I felt stubborn and optimistic. The Royal Insurance Company had just parted with the first half of the fire insurance. I could have used it to pay the bank overdraft and put a little by for the proverbial rainy day. Instead, I committed it to the new Middle East publishing venture.

– 3 –
No End to a Nightmare

– 1 –

Six months after the fire, *Middle East International* was about ready for launching.

It was when the magazine began to settle down, that Christopher Mayhew said one afternoon. 'There's a parliamentary group from the Labour Middle East Council going out to Cairo and Amman. All expenses paid by the Ariel Foundation. Why not go? Get more flavour of the Middle East.'

I checked out the Ariel Foundation and discovered it had been founded in 1960 to encourage 'by practical means understanding between countries'. Ariel was linked with the British Foreign Office and received from Foreign Office sources (including ambassadors) names of people to be invited to Britain and names of selected Britons to be sent on sponsored trips abroad.

Whatever the source of the funds I was all for it. I had already been on one quick trip with Pat to Beirut, Kuwait and Cairo to round up advertising revenue and subscriptions to support the new journal. A second trip would be a bonus.

We arrived in Cairo and were luxuriously billeted at the Nile Hilton. In the lobby, the Parliamentary delegation was surprised to find Christopher Mayhew. He had come to Cairo at the suggestion of the Foreign Minister of Abu Dhabi. Mayhew was to have a meeting with Sheik Zayed regarding funds for the foundation. He told me, to my surprise, that up to that point he had never met Zayed. 'Never set eyes on him,' he told me in the Hilton coffee shop. All his contacts with the foundation's benefactor had apparently been through representatives of the British Foreign Office, the Arab League in Geneva and the UAE Foreign Ministry. It was clear that Mayhew's meeting with the Sheikh was not of his own initiative.

I had asked Dennis Lyons, my guide through the Whitehall undergrowth, to look up Mayhew's foundation. It was called ANAF or 'Arabische Nicht Arabische Freundschaft' and was administered by a Dr Rene Weber whose address was c/o Mandatoria 23, 6301 Zug, Switzerland. It was said to have been established under Swiss law, apparently to keep its matters private from any Zionist activity.

Whatever the background to the founding of ANAF may have been, Christopher Mayhew's sudden appearance in Cairo was a pleasant surprise. We met a number of times and discussed everything from *Middle East International's* editorial policy to how much of an annual subsidy ANAF should request from Sheikh Zayed.

When the Parliamentary delegation finally left Cairo for Amman my respect for and curiosity about Christopher Mayhew had deepened, along with a certain inevitable irritation at his interference in editorial matters.

– 2 –

We settled in at the Intercontinental in Amman. It was to be a traumatic time for me. A turning point. In the Jordan valley I interviewed a Palestinian who had been deported from Israel after being charged with 'agitation'. He said the Israelis had taken him up in a helicopter and dropped him over a minefield. He had crawled through it to the Jordanian border and luckily got out alive. I had no proof of the story, but it haunted me.

Soon after meeting him, I visited Karami, now a ghost town in the Jordan valley. It had been blown to bits by an Israeli armoured division in a revenge attack against the PLO.

This visit to Karami would not have been worth a moment's consideration by a war-hardened Middle East hand. To me it was different. I wandered through that ghost town. I sat alone on a pile of rubble. It was my first sight of the reality of the Middle East conflict. I felt suddenly an enemy, neither Jew nor Arab, but the sickening world about me: the land grabbers, the manoeuvrers, the power players, the ignorant, the apathetic on all sides. How was this mess to be cured?

When I returned to England I felt both fascinated by the Middle East scene and immensely saddened by the Palestine problem and the world's indifference to it. A few weeks later I wrote an article about my trip and sent it to Christopher Mayhew telling him I would like to include it in *Middle East International*.

The article concluded with these words:

> Finally, the Palestinian fights because he feels himself cornered. In Jordan or in neighbouring Lebanon, breeding-ground of guerrilla fighters in that part of the world, you can see their beginnings in the refugee camps. Living in canvas or mud-and-straw hovels, a dozen human beings to a few square feet, there they are – short of food and short of hope, with breeding their only pitiful diversion. Unwanted by Israel, which has already occupied the land these people fled, thrusting themselves upon their brotherly Arab countries in which they now live, who wearily accept yet another problem. Regarded with prejudiced eyes if it ever comes to questions of employment, felt to be a statistical problem by the United Nations and a headache by the relief organisations, they have no hope. Go West, they used to say. Yes, with USA admitting a few hundred a month out of the tens of thousands clamouring to come. Yes, brother, go to Beirut if you dare, where some men still fight with their typewriters and others sit counting their profits from the Gulf Oil billions.

Christopher Mayhew was on the phone like a shot.

'Really, we can't print this. The editorial board would never agree. I see it was written with your heart. But it will upset too many. God knows what the bankers and businessmen of Beirut who are friends of pro-Arabs in Britain will think if this should ever appear.'

It wasn't the first time that Christopher Mayhew and John Reddaway through Mayhew had criticised my work on *Middle East International*. I got higher than a rocket and said a few un-recallable words. I was in no mood for seeing anyone else's point of view. It was the first demonstration to Mayhew of my appalling short fuse where my own work is concerned.

'All right, if I can't print my piece why don't you run the bloody paper yourself?'

He grunted patiently. 'Look, I'm sorry, but after you wrote earlier pieces John Reddaway said to me, "How can I tell Claud how naive he is about the Middle East?" He hadn't the heart.'

Never, as I was to reflect much later, was a truer word spoken. I was indeed naive. But at the time the comment lit me like a Catherine-wheel. The idea that I, the ex-Fleet Street journalist, the editor, the publisher, was considered naive incensed me. What did these politicos know about the business I asked myself. Nothing.

'I started the paper. I spend time running it, supporting it.'

Mayhew coughed apologetically. 'I don't think we can always print your articles. Of course, I'm open to contradiction if some other member of the editorial board feels differently.'

I was in no mood for any democracy. 'OK. Run the paper yourself, then. Take it! And don't complain if I go out on my own. Don't come in three months with a complaint from John that my articles are printed elsewhere!'

Mayhew realised I had offered him the editorship. Patiently ignoring my bull-headed reaction he said quietly: 'All right, I'll ring back tomorrow about that offer.' I suspected he was off to consult someone.

I still felt entirely insulted, taken down a peg by a school-master who, I felt, knew less than the pupil, at least about publishing and editorial matters. I didn't know at the time how deep the waters were. Christopher had the thinking of a trained Whitehall man, practised in avoiding bush fires. I was more adept at starting them.

I walked twice around our Swansea valley garden, in and out of the rhododendron bushes, and returned to find Pat in the kitchen. By that time I had realised what a shabby performance I had put up. Hell, it was done. I didn't regret a word. It had been a relief.

'You've just got yourself an article on Palestine and the Arabs for the next issue of *South Wales Magazine*,' I told her.

'It hasn't got much to do with the local affairs of South Wales,' Pat protested.

'But I must have it in!' I shouted.

The fact that I had dared in one of our Welsh papers, *South Wales Magazine*, to plan publication of an article which Christopher proclaimed was too sensitive for the pro-Arab *Middle East International*, was soon to bring the temple of all we possessed crashing down about the Morris family ears. It was to be another move with irreversible consequences.

– 4 –
DEATH OF A NEWSPAPER

– 1 –

I continued yo-yoing between Wales and Westminster. Some weeks later it was Jon Kimche who came to lunch at 4, Vincent Square. Middle East correspondent for the *Evening Standard* and at the time editor of the pro-Israeli magazine *New Middle East*, I had known Jon for twenty-five years, ever since he was editor of Nye Bevan's left-wing *Tribune* and I a columnist.

'Why not co-operate?' he asked. 'Amalgamate your pro-Arab paper with mine. We share the middle ground. Co-operation instead of war between Arab and Jew.'

I looked warily at him. His young brother was attached to the Israeli Foreign Office. David Kimche had been one of the brightest boys of Mossad Letafkidum Meyouchadim, the Israeli secret service.

Jon continued assuringly, 'I'm unpopular with the Israeli establishment. When I last went to a reception in Tel Aviv, Golda Meir turned on her heel when I came up. She was upset at my articles about Arabs.'

'How does your magazine operate?'

'Sigmund Warburg's[1] chairman of the editorial board. Backers are a group of Jewish businessmen. You should see Dan Gillon, my assistant editor, as well. He's a Dove. Son of an Israeli general, but wants a new deal with the Arabs. Just your cup of tea.'

'What are your publishing arrangements?'

'We're handled by Rupert Murdoch who does printing and mail-out. You'd take that over. It would be a good contract.'

At that moment the phone rang.

'Who is it?'

'Christopher. Sorry to interrupt. You seen this morning's *Jewish Chronicle?*'

'No.'

He was smooth on the phone, showing no memory of my occasional choleric temperament.

'There's a headline. "Four executives quit pro-Arab Welsh publisher".' My stomach knotted.

The story, as read by Christopher Mayhew, said that four leading executives of my Swansea company had resigned because I had thrown in my lot with friends of the Arabs like Mayhew. Vernon Thomas was leader of the group of rebels. Vernon was as courteous as a vicar proclaiming the last rites preparatory to lowering his old employer reverently into the ground. As Vernon said in his *Jewish Chronicle* obituary,

> I had recently been appointed Sales Director and my new post involved participation in the group activities with a pro-Arab paper ... My appointment would have involved meeting people concerned with this anti-Israel publication. I do not agree with its policy, nor could I bring myself to be supporting it. I had been offered future duties which would have meant that I had to associate with these people. This I have decided I could not do. Rather than do so I have resigned in order to start a project I have had in mind for some time – a newspaper of my own.

'Well, my staff's walked out,' I said to Jon, as I returned to the dining room. He was amazed.

'Look, let me ring the editor of the *Jewish Chronicle*, Geoffrey Paul, right now. I'm sure Geoffrey would print something about your side,' said Jon helpfully. 'Let's fix lunch. Geoffrey, you and I.'

I poured Jon a brandy and took a stiff slug myself.

'Well, no.' I was no longer in any mood for co-operation. A personal war had just been declared. Another phone call came the following day.

'Who's that?'

'Leonard Bloch.'

I hadn't seen Leonard for ten years. A brilliant Jew (another introduction of Dennis Lyons's into our Welsh circus), he had at one time been accountant for my papers.

'I'd like to come along with a proposition,' said Leonard. 'These days I'm accountant to Sigmund Warburg. When can we meet? I'd like to bring along a young Israeli, Dan Gillon.' I realised Jon Kimche wasn't giving up easily. Both Leonard and Dan appeared next day to put the case for my throwing in my hand with the Israeli lobby. Somebody out there, I suspected, was still trying to toss a rope. Whether to save or hang me I couldn't be sure.

I didn't say yes and I didn't say no. I just waited.

I rang Bryn Lloyd, one of my remaining ad. men in Wales.

'What the devil's happening?'

'You mean you didn't know? He hasn't told you? Lord. They were even talking about the *Jewish Chronicle* article at lunch at the Dragon Hotel today,' said Bryn. 'Somebody's busy. Photostat copies have been delivered to about thirty of our main advertisers.'

Others had obligingly circulated copies of Pat's *South Wales Magazine* giving my candid impressions of Israeli Defence Force activities on the banks of the Jordan. Then John Hogan, who edited a house magazine for us, came in to tell me that the chairman of another businessmen's club had called to tell him, 'That bugger Morris has criticised Swansea business for fifteen years. Now he's joined with Arabs. Everyone has left him. It's in the *Jewish Chronicle*. Somebody is about to boot him in the balls.'

'Were there any warning signs about Vernon's moves?' I asked Bryn.

'It was brewing for some time. A couple of months. Then that *South Wales Magazine* article came out. That did it.'

I soon learned that Vernon had taken three key sales staff and a bevy of circulation people with him.

Sylvia Lloyd, tele-ad. manageress for our papers and known as 'Auntie Syl' to all our children, was politely informed by the local Co-op, our biggest advertiser, that they couldn't advertise in any paper owned by a man who was anti-Semitic. Sylvia replied, 'I happen to be staring across my desk at one of my tele-ad. assistants, a charmer called Marilyn Miller, who wears a filigree Star of David as big as a horseshoe around her neck.' Also on our staff was Geoffrey Bowden, a nephew of Dennis Lyons and another import. He had a wry humour that made him a bright cartoonist and writer. If you made a roll-call, adding to it our Jewish solicitor, young Streull in Swansea, the paper facing the onslaught of Jewish indignation had more Jews attached to it than most of the journals in Wales. A second *Jewish Chronicle* piece dated 29 October 1971 which caused further furor was headed with the words 'ANTI-ISRAEL ARTICLES' and started off:

> Questions were asked at the annual meeting of the Swansea Hebrew Congregation on Sunday, about Voice Publications, following the report last week in the *Jewish Chronicle* about the resignation of four members of the firm's staff. Mention was also made during the meeting of anti-Israel remarks contained in the latest edition of *South Wales Magazine*, under the title of *Voice*, with the initials C.M. at the end. The editor of the magazine is Patricia Morris, wife of Mr Claud Morris, the group's chairman.

Dennis Lyons now pointed a howitzer of his own. He wrote to the *Jewish Chronicle*:

> I was surprised at a report from your Swansea correspondent implying that Mr Claud Morris is involved in anti-Jewish activities. I would point out that Mr Morris, whom I have known for many years, was the publisher of the book *Fascism in Britain* one of the most savage attacks on Oswald Mosley (or the National Front or Fascist idea) ever produced in this country.

I also wrote the *Jewish Chronicle* myself to put down implications of anti-Semitism:

> It is odd that a press devoted to the three following propositions should be attacked in your paper. These propositions are (1) We have no right to interfere with man's individual right of self-government; (2) We should not try erroneously to influence the thought of others; (3) We must not promote the obscenity of war and hate.

– 2 –

It was three weeks later that William and I waited patiently for the verdict of our accountant.

William, our eldest child and only son, had been brought up on the floor of our printing works. He could set type, operate the machines and at 18 was the youngest publisher in Britain when he produced a paper called *Career City*. It, too, was reeled off our machines. Now, at 21 he had become my right hand. We sat together watching the accountant's bland expression.

'Your Welsh local valley paper can't survive. It's losing too much,' he said.

'Is any recovery possible?' William asked.

'You've lost your key advertising staff. It's impossible for you to get others in place for months ahead. To hold out you'd need reserves of at least £100,000.'

'And no doubt a massive PR campaign to change our image,' I added.

The scene of the talk was our sitting room in Vincent Square, London. Outside were the magnificent plane trees. Night was falling. The lights of offices and buildings around the square were switching on. I sat back in my armchair surrounded by my familiar books, wondering what bloody next. William was totally depressed. He had been raised to inherit a Welsh print and publishing business. Soon there wouldn't be much left to publish. I had, by my insistence on publishing for all, brought about apparent ruin. Our 'flagship' newspaper was about to close. It was, I now realise, the one failure of guts I can remember suffering. I was tired of battling. There seemed to be no allies. Not even Arabs.

I knew that had I simply dropped everything else, made a single telephone call to Sigmund Warburg, Jon Kimche, or some other major or minor Israeli advocate, I could have saved the *Voice* and saved our auxiliary paper, the *Swansea Shopper*. Vernon's Swansea supporters would have welcomed the returned prodigal. I did not do it.

– 3 –

Almost with relief I lifted the phone from its cradle. The call, a heartbreaker, was to Mick Tems, then my editor on *South Wales Voice*, a spry young Cockney of Dutch descent, and one of the best young editors I ever employed. 'Sorry, Mick, we fold.' I could almost hear the pain on the other end of the line. 'When?'

'Now. Put this issue to bed tonight with an editorial on page one. Get me Doreen.'

Decapitations in the newspaper business have to be instantaneous. If I had waited, I could not have killed that paper. The death hangs over me now, more than twenty-five years later. It divided my family, although they followed me into the wilderness. It pushed William willy-nilly into an Arab scene which was to occupy a large slice of his life. It put a seal on the inevitability that I would be labelled pro-Arab although in my own mind I was merely pro the right-to-be-heard, and abhorred pressures to the contrary whether from the Abrahams or the Abdullahs, the Micks or the Limeys of this world.

'Here's Doreen,' said Mick.

'Hul-oo, Mr Morr-ees,' came the lilting Welsh voice of my secretary. She took down the death sentence for page one. It concluded:

> We will not censor, ban or refuse the right of publication to one group of people because another group would like to have such people boycotted. The *Voice* itself, known as a beacon of these valleys, will in future no longer offend, defend or denounce. It passes into legend, still clinging to the hem of truth. We have always given a fair hearing to every man and to every family. We have knowingly injured no man. We have worked for causes and for people throughout the West Wales coalfield. THE *VOICE* WHICH HAS ALWAYS WORN ITS OWN SCARS WELL, ENDS WELL IN DEFENCE OF A PRINCIPLE.

Timothy Maybe on BBC Radio 4 broadcast a reminiscence:

> This is more than an ordinary newspaper closure. It is the end of a great campaigning tradition. And now this campaigning newspaper ends, ironically enough, because of an advertising ban by traders who want to prevent the same presses that turn out the *Voice* from printing pro-Arab papers.

The *Guardian*, in a story headed 'Voice is silenced after 73 years' reported:

> The death of the *Voice* is rather more than the end of yet another newspaper. The fight put up for it by proprietor, Claud Morris, will earn it, and him, a small place in newspaper history.

I found an old miner's lamp, symbolic of the Swansea valley and the newspaper the people there had loved, and sent it to Christopher Mayhew to symbolise what I now felt was our common cause. We were yoked together in what seemed to be turning into a joint struggle and with my back to the wall I desperately wanted an ally and friend. I felt that I now knew how Mayhew had suffered in his own political career because of his support of Arabs.

Mayhew in response invited Pat and me to lunch and drinks at his Wimbledon home. The demise of the *Voice* was discussed. At the lunch was Nadim Dimeshkie, then Lebanese Ambassador to Britain. As I was talking to Nadim, Mayhew came up. 'We have some awful rows,' he told Nadim. He looked bewildered. He still couldn't put me in any conventional pigeon-hole.

– 4 –

The morning after the lunch and back in Wales I looked out of the window at the sheep grazing in the valley field opposite. I listened to the clip-clop of the farmer's boots as he walked down the lane, as regular as the seven o'clock BBC news. The background outside was limpid and tranquil. Nevertheless, it was the end of a chapter.

'Where do we go from here?' William asked. He came into my bedroom, tousled, in pyjamas, a cup of tea in hand.

Our son, with his tall slender figure, his wide smile and his mop of hair, was to retain his deep attachment to the Welsh people and to the valleys. He loved it all dearly, from the frenetic air of Swansea on a Saturday night to the valley coal-tip areas and the wild grandeur of the Brecon Beacons. In the best sense of the word this family publishing business was William's. The decisions were part of him. Together we had supported the right, as we saw it, of a minority to be heard. William possessed then, as now, an immense uncomplaining courage. To lose the *Voice* had broken a piece of his heart and I knew it. But we were, and are, a remarkably close-knit family. Not only had the *Voice* gone, my wife's *South Wales Magazine* and our Swansea money-spinning free sheet weekly were to follow. *Middle East International*, too, the cause of most of the trouble, was in difficulties. At every meeting with the editorial board, its collapse was discussed. Mayhew now headed that board and directed editorial policy. I had washed my hands of this side of it. 'We can't sustain the magazine with our own funds,' said Mayhew. 'I'd do anything for the Arabs except back them with money,' he said, not for the first time. So it rested for the most part on my own now precarious resources.

'Why don't you tell the *Middle East International* people to piss off?' urged Dennis Lyons when I saw him. 'You've lost too much. Kill the bloody thing.'

'No,' I said. 'That paper's the reason we stood firm. *Middle East International* has a right to publish. We're following principle, if I chuck it out it will die. The campaign against us will have succeeded.'

– 5 –

A week after the death of the old *South Wales Voice* there was a completely unexpected move which I thought at first would give me a wonderful new opening. Elizabeth Collard's weekly Middle East magazine *MEED* was in difficulty. 'Will you take it over?' she asked. The price was cheap. Just £30,000 for around 80 per cent interest. I felt in my bones that it was a good deal. I checked that despite the crisis in my own Welsh affairs I could borrow new finance from Leopold Joseph whose deputy chairman, my old friend Tony Berry, was enthusiastic.

Four days after the purchase had been agreed and balance sheets handed over, Christopher spoke to me. 'I hear you're buying Elizabeth Collard's business. She told me so at a dinner party. Why wasn't I informed?'

I couldn't understand what he was getting at.

'I would have told you, of course, in due time,' I answered, 'but it's just a publishing venture. It hasn't come off yet. I haven't mentioned it to anyone.'

'I simply don't think you should make this link-up.'

'Why not?'

'I can give you reasons.'

'What reasons?'

He coughed. 'I wouldn't do it with her. You would be ill advised.'

He gave his reasons. They were cogent, rational and political, based on his wide experience of Middle East politics. It was largely because Elizabeth at some time in her career had apparently been linked with the Communist Party.

Next day I sent a polite note of refusal to Elizabeth Collard. We had a last lunch at the Hyde Park Hotel. Elizabeth had guessed something had happened to change my mind.

'What did Christopher say about me?' she asked.

'Nothing important,' I parried, indicating that the board of *Middle East International* felt that a commitment to any other company might affect my work for them.

When Elizabeth Collard died a few years later after a long illness, Christopher Mayhew spoke from the pulpit of St Bride's Church, Fleet Street, at a memorial service and gave a generous tribute to her Middle East work, and her part in founding both the Labour Middle East Council and the Council for Arab-British Understanding. This only added to the strangeness of an incident which I still find extraordinary.

Exhausted and near bankruptcy, I stuck to *Middle East International* like glue.

– 5 –
THE CONSPIRATORS

– 1 –

Ahmed Anis's office was at Hay Hill, Mayfair. He occupied a suite with a sharp-witted assistant called Abdul Karim Al-Mudaris. When I was a Fleet Street hack, Ahmed Anis's office housed an institution called the Hay Hill Club. Lads of the Beaverbrook Press and sundry other topers with expense accounts once tipped their elbows there. Now, it was an office for the Arab League.

It was on a bright Monday morning that I presented myself at this address of many memories and faced an oak door marked 'Arab League – No admission except on business'. There was a gimlet-size spy hole set in the top panel. A girl's voice shrilled out through the speaker attached to the door.

'Who are you?'

I gave my name and the door clicked open.

Ahmed was the archetypal Egyptian diplomat. 'Come in, my friend.' He always spoke in almost conspiratorial terms, as if in a confessional. I immediately started talking about my need for more publishing work, but Ahmed took me by the arm.

'C'm on. Let's go around the corner for lunch.'

A few minutes later I was in a comfortable Louis XV armchair in a Dover Street restaurant, outlining the idea I had in mind with all the fervour of some latter-day Tom Paine planning another *Pennsylvania Gazette* crusading for the rights of slaves to be heard. Journalists inherit the gift of hyping everything. An apt enough publicist himself, Ahmed gulped it all down.

'What I want to do is to replace the old *Voice* with a new newspaper. It could equal the *Jewish Chronicle* in carrying news about the Middle

East,' I said. 'I want you to introduce people who might help me get it going by taking commercial advertising or buying subscriptions.'

'This is something all Arabs must support,' said Ahmed. 'I'll contact Cairo immediately.'

The idea for starting a new *Voice* came hot on the heels of the death of the old one. It was not only the need for more publishing and printing to fill the sad gaps left by closure of the *South Wales Voice*, but also a deep personal need to write about the Middle East without the shackles (as I saw it) now imposed on *Middle East International*. I was too long in the tooth to be fettered in my editing. I wanted to write freely, but with Reddaway and Mayhew looking over my shoulder that was impossible.

Having sounded out the family and some Arab friends, there remained only one last hurdle – how to explain to Mayhew my decision to start a new paper at a time when *Middle East International* was in the doldrums.

He was affable and said he appreciated my need to get another paper working to replace the lost work in Wales but didn't much like the notion of another Mid-East publication, however different it might be from *Middle East International*.

'I have to make a new start,' I insisted. 'That start must be another paper. Unless I get something going my whole business falls to bits. *Middle East International* will still carry in-depth articles on Arab political affairs. This new paper will carry up-to-date news items concerning commerce and tourism as well as current affairs. Furthermore, it will have to be profit-making.'

'I think you'd be better off doing books, or something of that sort,' Christopher argued. He was privately horrified, as he told me some years later, because of his fear that the new *Voice* would be too competitive with the shaky *Middle East International*, in advertising, in soliciting Arab support, and in using my own time and energy.

I again promised that the new paper would contribute to the overheads of *Middle East International* but I couldn't assess whether or not Christopher really appreciated the hole my firm was in. We were drowning. Even *Middle East International* owed us considerable money.

I next talked to John Reddaway. Reddaway admitted that he personally realised my best hope of survival might be more publishing work from the Middle East. He came forward with a proposal he thought might solve the dilemma. 'Why not share the profits of the new weekly *Voice*, when it starts, with *Middle East International*?' Believe it or not I agreed. I was leaning over backwards in an effort not to make waves.

'How will you finance the new paper?' William asked.

'We need some subscriptions, or grants, from Arab tourist offices, airlines and businesses, plus advertising,' I answered. 'And I hope I can get Arab embassies everywhere to buy copies. Then we'll collar any other work we can. PR. Training journalists. Printing. Anything. Ahmed Anis tells me there's a conference in Cairo that starts in a few days, which will be attended by Arab Ministers of Information.'

– 2 –

A week later, on a cold wet January night at Heathrow airport, William and I were sitting in an aircraft while the tannoy system thumped out a rather solemn tango, preparatory to take-off. Cairo lay ahead, and Shepherds Hotel was planned as the base of our immediate operation.

In the early hours of the next morning, we passed through the gilt-framed glass doors of Shepherds. From our room we looked out over the Nile. The scene was sleepy and unconcerned. Moored below the hotel were eight small sailing boats, waiting for tourists to take day trips down the river. Next to them was the *Nile Delta*, a three-storeyed river boat about 120 feet long, tour decks scattered with blue deck chairs. Just below, my eye could look out on the Nile Bridge. On the opposite banks were three Mississippi-style house boats. Although it was early morning, the Nile Casino lights still flashed on and off. Beyond, the Cairo Tower pointed 300 feet into the sky. Up river as far as my eye could see, the sludge-grey Nile continued to broaden and move downstream with its eternal dignity. Two skiffs spun along the river, propelled by furious oarsmen, fighting the current and the wind. Despite their efforts, they were blown hither and thither on a wayward course. The river of life, I thought.

Across the Nile Bridge at the Sheraton we found delegates from an information conference which was attended by every Arab state. Hesitantly we tracked people down by telephone and by personal call. When we finished we went to the Hilton, then to the Semiramis Hotel and on to Shepherds. We dug the Arab delegates out of coffee rooms, interrupted their meals, button-holed them in corridors, filled them with words about the need for a new newspaper, new books and publications to replace the old Welsh *Voice* press killed by fire and God knows whose pressure in distant Wales.

We assembled around us a support group of some of the more astute information men in the Arab world. One meeting led to another. William and I carried with us only the hope that we could still keep those Welsh presses rolling and that our dear old *Voice* would not have been sacrificed in vain. We were on a crusade.

At 2.30 in the afternoon a week later, the final meeting of the information conference was over. I stood in the hall of the Arab League, that great marble and sandstone monument to Arab aspirations, as the delegates left, shaking hands. 'Shukran, thanks for your support,' I said, using one of my few words of Arabic. 'Shukran gezeelan to you,' they chorused. 'Afwan. Afwan.' 'Don't mention it.'

At that time I met men who were to be friends for life. Among them was Dr Ali Khushaim. I had caught Ali Khushaim's eye and he invited me to the Hilton Hotel in Cairo for tea. I observed a man of about 5 foot 6 inches in height, wearing a light twill jacket immaculately pressed. He was the very epitome of an Arab gentleman. Aged then about 35, he had a doctorate in philosophy from Durham University. He knew England and English well having lived in Durham with his young wife throughout the years of gaining his PhD.

Ali was acting Minister of Information for Libya – a wise choice of Colonel Gaddafi's, for he had already written a number of books. His works on the philosophy of languages were outstanding, rivalling those he had written on the history of Libya. We chatted eagerly and happily. His humour was infectious. It was to me a fresh climate of intellectualism. Our talks have now covered well over twenty years. Each passing year has been a milestone. I owe all my knowledge of Arab literature to this remarkable man, rightly regarded as a giant in his own land and an expert on the Sufi.

At the time that we met he was fascinated by my thought that I must give my life to the Arab world. I shared with him my almost impossible ideal of socialism, that one should always put the other fellows first. He explained to me that this was also Gaddafi's high ideal of socialism. There was no doubt in his mind, though there may have been in mine.

He soon handed over his duties in the Ministry of Information to the enterprising Abu Zaid Durda and he himself became Minister of State for Libya in Cairo at the time when these states were trying to create a union. Like many of my Arab friends, he was a frequent visitor to London.

We shared one thing – a belief in God. And all that followed, come ups and downs, was part of that unshakeable faith.

– 3 –

William and I went off to Cairo International Airport full of confidence. What could go wrong? 'Nothing,' I told William. 'We've gained the backing of new friends.' The ministers and under-secretaries of the Arab states had finally made solemn promises to help by suggesting that the biggest industrial companies in their countries support the new paper. If we all stuck together a new era would open for the chaps in Wales. We would have another paper to replace the old *Voice* which we would print alongside *Middle East International.*

Now, armed with a round-trip ticket from Cairo to Baghdad, down the Gulf to Muscat and all points en route, William and I set off again. In my pocket was a letter addressed to every Minister of Information we were to visit, asking support for the new *Voice* as per the unanimous resolution of the Cairo meeting, plus scores of advertising and editorial contacts. What could go wrong?

– 6 –
Unforgettable Friends

– 1 –

William and I were in the middle of nowhere. We were in the desert, one hundred miles inland from Abu Dhabi in the United Arab Emirates. We had a rendezvous with Sheikh Zayed.

The meeting, which had been arranged by the Minister of Information, Sheikh Ahmed bin Hamed, was to prove the most significant of all the meetings that my son and I had that spring. It came towards the end of our long trip down the Gulf. We had already visited Baghdad, Kuwait, Bahrain and Qatar and had received promises of £160,000 in advertising and subscriptions for the new paper and for *Middle East International*. All seemed set fair. Now, in the final days, we were to meet the legendary Zayed.

Suddenly, after two hours' driving across the undulating desert, we came across a big black Mercedes. Zayed was at the wheel. Four of his children were in the back. He had parked his car strategically half a mile from the starting point of what was to be the greatest camel race of the season.

With a yell like Bronco Bill our own driver announced that the camels were coming. We looked behind us. There, coming up fast, was a long line of Hejin racing camels, long of limb and graceful of neck, a beast that easily outruns a horse over a distance. Spreading out on either side of the camels like a vast fan were at least twenty trucks and cars, menacing, roaring and full of screaming, shouting Bedouins. Our driver, to escape the irresistible tidal wave of camel and mechanised menace, got into top gear. We now raced ahead with Sheikh Zayed's Mercedes pounding alongside us across the desert. We were like two charioteers chased by this fantastic Arab Grand National. Through the rear window we could see the camels, licking along at

35 to 40 kilometres an hour. Their front legs were going like great pistons. They pitched like ships. The boy jockeys clung to the wooden saddle frames. At one point I shouted to our driver, 'Can we do it?' 'Insha-Allah' (God willing), he screamed back.

At that precise moment our vehicle leapt three feet in the air as we bounced over a hillock that must have been our Beecher's Brook. With screams of demoniac laughter from the driver and his mate who shared the front seat, the front wheels suddenly pointed skywards again. My stomach was left three dunes behind. It was bump, bump. Woo-oosh! Sometimes we hit the sky. The driver shouted and laughed with a glorious sense of happy irresponsibility. His foot was flat on the accelerator, regardless of terrain. I nervously eyed the speedometer and found we were clocking 70 kilometres per hour – which in this desert is like doing 500 on Daytona beach.

Suddenly we stopped. By brilliant driving we were well ahead of the race, and were drawn up at what was clearly the finishing post. Sheikh Zayed's Mercedes came roaring in. Then the camels, their movements blended together now. The first three arrived. I saw they were ridden by little boys of not more than eight. Pint-size Lester Piggotts, all sweating, dishevelled and desperate, clinging firmly to their seats at the back of the humps. No saddles here. Their faces were shining with broad smiles in the unforgettable way of Mickey Rooney in old-time movies – a triumphant look worn by a kid who has chased a king across the desert, who knows that he, the rider, is the 'greatest'.

The big slender beasts were specially belted beneath the belly. Fed, trained and groomed to the nth degree, they hardly showed the strain of the race.

Sheikh Zayed got out of his Mercedes and walked to a tent that had been erected not far from the finishing post. It was big and looked cool. As he turned to sit near its entrance he saw William and I coming towards him across the sand. He beckoned us to sit with him. With words of welcome he offered us coffee and the three of us settled down with his men and supporters around. Saif Ghobash, a trusted friend of Zayed's who in time became a true friend of mine, as well as Minister of State at the UAE Foreign Ministry, acted as interpreter. We were about to watch desert democracy at its best.

A wizened old man followed by a turbanned boy came up to Zayed. The old man put his nose to the ruler's nose, gently. The old man passed to me. I shook his hand. As I took hold of him in a firm grip he pushed out his chest against his bandoleer. The silver-handled dagger in his sheath-belt poked into my stomach. With a slow, dignified smile he passed on to William. In the background Sheikh Zayed's troops were watching. Three or four stood there, guns in black holsters, hawk insignia on their head-dress.

Next came a Bedouin with a thick envelope, which he showed to Sheikh Zayed. The ruler nodded. The Bedouin, with a flick of the wrist, poured the contents of the envelope on the sand in front of us – thousands of green dinar notes, in bundles. Now the guardians of the boys who had ridden the first three camels approached. They sat, squatting on their haunches, looking at the greenbacks, occasionally flashing quick, proud glances to the Sheikh. At a signal the three boys appeared. Sheikh Zayed walked forward and sat on the sand with them. I was beckoned to follow. I asked how much the prizes were and was told the first camel, 1,000 Bahraini dinars (£1,100 sterling), the second camel, 600 dinars, and the third camel, 500 dinars.

As we were sitting there in the desert dust, almost encompassed in it, someone came up with Pepsi-Cola and lemon drinks. Sheikh Zayed took his Pepsi and nodded gravely. I took mine. Then William. Then the three guardians and the prize-winners. Sitting there, smothered in dust, a cool drink at his side, Sheikh Zayed began talking quietly to each and all of us, preserving his foothold in the minds of people by an act of grace, of democracy, which was a rare sight. There was no one here to see him. He was not on show. This was no state 'occasion'. A camaraderie developed among us all, an acceptance of one another which soon had little to do with tribe or place, East or West.

'Let us have your son,' laughed Zayed. 'He'll make a good camel rider.' He spoke through his interpreter.

I laughed back, 'How much?'

William shouted in my direction, 'Be careful, he means it!'

It was my first chance to study Zayed. I remember the comfortably sandalled feet, his loose robe surmounted by a strong pillar of a neck, the black beard with the moustache filling the upper lip. The charisma of the man was like an electric charge. The lean, bronzed, weather-beaten face, spare and muscle-hard, was dominated by the eyes which focused hard and strong into mine whenever he looked my way, and then held on target so that we were giving each other a penetrating eye-fix, a mark of contact, an assessment customary in this desert. He looked powerful and agile, with the glowing, burnished health of a man in his prime. Neither time nor despair had ravaged him, and it seemed that they never would. His hand as he held it out was rough and strong, surprisingly thick and knobbly, the hand of a man who has dug in sand, shifted his own rocks, caught his own game, planted for himself where he had to and squeezed his own triggers. A man of the soil as well as a great hunter, I had been told. It all fitted.

The occasion was more social than business, but I managed to tell him about our new paper. 'The *Voice*, eh?' he said. 'I hope it's not the Voice of the West!'

We talked of philosophy, religion and life in the West. What do you think of the Arab states you have visited – Kuwait, for example, he asked? Do you suppose we shall all go the same way? What is the future for our children here?

Finally, at sundown we left. He was ready for prayers. He had given us the assurance of his country's support.

We drove away across the desert, back to a meeting with Sheikh Ahmed bin Hamed, Zayed's Minister of Information.

Years later I was to say to Sheikh Ahmed, 'We began as friends.' Ahmed was to reply, 'Yes, we began as friends but we ended as family.' Neither William nor I knew it then, but links each side made with the other at that time were to be strong enough in the years ahead to remain unbroken. Four of Sheikh Ahmed's sons were to spend their summers with us in Vincent Square. My children would grow up with his. The vicissitudes of Western and Middle Eastern economics and politics never affected that friendship up to the present day.

– **2** –

William returned direct to London, but I decided on a stop-over in Lebanon and took an MEA flight to Beirut, booking into the Vendôme Hotel. My plan was to contact an Egyptian journalist whom I had met, a wiry, black-haired writer with a distinctly anxious face called Jelal Keshk. He worked for the famous Arab picture magazine *Al Hawadess*. Having heard of my attempts to win support for a Western pro-Arab press, Jelal had arranged a picture spread in *Hawadess*.

Martin Buckmaster[1] who was at the time Information Head at the British Embassy in Beirut, came to my room at the Vendôme just as I was ending a photo session with the *Hawadess* cameraman. An intelligent, kindly Catholic, Buckmaster had an encyclopedic knowledge of the Middle East. He offered his help in promoting *Middle East International* and *Voice*.

I called on Hasseb Sabbagh.[2] He ran a large outfit in Beirut called the Consolidated Construction Company, and was known as a businessman who helped in Palestinian affairs. His financial tentacles extended throughout Lebanese banking and industry, as well as the Gulf. I spoke to him about my new paper, and also told him that *Middle East International* needed help fast or it would close. As I had agreed to split the profits of my new weekly, the more funding I could get for *MEI* the lighter my own burden would prove. 'Unless someone helps *Middle East International* it can't hold out,' I told him. 'There's no money unless people like you come forward.'

When Jelal's *Al Hawadess* article appeared I sent a copy to Hasseb Sabbagh, punching out a letter on the stationery of the Vendôme Hotel to emphasise the urgency of the position. Jelal had concluded his plea for the salvation of *Middle East International* with the words: 'Oh, Arabs, shame on you Arabs!' I felt the cause of the two papers had been driven home to the financially formidable Mr Sabbagh.

- 7 -
THE HORNETS' NEST

- 1 -

Arriving back in London, I gave an optimistic report regarding the new *Voice* to Ahmed Anis adding some very positive sounding figures. And since under the John Reddaway plan *Middle East International* was to share in the profits, the future for both publications seemed bright.

'Great,' said Ahmed. 'I'll spread the word around.'

It was a fatal idea.

That week the amiable Michael Rice, then Public Relations Consultant to the Arab League in Britain, called. Michael was also PR consultant to the state of Bahrain. He employed some ex-diplomats, and his links with the Foreign Office gave him considerable influence abroad.

Michael said that there was a lot of talk about my success in selling the new weekly in the Arab world. Ahmed Anis had been talking. A few people with existing publications were more than a little concerned that I might overshadow them.

'Who's concerned?' I asked.

The cautious voice of Michael continued. Apparently he'd had approaches. John Reddaway of CAABU was one and there were others. Elizabeth Collard of *Middle East Economic Digest* (*MEED*) was furious. She made protests to ambassadors all over London asking them to write to their home governments to hold up support for my own publishing activities until they had the opportunity of considering the needs of others who had been longer in the field. All to some degree were getting subscriptions for copies from Arab embassies and contacts, or appealed to Arabs for funds and support.

Michael had visited the Arab world and confirmed in a follow-up talk later, 'I think that a certain amount of "knocking" has gone on . . .'

I asked Michael whether any action was proposed. He answered that he'd been asked by one or two to compose a letter to the Secretary General of the Arab League expressing the hope that my success would not be allowed to affect the future of other pro-Arab publications in Britain. The Secretary General was to be asked to come to London and guarantee help for other publications.

'What about us?' I asked.

'Oh, there's no mention of you,' said Michael. The person who had started the drive for an Arab press was now forgotten. The tens of thousands of pounds of advertising painfully collected were set aside.

I then heard from Mayhew who asked me to dinner at the House of Commons. I showed him the first advance page proofs of the new *Voice*. He was clearly expecting a paper that confined itself to commercial and tourist affairs, rather than delving to any extent in politics. 'Look,' he said, pointing to a front-page item. 'That's far too political!' I said it was impossible to produce a regular weekly paper and avoid reporting politics entirely. 'I object to anything political,' he argued.

'Do you think that you and you alone control or influence whatever people in Britain might read about the Arabs?' I asked testily. 'If you say stop, does the Anglo-Arab world grind to a halt? Do you really think no one can do anything for the Arabs without your say-so?'

The angular English face bent crane-like across at me. He was perfectly serious. 'I do,' he said quietly.

I rapped the table in anger.

'You have the gall to tell me no one except you should influence policy, not only on the magazine I started for you, but on my new newspaper and everything else published in the UK about the Arabs. Don't you realise I rely on publishing for my livelihood?' I was furious. 'I've been carrying your debt on my back for months. Without that credit you could not publish *Middle East International* at all. You warn me off buying *Middle East Economic Digest* at a reasonable price with dire predictions of the consequences. You won't allow me to originate a line in *Middle East International*. I've played along. Now you poke your fingers into the rest of my business!'

Mayhew looked around with alarm at the danger of a scene. Afterwards when we walked out into the central lobby I half-apologised. I had been unbearably rude, whatever my case. I had eaten the man's dinner, drunk his wine, welcomed his contacts, and embraced his cause.

'I hope you understand,' I said as we proceeded towards St Stephen's lobby.

'I understand perfectly,' Mayhew replied. He stood there in the outer lobby, tall, distinguished in a grey suit, lips drawn in a tight line, unsmiling. 'I think you've made yourself perfectly clear.'

'I'm getting to be a cantankerous old bastard,' I told Pat the next day and phoned Mayhew my regrets, following up with a note of apology for losing my temper, which he accepted easily enough, it seemed. But the truth as I saw it had been laid on the table.

– 2 –

In the weeks following there was a sudden unexplained silence on the Arab scene. My team in Wales started producing the new *Voice* in June 1972, but it was as though a giant switch had been turned off concerning our contacts with Arab capitals. In desperation William and I sallied forth again.

In Kuwait, Sa'dun Al Jasim, Under-Secretary at the Ministry of Information, looked at me with weary eyes. He was a man who had become a sympathetic friend and would remain so. Now he was like a man who had pledged his troth only to be told his new love was flawed. 'We've been instructed by our Foreign Ministry not to support you.' The message had come through Kuwait's Cairo Embassy where the Ambassador was reputed to be a close friend of Elizabeth Collard. It was like the verdict of God.

Then an odd article popped up in the *Arab Times*, intimating that an unnamed 'fortune hunter' was touring the area promoting the Arab cause for cash. A similar piece describing my sycophantic ways of influencing people appeared in the *Gulf Mirror* in Bahrain. To my amazement it coupled my name with that of Margaret McKay, the former Labour MP and enthusiastic pro-Arab, about whom at the time I knew nothing. I complained to Ahmed Jeralah, editor-in-chief of the Kuwait English daily *Arab Times* and *Dar Al-Seyassah*, its Arab-language twin. He discovered the offending piece in his paper had been planted by an English journalist then in his employ.

I was being haphazardly tarred and feathered. Someone, somewhere was enthusiastically poisoning my reputation in the Arab world.

Back at the Kuwait Sheraton I wrote Mayhew telling him what was happening despite our agreement that the two publications could run in tandem. Someone had thrown a spanner in the works.

We flew down to Muscat to see Nasser Saif Al Bualy,[1] then Director of Information. Diving into Muscat was a nightmare. We came in from the Indian Ocean. Suddenly a gap opened up in the jagged, brown stone cliff. The wing tip of our tiny Fokker seemed almost to scrape the surface of the mountain rock as we flew in at slightly above stalling speed. Then after a breathtaking five minutes the Fokker touched down.

The aerodrome, if it could be called that, consisted of an empty sandy floor with a couple of wooden huts with galvanised heat boxes, old-fashioned air coolers, pumping air in, fighting against all odds to withstand the excessive heat.

When we saw Nasser Saif, he said, 'I'm sorry. His Majesty the Sultan has had an approach from the British Foreign Office suggesting a famous name handle the work I intended for you. Michael Rice. There's nothing I can do.' He was most upset. Out of the window went a large order for subscriptions and consultancy services for my small press. Apparently a Foreign Office nominee, in this case Michael Rice and Company, was to get any publishing or other work available in Oman. An engaging Anglo-Arab called James Belgrave,[2] a partner of Michael's whom I had met on my tour, was already hot-footing it to Muscat. He was the influential son of the former British Resident in Bahrain. In spite of our losing the contract, James and his wife were to be kinder to me than I can say.

While in Muscat, William took a walk in Mutrah and stayed out for about two hours. He climbed up to one of the forts in the noonday sun. Mad dogs and Englishmen. When he came back he was sweating. Coming into the cool hotel, he fainted. He was shivering with cold and sweating with heat alternately. I kept him in bed for a day and then, no medical advice being readily available in Oman at that time, we caught the tiny Fokker up to Bahrain, a flight of about two hours.

William refused to go into hospital there, but Mrs James Belgrave took over. With a practical loving hand she nursed William for days without stint, a fact for which his father and mother are forever grateful. You would not have thought that Michael and James were competitors of ours. When William returned to London his eyes were as yellow as a canary and we put him to bed with jaundice, a side effect of the virus attack comparable to meningitis that he had had on the Gulf. He recovered within days.

After putting William on the plane to London, I went to Cairo where Bahi Nasr told me, 'Mohamed Riad (Secretary General of the Arab League) has got a red light from London. The lobby there describes you as some sort of over-successful business monster to be curbed.' He laughed. 'They want a big share of your loot. What the hell's happened? We were all set for a big advance for both *Middle East International* and the *Voice*.'

Whoever or whatever it was, I was not to be allowed to succeed.

– 3 –

I was beginning to feel the need for a little 'inside' counselling. Journalists wherever they are on this globe are a unique old boys' network and as long as you're not working on the same story, are great swappers of information.

At No. 2, Courtfield Gardens in South Kensington lived Colin Jackson, a fellow journalist who had already been helpful with *Voice* as well as *Middle East International*. Colin had been admitted to Lincoln's Inn after leaving Oxford. He won Brighouse and Spenborough for Labour and became chairman of the Parliamentary Labour Party Foreign Affairs group. He had a flushed, choleric appearance, and a basilisk stare which could freeze hostile advances. And he enjoyed a drop of Scotch. He was a ready enemy of tradition and of Whitehall or Westminster cliques and was a man after my own heart. At the time deputy-chairman of CAABU, he frequently leaked stories from CAABU's inner councils.

'Your latest headaches,' pronounced Colin after the second scotch. 'Well, you might blame the Zionists. On the other hand, God knows, it's bizarre enough to put your troubles down to someone being told to upset you. Maybe it's CAABU – John Reddaway. They are all dependent on John to do their homework. Or maybe Christopher Mayhew's IRD is partly to blame.'

'What's IRD?' I'd never heard of that one.

'Don't you know?'

'Not a whisper.'

'IRD – Information and Research. It's a special department down on Vauxhall Bridge Road. Concerned with disinformation. Keeping in touch with the Middle East press. It's supposed to combat Soviet media infiltration in the area. Quite a few journalists work for it. I do occasionally. It has involved various foreign affairs and study groups. Not all know – in fact few do – where any strings are pulled. They like to control UK Arab information links. They feed things into the system – to MPs, to news agencies, to opinion formers. Clever stuff. Some of them don't love you, brother. I heard that. They hope you'll fade away never to be heard of again.' He laughed.

Colin rambled on, slightly incoherently. 'They also have a good line in smearing colonial revolutionaries who might be tilting towards Moscow.'

I thought back to Sultan Ali Abdul Karim, my introducer to the Arab world, chucked out of his homeland.

'You approve of this – of IRD?'

'It's done some good work. They have some excellent people. Unfortunately, they have Caesar's disease.'

'What's that?'

'Caesar didn't know when to stop.'

A few days later I ran into Tom Little. We hadn't seen each other for some time as Tom had resigned from *Middle East International*. He said it was in order to do more writing.

'You know anything about IRD?' I asked him.

Tom smiled. 'Yes. I knew it in Egypt. In effect, it ran the Arab news agency which I founded.'

The Arab news agency had operated a network that stretched to Baghdad, Damascus, Beirut, Jerusalem and Amman. It had been subscribed to by about every Arab paper that existed.

'Could you tell me something about it?'

'Oh, I was only a cog in the wheel,' said Tom modestly. 'You should ask Christopher Mayhew. It's more Chris's line,' he added cautiously.

That was as much as he'd say. More in Christopher's line? I was beginning to feel like a fly caught in a web that went on and on. Was there no way out? Then Colin's words came back to me: 'Some of them don't love you, brother . . . they hope you'll fade away never to be heard of again.'

Why? What had I done?

One thing was certain. I had no intention of fading away.

– 8 –
ABANDONED

– 1 –

The next chapter opened with a letter from Mayhew, who was on holiday in Cornwall. He wrote that he had met an Arab who 'preferred to remain anonymous' but who had offered £5,000 immediately and more to follow to support the ailing *Middle East International*.

After protest from myself and Tony Nutting the anonymous supporter was eventually revealed as Hasseb Sabbagh, the tycoon whom I myself had seen in Beirut.

Christopher Mayhew concluded with the, to me, surprising words that if finance was now available he seriously doubted that printing and publishing could be split between London and South Wales. In other words, now that they had the promise of money they would end the printing set-up that had given them birth and that had stood by during hard times. It was to me an incredible suggestion.

But he ended his letter, reassuringly enough, with the words: 'Whatever we decide we must all maintain a friendly and helpful attitude to both *Voice* and *Middle East International* – otherwise both will go under.'

The weeks passed. The next board meeting of *Middle East International* was held as usual at our Westminster home. After we had swallowed a preliminary cup of coffee, and had a discussion about Sabbagh's contribution, Mayhew said in his usually crisp intonation, 'If more cash comes consideration will now have to be given to printing the magazine somewhere else, for central convenience, away from Wales.'

I answered that the people down there in my plant in Wales were doing their best. 'We've not had a penny from *Middle East International* for four months or more,' I said. 'It has to be produced in down time.

We're doing it at a fraction of the price of printers elsewhere, plus providing offices and all services. What do you expect?' I was furious at the slightest suggestion that the printing work be removed.

Tony Nutting interjected. 'It would be unthinkable to print the magazine away from the Welsh works,' he said, 'Claud started it and maintained it.' I felt reassured and grateful to Tony. With his 10 per cent vote on my side nothing could happen. If 50 per cent wanted to move the printing 50 per cent would now oppose it.

John Reddaway and Christopher Mayhew made no further comment. The rest of the meeting struck me as being as humourless as a vicar's tea-party. However, reading the silence as agreement, I thought the matter disposed of. To take the work away from the printing works that had originated the idea and financially backed the project was a notion so incredible to me that I felt it was a kind of joke.

As they filed out John Wells, the *Middle East International* auditor who had joined the meeting, turned to me. 'They still want their fun at your expense,' he observed. I realised he was right. To them it was all a game. Outside the door he said quietly, 'They're railroading you. But it's Reddaway you have to watch. He's your real problem.'

– 2 –

All went quiet. It would be a disaster if two of the little group I had been instrumental in bringing together gave the Welsh works the sack. Morale everywhere would collapse.

Forgetting the matter, I now designed a brochure for presentation to the Arab League and to Mohamed Riad, its Secretary General who, apparently at the suggestion of the Beirut millionaire Hasseb Sabbagh, plus numerous appeals from London, was now to organise fresh support for *Middle East International*. Also involved in fresh support were to be the governments of the UAE and Kuwait.

The intermediary in much of this was Basl Akl. Out of curiosity and self-interest I invited him to lunch at the Hyde Park Hotel. Basl was a Palestinian unofficially running the PLO in London while the Foreign Office 'looked the other way'. He told me that he had run into Hasseb Sabbagh and Hasseb had mentioned *Middle East International*. Hasseb knew that Basl, as a politician, was in turn currently devoting his attention to those whom he felt could exert political leverage, particularly Christopher Mayhew. 'Of course, I might have contacted you as publisher when I found Hasseb willing to put up money. But that was difficult.'

'Why?'

'Because of the stories being put about over the past couple of months that you were quarrelling with the powers that be and that you were even thought of badly by certain people who have been repeating gossip about you. These stories went out to Cairo, Kuwait, everywhere. What was anyone to do?'

I lamely dismissed what he said, although all the facts pointed to it being true. I was being chastised for being too successful operating on my own. The message was obvious. Play with us or don't play. One person was being set against another, the old intelligence game of raising suspicion. My new *Voice* which would replace the old *South Wales Voice* was anathema.

– 3 –

Tony Nutting did not show up for the next board meeting. John Wells, our accountant, was also absent. I was faced with Mayhew and Reddaway. Fifty per cent of the votes against my forty.

Mayhew announced that through fresh efforts he had obtained a donation from the Kuwait ambassador for £20,000. A further amount was in the pipeline, money supplied by Abu Dhabi and cycled through the Arab League. The paper was now as good as saved.

Then came the body blow. 'I still think now that our future is assured we should print *Middle East International* more conveniently, away from Wales,' said Mayhew. I realised to my astonishment that there had been no change of heart.

'With whom?' I asked.

'John has got a quotation,' said Mayhew.

It was amazingly enough from Elizabeth Collard and *Middle East Economic Digest*.

I couldn't believe it. Unknown to me as publisher, it appeared that John Reddaway, following receipt of new money, had as a director gone out to search for a printer to replace me. I cursed the air and the world in general.

'But for the workers in that Welsh plant, neither of you would be sitting around this table!'

They were silent, waiting for the anger to run out. No one said anything. They made not the slightest move nor expressed a single opinion. Mayhew fingered his pencil, head down. Reddaway eyed the ceiling. They were without emotion or reaction. I don't believe Christopher quite realised what the loss of the contract meant to our works.

A day later Elizabeth Collard, who was now to typeset the paper, rang me. 'I wanted to let you know I had nothing to do with this. John Reddaway contacted me, asked for figures if I was to take over the work from you. He said it was all most private, to be done without your knowing. I'm most embarrassed.'

I wrote Christopher a letter on 5th September with all the facts of the situation in Wales and tried to persuade him to withdraw. At the very least, I wanted him to know what he and Reddaway together were about to do. I concluded:

> I am sending a copy of this letter to John and Tony. Incidentally, I think Tony should be present at any Board meeting making decisions as to the future. He was good enough to say at the last meeting that he felt it would not be right to continue *Middle East International* without my company's printing aid.

Tony Nutting was the first to ring. I reminded him of his remarks at the earlier meeting supporting the Welsh plant. He said 'Since the magazine seems to be so much in Christopher's hands and the ANAF Foundation people now, and they want production in London, I'm afraid I've no option but to agree with him. It's Chris Mayhew's show now,' he remarked cheerfully. I said nothing. The man who to me represented 'my side' of the 50–50 arrangements had switched. He had changed his mind.

The Welsh interests had been floored. The three *Middle East International* directors were now no more in my world than Banquo's ghosts. There was to be no reply to my letter of 5th September. At further meetings, there was no comment. Questions were avoided. As far as they were concerned, the matter was finished.

When the money finally came in there was a celebratory lunch of *Middle East International* directors held at Locket's[1] restaurant on the ground floor of Marsham Court in Marsham Street, Westminster, to praise the attitude of the Palestinian millionaire and others, in promising backing for the journal.

I was foolish and went along. My wife, Pat, said I was too forgiving.

It was all a bit of an Irish wake. I could think of little to say. My companions were gossiping with the cheerful but artificial benevolence of a trio whose company was suddenly a sure-fire success. I stared rather mechanically at the red candles on the table, the blue irises in little glass vases, the ancient prints of medieval battles on the walls, hating them, hating myself more, my mistakes, my predicament.

The waiter dropped ice in my glass and a very large measure of whisky. 'Come again,' I muttered in a few minutes. I took four doubles in succession to keep an even keel. My mind was obsessed with the boys back in Wales who would now lose the particular *Middle East International* printing work we had been through hell and the loss of two local papers and several printing contracts to defend. Well, I thought, too late now. An unforgiving inner voice told me I had laid on the altar an entire Welsh press. I had not even the satisfaction of getting any money out of it.

One strange by-product of the affair was my application for membership of the Council for the Advancement of Arab-British Understanding (CAABU). John Reddaway, through whose hands the application had to go, replied time after time that the matter was in 'processing'. It stayed in 'processing' until after his retirement. Indeed, as far as I know it's still 'processing' twenty-five years later.

– 9 –
THE CRASH

– 1 –

At 10.00 p.m. on the day after the loss of *Middle East International* printing had been finally confirmed and I had resigned as publisher, the phone rang. It was Dennis.

'I was told you were in trouble, *Middle East International's* been taken away from you.'

I was flabbergasted. How could a meeting at which I lost the printing and surrendered the publishing be signalled within hours to Dennis Lyons?

'Who told you?'

'Burton's PR Department. The management of *Burton Contact*, the newspaper you print for Burtons, were approached. Burtons have got the message that your Welsh business is crumbling. You could go to the wall. They were also told your pro-Arabs had deserted you and you might soon be bankrupt. It was neatly suggested they should quit your sinking ship and remove their own paper as well.' He laughed. 'It's a hell of a story to go to sleep on. But I thought I'd let you know that some buggers are after your hide.' Burtons was one of the many companies we printed for.

'What can I do?'

'I'll ring Ladislas Rice for you, or Richard Stokes or Clifford Jupp.[1] Whoever's available,' said Dennis.

The only thing I could think of was that a few hours after I had been sacked, 10 Downing Street's PR office had been privy to the close secret that I was no longer wanted.

The next night it was Pat who received an unexpected call. It was from Margaret Williams, wife of an old friend, George Williams, a workers' director of the British Steel Corporation, of Port Talbot, for whom we printed *Steel News*.

'I'm sorry to break bad news, but George was at a meeting of British Steel today, and they decided to centralise the Welsh edition of *Steel News*. He couldn't do anything about it.'

'It was our biggest job – our finest contract,' I reminded Pat when she broke the news to me. 'It's the underpinning, the bread and butter. Good God, we haven't had a hitch with British Steel in years. What's wrong?'

I rang Dennis again.

'Could you find a way of approaching Monty Finniston?'[2]

Dennis chuckled. 'Don't jump to conclusions about the Zionist lobby.'

'Who then?'

'It could simply be coincidental.'

I then found that Christopher had decided that all large subscriptions for *Middle East International* would in future be channelled through the ANAF Foundation in Zug, Switzerland. This meant that all power now rested not with the *Middle East International* board but with the ANAF board with Christopher as chairman. The journal was now in effect controlled by a Swiss foundation.

Four days later a new blow came from the bank. My current arrangements were that we would not exceed agreed overdraft limits, while waiting for our business to recover its old vigour and revenue to appear from the new Arab *Voice*. These arrangements were meticulously kept.

I had been in financial holes before but knew how to dig my way out with the help of a co-operative bank manager. I regularly paid in amounts to meet plant wages. I watched cash flow intently. And I knew that despite recent blows which had led to big cuts in staff, we could, in the end, survive. On the Wednesday, half-way through what can conservatively be described as a traumatic week, I paid in funds earmarked to more than cover wages for the printing staff in Wales.

On the Thursday morning I telephoned the bank. 'I'm sending around my clerk in Wales to the local branch to collect the wages.' The manager's clerk coughed apologetically. 'I'm sorry. We've just had a message from our main board. We have to withdraw *all* your facilities. We've been unable to transfer funds to Swansea to pay your firm's wages.'

'What?'

'Withdraw all facilities,' he repeated mechanically.

'Your company's loans are recalled immediately. Everything.'

'But I only just paid credits in to more than meet wages. You can't pull the rug from underneath me like that!'

'Sorry. Any future cheques will not be honoured.'

'Can I speak to the Manager?'

'The Manager's on holiday this week. He's taken an unexpected break. Sorry.'

It was a Kafka-esque nightmare.

'Surely these sort of things are normally discussed?'

'It's the main bank board, I am afraid. Quite impersonal. I wasn't expecting anything like this when we accepted your London payment in to meet your Swansea wages. Nobody was. Nobody here could have advised or warned you. Not even the manager. The board met this morning. After the meeting the branch was told to contact you.'

'I can't understand it.'

'It's just the luck of the draw. I know the relationship you've had here. I should warn you, though, you'll be getting a demand that you pay your guarantees. They'll no doubt give you a chance to see them and discuss how you go about it. It's come from much higher up than this branch.'

I wrote a detailed three-page letter to the bank's chairman at his home in Surrey. He was a man with a sympathetic interest in the developing world and the Arab world's affairs. Ironically, too, the bank, on the recommendation of their public relations adviser had recently invited me to plan and publish a new paper for employees. The chairman himself was soon to receive a title for his support for the under-privileged. However, his undoubted talents did not on this occasion include the rapid acknowledgement of personal letters. There was no reply.

– 2 –

Manuela Sykes came round to Vincent Square. I told her my tale.

'Look,' said Manuela, 'why not try one of the big Middle East banks to take over your account? After all, you have securities.'

'Of course. Buildings, machinery. But I don't know any Arab bankers.'

'I'll have a word with a friend. An executive in the Kuwait bank. I'll pass him your number.'

The following day the banker rang from the city branch of a Kuwait bank and invited me around. He was a Palestinian.

'I don't think I can put up your case here,' he said, having patiently heard me out. 'Although ours are Arab funds they're in the hands of English managers. I'm only a cipher myself, if I may put it that way. If your case is handed to these money managers they'll consider the fact that you printed political papers like *Free Palestine* and *Middle East International*. And you now publish *Voice*. Our funds in Britain are loaned to British institutions and businesses. There would be something wrong in their view if our bank took over your account. In fact, the board here are not really friendly to Arab politics of this sort. You've been too pro-Palestinian, and although I'm one we're not popular. I'll be frank.' He waved his hands apologetically. 'They would sink through Threadneedle Street if asked to lend to someone with the kind of pro-Arab record you now possess.'

'But I have the plant, the building. Collateral. I'm not simply a political case. It's true that my present bank holds these securities, but they can be transferred. I'm a publisher – a businessman. What's the use of Arab banking if it can't once in a while back what everyone thinks is the Arab cause?'

'Well, I'll put it up. However, I can tell you what the answer will be.'

It was useless. I thanked him and walked into St Paul's Cathedral nearby and sat there trying to erase from my mind the deep trenches of international finances – whether Christian, Muslim, Jew or Hindu.

Tony Berry now suggested that I might get some financial advice from Leopold Joseph's.

'I heard they were throwing rocks at you,' said Louis Heymann. He had helped when Tony and I had planned the purchase of the London *Times* and was one of the City's acutest financial brains. 'You've upset some tough ones.' The City of London grapevine is quick and abnormally accurate.

'Who's throwing the rocks?'

Louis smiled across the polished mahogany table in the Joseph board room with its immaculately positioned pads of notepaper in front of each chair. He shook his head. 'No comment. No comment at all. I don't think I can recommend anyone else to pick up the tabs, either. Somebody up there doesn't love you. You've been dropped in it. You put yourself on the side of unpopular people. But it's your battlefield. You chose it.'

I appealed again to Ahmed Anis, the Arab League director who originally encouraged the publication of the new *Voice* as a British alternative to the *Jewish Chronicle*.

'It's my last chance. Our firm may now go to the wall.'

'Submit a memorandum. I will put it up to the meeting of the Arab ambassadors in London, all twenty-one of them,' he said.

'A commitment of a few thousand each – subscriptions or orders for work – could see us around the corner,' I said.

William, Pat and I got down to preparing the memorandum with background material.

After the ambassadors' meeting, I rang Ahmed. 'They all praised your work for the Arabs,' he said cautiously. 'Everyone spoke highly of you. You have the name of being their great friend. You are producing a good paper. You do so much.'

'Yes, but what was the outcome?'

'Ah,' said Ahmed. 'While they appreciate all you do, the ambassadors have received messages from CAABU that when you started out you said you would use commercial means to support your paper, advertising and that sort of thing. That meant you would be independent.'

'What are you trying to tell me?'

'Well, my friend, they decided they couldn't assist you. That you were all right.'

'But all those promises!'

– 3 –

When I next visited my bank I told a new manager that all I wanted was to come to an arrangement whereby I freed my securities and repaid every penny of the overdraft created by the *Middle East International* débâcle and all its surrounding consequences. I was on my own, broken but not down. No more arguments.

'But you will have to give me time,' I added questioningly.

'We never had the slightest doubt you would repay. We knew your word was always good.'

'I will use any money my company might yet earn from the Arab world to repay our other creditors first, not the bank itself. So far as the bank is concerned, I'll have to handle repayment of the overdraft on a long-term basis out of personal work and my private pocket, as best as I am able.'

'How?'

'By consulting work. Any means. I'll have to work for Arabs. Ironically, my independence has been partly destroyed. Most of my English clients have left. I might have to write books or pamphlets. I've been knocked down. You know, I'm beginning to get paranoid about it.'

'What do you mean?'

'I don't know. It might be commercial rivalry or politics. Anything. I feel somebody or something wants to destroy all links between influential Arabs and myself. It seems to me there have been remarkably successful attacks on us from a dozen angles.'

A white shaft of winter sunlight came in through the window behind him. He looked surprised, his eyes suddenly focusing up to mine like rifles at close range. He sat back in his chair, pushed the papers on his desk aside, and took what seemed to me to be an offended gasp at the surrounding air space. He remained silent.

'I'm not suggesting it's you,' I said. 'Your Head Office. Some director. Some major customers. Some government outfit with influence over banks. Why doesn't your chairman reply to my letters?'

'Look, I'll show you the names of our directors. All solid English country names,' he said.

I started to smile, thinking of his definition of respectability.

He began to fumble in his desk drawer. However, he was saved any concern about the path of future discussion by saying, 'Sorry, I don't happen to have the list of directors here, but all English names, I assure you.' The phone rang on his desk at this moment. He lifted it, then pressed a button. 'Please hold all calls,' he said. 'Everything. Please!'

He dropped his eyes and then closed the file in front of him. Utterly weary. To me he was only the executioner, not the sentencing judge.

I did not like to see a man in such concern, his face suddenly sunken as though in the dock for the mistakes of others. I did not know who it was. I knew it could not be this sad man attempting to be as charitable as possible in an awful, bloody job.

'It's been a decision from above,' he said suddenly. '*Middle East International* was being taken from your works. You'd been in here with letter after letter showing promised Arab support. Your last big trips to the Middle East, supposed to save both *Middle East International* and *Voice* meant an increased overdraft for you. Now the *Middle East International* publishers' account which you placed with us has £25,000 or so in credit. They're doing well, as you know. But your own accounts, company and personal, are over twice that sum overdrawn.' He paused, thumbing the file. 'Way back after your fire you had a substantial insurance cheque. Yet you admitted to using this to back your Middle East publishing in general instead of reducing your bank overdraft to the kind of figure we were looking for. We waited patiently after your last money and order-collecting trip in the Middle East. The result of that trip seems to be prosperity for the people who have, to put it frankly, dismissed you.'

'Why are you so certain of all this? Did you check with anyone?'

He pursed his lips. 'Enquiries were made. Head Office looks carefully into these things before taking action. I suppose we checked with the usual sources.' He fingered his papers. 'Let's leave it that we were thorough. I've been through your record. We've enquired. Banker to banker, confidentially of course. But we got a report.'

My protest was landing me nowhere. The man had logical explanations. I rose and held out my hand. 'I'm sorry if you think I blame you. It's not personal.'

He in turn took my hand, shook it, then held my arm, and led me from his room to the door of his suite. He clicked open the security lock and saw me out to the street door. It was the first time in twenty-five years of up-to-then cordial business with the bank that any manager had ever walked me out, almost to the pavement.

I went down the street, staring into the shop windows. The truth was I didn't know what the devil I was at, who was doing what, or who was doing who.

There were a few final pangs, despite the sad but cordial enough meeting with the bank manager. The Board of Trade had a second mortgage on our valley building. The bank, now satisfied because of my assurances to my branch, and my guarantees to cover their loans, in one of the unkindest acts of all, released the deeds of the building to the Board of Trade. The Board then proceeded to sell the building and the plant that remained to cover the government's small loan of £7,500. A small fortune in assets were sold at knock-down prices to satisfy a £7,500 commitment. The auctioneers were happy. The Board of Trade was delighted. The eager vultures who came to disposal sales had a bargain-hunting day.

In the end, however, almost everyone was paid. Although the once prosperous company was crippled, we even paid to a full pound per share the few local shareholders, including as it happened some of the staff who had left us on the basis that we were 'anti-Jewish'. Vernon Thomas had his share. 'Thank you for your client's most generous and unexpected gesture,' Vernon wrote David Harrel, our solicitor.

My family were left with £250,000 and my good friend Tony Berry with £30,000 in worthless shares. Dennis Lyons called. 'I'd think you'd be pissed off playing silly buggers.'

– 4 –

Driving to Swansea, I now had to see the men who had kept our presses rolling for my family and for the so-called Arab interest. Some of these fellows had worked themselves into frenzies of involvement that meant sacrificed weekends, nights and the good opinion of society about them, even opposition from some members of the NGA. They had faced the psychological destabilisation of Vernon, two sales managers, a circulation manager and a distribution team walking out. They had stood like a rock because I had asked them. One by one I had to talk to a procession of workers, most of whom now faced the sack.

'What nobody guesses is that the men now face a penniless boss,' I told Pat later.

After the last of the staff had left, I sat there in my office and made pencil notations. I took momentary stock of myself and the necessary actions. Some of our men had worked with me for over twenty years. The majority had known no other employer from the time of their apprenticeship. I needed to help a few into alternative jobs in the print industry. They were a fine team, and would have no difficulty in finding work. Several were going to start their own co-operative press, like John Jones the compositor, Neil McLeish the machinist and Tal Phillips the lino operator. It was the carving-up of brothers, the end of a lifetime of daily relationships between boss and staff. But where was the money to be found to bring a relatively painless end to it all? Should I have to confess to a practically empty pocket and ask my own men to give me time to meet the redundancy payments they were entitled to by law?

I locked up the old doors to the building and motored up the valley to my home. I sat there in my study wondering if I weren't into something so diseased that I would soon go completely mad. There was no one else around. I sat there, letting my coffee go cold, my stomach rumbling, gazing silently at nothing. We had staked everything on a principle. I reminded myself of John Stuart Mill who said: 'If all mankind were of one opinion and only one person were to the contrary, mankind would not be justified in silencing that person.' It sounded hollow. I had not much, if any, faith left. 'God help me,' was all I could think. 'God help me!' I am not always or easily a praying man. Often, true, I attempt to meditate, to 'get in tune' with an infinite source, but that night I prayed until my kneecaps felt raw. When I got up from my knees I opened the Bible at random, as was my habit first thing in the morning and thumbed the words in the book of II Kings Chapter 25 Verse 30: 'And his allowance was a continual allowance, given him of the King, a daily rate for everyday, all the days of his life.'

– 5 –

I came down to breakfast next day at 7.30 a.m. I had been up since 6.30, trying to prepare for the crunch. I didn't quite know how I was to face those men who had trusted my assurances that Arabs were honourable and that guarantees of work and security were certain. At 9.00 a.m. William and I were to pick up my London solicitor, David Harrel, and drive to the works to deal with the redundancy payments and the cash pay-out of wages in lieu of notice. It was cash I didn't have.

I went to the letter box. There was one little brown envelope in the post marked 'Midland Bank – External Account'. I turned the envelope over and noted the small printed words 'NOT A CIRCULAR – NOT TO BE THROWN AWAY'. I opened it. Out fell a single cheque for £5,000 with a printed compliments slip and name attached. The sum was exactly enough to meet redundancy and wages.

On the slip was the information that this was payment for subscriptions to the publication *Voice*, the first we had ever received. It was intended to cover the dispatch of copies of *Voice* for a year to Arab students at various universities and schools as well as to tourist offices in the United States and Britain. It was sent by Sheikh Ahmed bin Hamed, Minister of Information of the United Arab Emirates and by

Rashid Abdullah, then Under-Secretary of Information who was to become UAE Minister of State for Foreign Affairs. The cheque was by order of Abu Dhabi National Bank, Sheikh Zayed's account. But that morning we had to pay out all of it. The payment was approximately to our needs for the single day ahead. I could hardly believe it and shouted out to William and Pat.

The friends William and I had met in Abu Dhabi had rescued us. We had been saved in what had looked like being the last round.

PART TWO

– 10 –

THE GREAT KING OF ARABIA

– 1 –

I was in a Boeing 707 rapidly approaching the Saudi Arabian coastline. The Boeing dropped to four or five hundred feet. There was the almost imperceptible, sturdy click beneath the aircraft as the landing gear dropped. Below a white dhow looked deceptively near. Beyond were scattered ships like toys on a glassy sea. A modern jetty flashed beneath the wing tip. Beneath us, a haze of dark sand. We were coming in low, over large dusty villas surrounded by greenery. Suddenly, bump. The shock absorbers responded as the tyres hit the runway. I was landing in Jeddah, the commercial capital of Saudi Arabia on the Red Sea, on my second mission 'to the top'.

I had placed my hopes in the hands of the lanky Salem Assam, then Press Counsellor at the Saudi Arabian Embassy and later to become Secretary General of the Islamic Council of Europe. I explained to him that I wanted to see King Faisal as I felt he would be interested in some publishing plans that I had.

'I am sure he will help,' said Salem. 'I'll telex the Kingdom.' He was as good as his word. Within days I received a visa.

At Jeddah airport a polite escort, Abbas Sindi, was waiting. After escorting me personally to my hotel bedroom, Abbas said, 'Have a rest. I'll leave a driver with you in case you want to go anywhere tonight. Otherwise, be ready at ten in the morning and I'll take you to see His Majesty.'

Any of his subjects could at that time go to see the King from 10.30 a.m. on any working day of the week. 'Makes it awkward at times,' Abbas told me. 'You never know when some fellow will walk in to the King's majlis[1] and complain that he's being pushed around by a government official.' But that was the desert democracy of Saudi Arabia in those days.

Next morning at 10.15 a.m. we swept through the gates of a great pink pile of sandstone. The palace had some towers and domes but there was nothing ornate or flashy. It looked plain, serviceable and unpretentious. It would not be at all out of place as a good-looking government building in Birmingham – or for that matter, Boston.

I stepped down from the car. Two troopers wearing berets made the most casual inspection. I walked up some twenty steps to a large open hall. There was another pair of the blue bereted soldiers who I learned were royal guards. They were standing very much at ease.

'It's very casual,' I said.

'Ah, yes,' said Abbas Sindi. 'Like his father before him, King Faisal does not believe in military stiffness. He wants people to come to see him. Not too many guards, you see. Practically anyone can come in.'

In the background was the green Saudi Arabian flag. On it the words in Arabic: 'There is no God but Allah. Muhammad is his Prophet.'

I walked out of the 40° centigrade heat into the entrance hall. It was like a sudden cool bath. Very cool. I had become something of an expert on air conditioning since travelling around the Arab world. King Faisal's air conditioning was perfect. Absolutely. The people in the great hall were chatting quietly to one another. There were about thirty in all.

'All these people waiting to see the King?'

'Yes.'

'Surely he doesn't see everyone who comes?'

'Yes, indeed. Why, the other day I was outside the palace when the King came out. He had one foot in his own car, about to get in, when a Bedouin appeared shouting "Faisal! Faisal!" and started screaming some complaint to him.'

'What did His Majesty do?'

'The guards tried to push the Bedouin aside, but the King said no. The King just stood there, one foot inside his car, the other on the street. He stood for a full six or seven minutes while the tribesman argued with him.'

At that moment Abbas Sindi tugged my arm and led me into an ante-room. 'You must meet the interpreter.' Abbas Sindi introduced me to a reed-like Arab who greeted me with a firm handshake. It was

Mansour Al Khuraigi, interpreter to His Majesty at the Office of Royal Protocol.

'Could you tell me what you are likely to talk to His Majesty about? It will help me in my interpretation,' Mansour said.

'Certainly,' I answered and explained my purposes.

'You appreciate this is not an interview?' questioned Mansour.

'Yes. Shukran.' Thank you.

'It is we who should say Shukran to you,' he replied with exquisite courtesy.

Suddenly Ahmed Abdul Wahbi, the King's premier courtier and Chief of Protocol, beckoned. 'Come. The others will have words with the King. Then when they go, you will have time to chat privately.'

I was now a strange black-suited fish, leading a swaying white-clothed crowd that walked a dozen or so steps down the corridor into a larger room. It was of ballroom size, more than six times as large as the ante-room. There were easily seats for over 100 around the walls, the same soft, deep couches that were in the ante-room. Six glittering chandeliers hung from the ceiling.

We walked across the floor, across a large empty space. It was at the end, in front of a couch like every other in the room, that King Faisal stood.

He was all of six feet two or three inches tall. He wore the *egal* head-dress, its golden stripes surmounting his craggy face with its deep clefts that resembled dried-up gullies or crevices from which all water or moisture had been drained. Faisal had big shoulders; his back was heavy and strong. The body was a trifle thickened, but there was still great virility there. The brow was wide. There was the striking, splendidly Semitic nose. There were wrinkles like a score of bracket signs on his forehead. The skin was not flabby. It clung to the bone structure. The eyebrows were thick and strong with powerful lids that furled down at the corners. The eyes as I stood in front of him were scrutinising me. They were agonisingly tired, washed-out, as chilly as the Antarctic. There was a moustache, an unsmiling, coldish mouth, a slight tepee beard.

Faisal held out his hand and I took it, noticing that there was only one item of adornment, a plain and undramatic signet ring. Greetings exchanged, he beckoned me to the couch beside him, on his right hand. He made no effort to impress, to smile, to express any warmth at all, not even by as much as a twitch of face muscle. Throughout the earlier part of the time I was present he showed a cold, professional indifference to me and to everything in sight.

I sat there on his right hand. The others, who had come in with me, dispersed around the room. I looked out of the corner of my eye at Faisal and noticed how he held himself with total stillness, as though he were not responsible, as though he were a vehicle of some sort. There was a huge dignity about the worn, old man.

He continued to ignore me completely. His eyes were fixed now on a late-comer who had entered the room. This was an old man who could scarcely walk, wearing a billowing cloak. The old man moved across the room taking what seemed like an age. It was a physical struggle, with the eyes of the entire room upon him. It was like some test of mind over matter. When the old man finally reached Faisal he could hardly stand. He dropped on his crippled knees and began kissing the King's foot. A look of tremendous pleasure suddenly expressed itself in every line of the old man's face as he performed this act of symbolic devotion.

I looked now at Faisal. His features were still, almost as expressionless and cold as before. But not quite. Faisal reached out a hand and touched the old gentleman gently on the shoulder. He rose and pressed into the King's hand a piece of paper. Faisal did not open the paper. He dropped it carefully in the space between us. I was sitting less than a foot away from him, but in between us was a box intended to contain written requests for help.

Suddenly, to my right, a bearded Bedouin began to ask questions. His voice rose in volume. He became impassioned. Mansour knelt before me on my right, acting as my interpreter, explaining *sotto voce*: 'The man is from North Yemen. He is asking some questions about disputed border land.'

Faisal, I saw, was listening intently. Then a reply came. Firm. Clipped.

As Faisal's question and answer session continued, eight coffee servers, each carrying silver coffee pots about two feet in height with necks like swans, entered. One coffee server moved in front of me, smoothly and swiftly. In his hand he was holding not only the pot but juggled between his fingers half a dozen small, Arabian coffee cups.

Another question came, then another.

Just as rapidly as they had arrived, the coffee servers were marching out again, then back in again. This time they had silver trays balancing in the palms of their hands, ready to serve the traditional 'red' tea with sugar in tiny glasses.

Unwittingly, at this point, since I was getting stiff from sitting with my two feet planted so squarely in the one position, I crossed my legs. Mansour looked at me with horror. He had been squatting just at the feet of King Faisal but now he lifted himself to whisper in my ear: 'Please, do not show the sole of your foot to His Majesty!' I had shown a great discourtesy.

Suddenly, from the far corner of the room, a young Bedouin of about 23, wearing a red head-dress, but otherwise clothed rather indiscriminately in a pair of dusty flannel trousers and a torn, flapping shirt, open to the navel, rushed forward across the room with a lunatic cry. Every article of his dirty clothing was in flying disarray. He was propelling himself towards Faisal like a tipsy greyhound, aiming straight for the point between the King's seat and mine, shouting as he came.

Momentarily, I was hypnotised by the sight. It took perhaps some ten seconds for the young man to hurl himself across the room.

The people around were frozen. I looked at Faisal. His face was expressionless, except for a single muscle which I saw twitch in his jaw. The young Bedouin, eyes like huge brown saucers, pulled himself up with a jerk scarcely eighteen inches away from Faisal and suddenly sprawled down to tug at Faisal's hand. His face shone up with an eager, ingratiating but frightened smile.

Suddenly, Faisal spoke. Just three words like the crack of a whip. The Bedouin lay there grovelling. Two guards advanced from the corner of the room and seized the man. He was escorted, trembling, back to his distant seat. Faisal's right hand clenched the bit of paper the boy had given him and instead of putting it in the pile between us, dropped it on the floor with an obvious gesture of disdain.

I had heard before that nothing disturbed Faisal. There had been no confusion about him as the young Bedouin rushed at him. It might have been, for all one knew, an assassination attempt. So far as I could see, there was no security at all in the entire palace. Nobody had been searched on entry.

The Chief of Protocol now stood up to indicate that the gathering was at an end. Faisal had apparently given him a sign which I had missed. The majority of those in the room – about 100 Bedouins – had not spoken. Now, however, as they filed out, shepherded by the

Chief of Protocol, they passed the King, dropping their paper petitions into the box between us.

A young man in an open-neck shirt who had sat beside me in the ante-room before coming in, handed an airmail letter to Faisal. An old gentleman carrying a black umbrella handed what was obviously a small bundle of deeds for examination and possible advice. Another put into the King's hand a faded document. They had all brought their problems to Faisal. Now, on leaving him, they looked satisfied as though the very fact of communion had soothed them, had lifted some vast weight from their minds.

I noticed that the King did not like them touching or kissing his hand, which some of them did. There was a slight twitch of evident annoyance in his face. Most of them clearly idolised him.

One by one the people left. The great room was now empty. I was left sitting there, beside Faisal. He said nothing. Made no move. Mansour stood in front of us. A full minute passed. Silence. I asked Mansour whether I should stand. He shook his head. 'No. Just speak – what you will.'

'I thought you might like to see our new newspaper, your Majesty,' I said, handing him a copy of *Voice*.

Somewhat to my surprise, out came an articulate stream of comment. Each 'flow' in Arabic (although Faisal understood English he preferred to use his own language), was then interpreted by Mansour, who opened every phrase or so of his interpretation with a six-word introduction, 'His Majesty wishes to say that . . .'

The interpretation into English might appear slightly stilted, but it was as perfect a job of intelligent interpretation as I had yet come across. Later I was to know other interpreters of Arab leaders who had great brilliance, possessors of the art of 'free flow' in relation to the ideas of their masters, such as Zaki Nusseibeh of Abu Dhabi. The best compliment I can pay to Mansour was that he was in this class.

'There is a giant conspiracy in the world,' the King began. 'It is to overthrow both Islam and Christianity. It is against all men of faith, so it may well have been operating against you. The people behind this conspiracy can be found in the most unexpected places, holding the highest positions in governments, close to the sources of power. So it is easy for them to pick their targets.'

He paused, a crack again showing in that age-lacerated face. 'You must recognise this conspiracy as inhuman, without humanity. One must be prepared to face it and suffer it.'

'Is it Communism?' I asked, thinking momentarily that this was the conspiracy Faisal referred to.

The brooding face shot me a sideways glance, cricking his neck to the right so that the beetle brows levelled with my eyes. For the moment Faisal did not speak. Then his left hand reached over the pile of paper that lay in the box between us. The hand, in the first and only indication of any intimacy or sympathy, touched me lightly. It rested there on my sleeve, as though he were trying to signify some closer contact.

He spoke, and Mansour swiftly interpreted: 'There is a force in the north, threatening to devour us,' continued Faisal. 'It descends upon the deserts. It is also planted deep in Israel. They are there in their hundred of thousands. Did you know? Even many Israelis will one day be surprised. People are moving into positions among us in our societies who bear false labels, but they do not all belong to the force from the north.'

'Where else do they come from?'

'Some of them serve American imperialism. There is little difference between the Soviets and America. Both seek our discredit. They are dogs and we the bone. Our only Arab chance is independence. We must keep free from both camps. We wish no interference. We advocate nothing against them. We must be careful not to provide the opportunity for their jousting or contesting together while we pay the bills.'

'But who is directly behind all this?' I asked.

'There are people who serve the ends of materialism. Communism is one extreme. American colonialism is another. You get mass thinking. People are made the victims of the poisoned thoughts of the few. The end is the same. War. Division. Invasion. Meddling by outsiders. Theft of resources. Manufactured hate. Corruption of people.'

Faisal paused. Mansour continued his translation.

'But surely there are good political forces in the world, statesmen who work for peace and harmony and understanding?' I questioned.

'An attempt is being made to control the world. It is a conspiracy. A conspiracy to rule the earth.'

'Is this conspiracy carried out by agents from within?' I questioned.

'Yes. By all means. Everything's possible. The Arabs themselves are sadly inadequate in combating this field.'

'What can men do about this?' I asked.

'The call is for Christians and Muslims who believe in God to realise the dangers of anti-God. In the press, in politics, in industry, I see the dividing line in the world not between East and West, North or South. I see that there are men who stand for the forces of life, truth, humanity, compassion and love of God. Now there are other men – often duped men and betrayed men – who believe in nothing beyond self – who stand against God. The men who are against God I see exerting some double-standard in their judgement.'

'What kind of double standard?'

'Do you think the world sees the picture of the true Arab? The enemies of the Arab are waiting for his mistakes. If he makes no mistakes they invent them.'

'What can the Arab do?'

'I think it is the duty of Arabs to promote a policy that will win friends for Arabs, and indeed for Islam, everywhere, not ill-will. Unless we do this our cause will die in these deserts. There are those near and far who threaten men who speak the truth.'

I was fascinated by what he had to say and the way he said it. He turned sideways again to cast me a sharp glance. Mansour interpreted, with an expression of gravity. 'Believe me. All who speak against the corruption are under threat,' Faisal continued. 'The Americans, friends of the Zionists, ask us to give up our claim to Jerusalem. They threaten us whilst pretending friendship. The Communists also threaten us. Both seek to operate against us from inside, in their different manifestations.'

There was a pause. Mansour Al Khuraigi who, in his endeavours to interpret what the king said, was on his knees in front of both of us, now semaphored me with his eyes. It was time to go. Mansour glanced pointedly at his watch.

'Your Majesty, I am most grateful for this talk. I'm grateful for what you have told me,' I said.

Mansour was standing beside me, ready to bow in departure.

'His Majesty says he enjoys a dialogue on serious matters. In his busy life he has little opportunity. He respects the view of the stranger but few strangers listen. He welcomes you as a good messenger of hope. He says to come again.'

I stood and said goodbye, shaking Faisal's hand. We stood silent for about five seconds, staring into each other's eyes. Then I walked the long walk across the empty room. Turning slightly I looked back at Faisal. He was examining his papers – his messages from his constituents, if you will, his people, his brothers, his tribesmen.

In the ante-room I stopped to say goodbye to Ahmed Abdul Wahbi, the Chief of Protocol and Mansour Al Khuraigi. As he shook hands in farewell Mansour said: 'His Majesty felt you made your case well. Yours is now his cause, be assured.'

'How often does he talk as he did today?'

'Not much. They come in delegations, you know. Groups. He cannot talk easily to a group of MPs, congressmen or diplomats, although he tries to convey much the same message he gave to you. He's single-minded.'

Abbas Sindi, my guide, was there to escort me to the car. In the car I reached for my notebook to record my impressions. I felt somehow lightened by my visit to Faisal. On my own long road some new perception suddenly reached me which had not been there before. If I had come to Jeddah with some load, some hump on my back, I realised going out of the palace that it did not matter too much. I had found a most unlikely friend.

'The King was working at his papers when you left?' Abbas Sindi asked me, suddenly interrupting my thoughts.

'Yes,' I replied. 'He seemed not to waste a minute.'

Abbas Sindi smiled. 'Faisal says if he doesn't work he gets sick. His work is his health. He wakes in the morning at five in order to authorise even visa applications. Nothing escapes him. He cannot afford to trust his work to others for others do not care.'

– 2 –

The next day I took off for Riyadh, the Saudi capital which lies in the heart of the desert kingdom. There was an early-morning meeting with the thin, elegant Deputy Minister of Information, Sheikh Fahd Al Sudairi who spoke impeccable English. He listened with interest as I told him of my visit to Faisal.

'Oh,' he said, 'you saw His Majesty.'

It was quite clear he knew nothing of it. I had supposed that he would have been informed.

'I hope we can work together, that you will work with me commercially to help us develop our newspaper *Voice* and other projects.'

He smiled, rather enigmatically. 'You've spoken to the King now.

You detailed your requests in the letter or memorandum you gave him. There's nothing to do but wait on His Majesty.'

I nodded. 'Could you take some advertising in the paper to encourage British–Saudi and US–Saudi trade? I was thinking of Saudi Arabian Airlines.'

'Of course. I'll send a telex to them today.'

'Could you influence others to advertise in the new paper? Such as the Saudi banks with branches in the West?'

'Certainly.'

– 3 –

Before finally leaving I rang Alan Rothnie,[2] the British Ambassador at that time. I joined this goatee-bearded experienced Arab hand for an evening nightcap and confided my mission to him. He said he would help in any way he could. I had seen the King. There should be no difficulty.

Back in London, and after a discreet interval, I called on Saudi Arabian Airlines about the promised advertising. They had received no instructions. Reminder telexes to the Ministry of Information in Riyadh proved fruitless. The Regent Street manager of the airline became irritated at my persistence. Calls to Saudi banks resulted in a similar string of negatives. No-one had been instructed to advertise. Finally I telexed Ambassador Rothnie and asked whether he could help by taking up the matter.

Four months passed. I was still awaiting the fulfilment of Faisal's promise when a call came from the Saudi Embassy in London. I entered the Embassy door and mounted the stairs. I was asked to sit in an ante-room. I caught sight of the Ambassador hurrying out and down the stairs, with just one rather startled glimpse in my direction as he hurried away. Another man came in. He pushed a ledger forward: 'Would you sign to say you have received this?' I signed. He handed over a sealed envelope.

I fingered the envelope thoughtfully under his almost scrutinising gaze.

'This is for services to our Kingdom,' he said.

I did not open the envelope until I was in the street. I told myself that here was the promised investment from Faisal at last.

It was a cheque signed by the Ambassador for a modest amount of £2,000. It was just about enough to buy a copying machine, certainly not a printing press, but it was a gesture, a beginning that established a link which was to continue unbroken through the years ahead and I was grateful.

I was never to see Faisal again. He was assassinated in his majlis by a 26-year-old nephew, Faisal ibn Musa'id. The King who suspected a world conspiracy now lay in an unmarked grave in Riyadh's Central Cemetery, less than twenty feet from the remains of his assassin.

– 11 –
THE YOUNG MAN IN GORDON'S PALACE

– 1 –

William and I sat by the coal fire in our London living room. He enjoyed a real fire and lit it every day when he came back from the office. Its bright glow warmed the heart.

'You think we can recover?' William asked. His young face had grown older over these weeks and a depressed tiredness was reflected in his eyes as he watched the low flames.

I told him about the last talk I'd had with Michael Adams. Michael, the kindest of men, was an assistant to John Reddaway in his Strand office and had been appointed editor of *Middle East International* after Tom Little resigned and I had departed. Michael's last remark was on the perils of pro-Arab partisanship. It was made when I tried to explain that we were still defending the right of a minority to be heard – even if that minority hadn't at all times appreciated it. My brain sometimes screamed to pack up and get away from the scene. But I knew that we would go on communicating – even if reduced to one typewriter and a copying machine. Furthermore, we had managed to keep the title *Voice* from crashing with the company. We still had a paper.

'You're going back to the Middle East?' William queried, poking at the smokeless chunks of Coalite.

'There's nothing else to do. We may have been cut off in one direction, but if anyone thinks we're dead and buried they're mistaken.'

'Who will you try to see now? What's next?'

I thought a moment and then said, 'Brondesbury Park. Yes, Brondesbury Park.'

The Young Man in Gordon's Palace

– 2 –

In Brondesbury Park lived the flamboyant Colonel Kamel Hassan, at that time military attaché at the Sudan Embassy in St James's and reputed head of the Sudanese intelligence in Britain. A former football hero in the Sudan, he enjoyed parties and the *dolce vita*. As a member in his early years of the same football team as General Jaffar Numeiri, Hassan was still close to his Commander-in-Chief. He was a direct appointee of the President in London. I had recently done a favour for him by finding work for an unemployed relative of the Colonel's who had been stranded in Britain, Kamil Hassan Mahmoud.

The Colonel and I had become friends. His modest suburban house, where he was certainly the only man in Brondesbury Park to enjoy two jolly, official wives, was an unofficial Sudanese embassy. Following my so-called 'good turn' the Colonel had invited me to parties to meet visiting Sudanese ministers. Through the Colonel I had met Ali Mohamed Shummo, Sudan's Under-Secretary of Information, a brilliant man who was to become a close friend. I also met a merry 'Mr Fix It' called Dr Khalil Osman, a one-time Khartoum veterinary surgeon who had built friendships with the Gulf oil sheikhs. Khalil had linked the Sudanese government in profitable deals with Lonrho, the African-based corporation run by R.W.(Tiny) Rowland. Now I wanted to meet General Numeiri himself.

'Why not?' beamed the Colonel. 'I'll have you sent a first-class ticket from Sudan Air. You are our guest.'

I was eager to go anywhere, follow any path that would help to turn the tide that seemed to be flowing against my future.

– 3 –

'I don't understand it,' said Guy Etherington-Smith, CMG, HM Ambassador to Sudan. He waved his hand loosely and forlornly. 'You arrive at the airport and then straightaway spend all night talking with the President. I've been waiting for an appointment for two months.'

'I think the President may like to talk to old journalists,' I said.

He smiled. 'Well, yes. I realise these chaps may be keen to see reporters, to gossip.'

I nodded. It was an acceptable explanation.

'Of course, Numeiri's after a loan. Aid. Not a chance, I'm afraid.

He's talking ten to fifteen millions. Not a chance. The country's a basket case.'

'Well, we talked. It didn't do any harm. Perhaps some good.'

'An ambassador couldn't, of course, breeze in for a chat like that. Protocol, you know. Must go through channels,' he added, quite correctly. The lean, mahogany-faced Etherington-Smith was a chip off the Downside public school block.

I always avoided 'channels'. I drove up, always dressed in a formal dark blue suit, white shirt and tie, carrying a briefcase or papers in a folder. If there were guards I just walked through, eyes neither left nor right. In those days no one challenged a grey-headed Englishman. To most Arabs I was as anonymous as any of the stereotyped English advisers they were pretty much accustomed to.

I frequently sat in an ante-room for long periods – hours, whole afternoons, returning the following morning in the end. Patience always opened doors. I armed myself with stationery and something to read for these long waits. My Bible, old and battered, was never out of reach. I opened to a certain verse and chapter each day, completely at random. Every page was marked with ink marks and date, like 'Cairo, 14th May' the year and the occasion. My portable office went wherever I travelled.

– 4 –

It was the day before my call on Etherington-Smith that I had seen President Numeiri. I met him, after a two-hour wait, in the simple old wooden building that at the time served as the home of his Council of Ministers in Khartoum. He was behind his desk and rose to greet me.

'Assalamu alaikum.'

A grin spread across his leathery face at my appalling phrase-book Arabic.

'Alaikum assalam.'

He had a square, powerful nose. There was determination in every line of the face. His whole body was held slightly forward as he spoke. From time to time he bounced slightly up and down in his chair, like an athlete tensing his body. He was what I would call distinctly bouncy. He had what the Americans call 'style'. It had no doubt helped him as one of the longest survivors in those days of the turbulent torrents of

African politics. Endurance was the one word which I felt instinctively summed up Numeiri. Hard to understand, a fighter of lost causes, a maker of enemies, a bit too much of a day-dreamer. All this, perhaps. But a real survivor. Being something of a survivor as well at this point, I warmed to him.

He was 43 when we met, an ex-footballer with a frame that would be no disgrace to Liverpool FC. There was a plain silver ring on his right hand and on his desk a variety of pamphlets and books. A man of endurance, if not one of tolerance. I had been told that morning that his officials had just gaoled one Ministry of Information department head simply because a cousin of the man concerned had voiced a few modestly disloyal thoughts. Guilt by relativity. However, as a seeker for work I was not at that precise moment going to remind Jaffar Numeiri of his warts.

'I see you keep studying.' He had all sorts of books on his desk and it was obvious that he wanted to keep himself up-to-date on the outside world. It was unusual to see so many books about.

'I take my own refresher courses in everything,' he laughed. 'Why have you waited to see me?'

I took out a photograph of my burned-out press in Wales. My calling card.

'I want work. Publishing work. Advisory work. I would like to explain Sudan to the West. Possibly a book about you.'

'I wish you would tell me how the West really looks at Sudan,' he said after we had briefly discussed a few ideas.

'To many it's a vast bureaucracy. True information about the real qualities of the people never emerges. All the West sees is a forest of officials. Bureaucrats!' I replied.

'For example?'

'I met an English manager here on holiday. He told me he once had twenty Sudanese doing the paperwork in the days when he ran his privately-owned British company in Khartoum. Today that same company as a nationalised concern under the Sudan authorities has quadrupled that number. One hundred people are doing the same office work. The company no longer makes a profit but a loss.'

Numeiri clasped his hands together. 'It's a matter of education,' he insisted, 'educating managers.'

'But I've seen plenty of able Sudanese managers elsewhere in the Arab world. They all run off abroad.'

Numeiri smiled suddenly as though in tolerant memory. 'I know.

Their reputation as workers in Arab countries and Africa is pretty good. Once abroad they are not interested in anything but work.' He grinned at me and leaned forward. 'But the same people don't work here in the Sudan. Most Sudanese who come back don't work as well here as they do abroad. But as a country we're as efficient as others in the Arab world,' he added. Then he suddenly said, as though trying to make a point, 'It is part of my policy to deal direct with the people everywhere. I visit almost every village in Sudan every six months or so. Come with me on the next tour if you like. See for yourself.'

The invitation was as unexpected as the man himself. It was an invitation I would eventually accept. Now, perhaps rudely, I wanted to make a point.

'Do they ever tell you the system's not working?' I asked after thanking him for his generous suggestion.

'No. Nobody ever tells me that!' He grinned again. 'Perhaps I'd be the last to know, if those around me had their way! You think Britain gets the wrong picture of Sudan?'

'Yes. You must decide how to present the best image to the West. What do you want in aid?'

'Ten million. Maybe fifteen. Do you know Tiny Rowland? He's helping us. A good man.'

I didn't know Mr Rowland, but Numeiri was very open. He showed me his wall maps of the country's future development.

'Look,' he said, 'I've a cabinet meeting in half an hour. Would you like to sit in on it?' That afternoon I became probably the first and last Englishman to attend a meeting of the Sudanese cabinet.

Numeiri and I met again the same evening at around ten. The Secretary of the Sudan Socialist Union came to sit in and listen while Numeiri and I batted the communications ball but at midnight he asked to be excused. The President and I carried on talking. We talked of socialism, of efficiency versus bureaucracy. We talked of coups and counter-coups, of the help he said he had received from Britain and Libya in surviving the last attempt to overthrow him. Jaffar Numeiri talked frankly, as though glad to find a sympathetic ear. He had survived more attempted coups than any man alive.

'I hear that Gaddafi helped you escape following that last attempted coup. What do you think of him?' I asked.

'Ever since then he's been coming and telling me things,' said Numeiri. 'He wants a big road between Libya and Sudan. Unity.'

'What's your reaction?'

1 Claud Morris, the author

2 HH Sir Sultan Ali Abdul Karim of Lahej. It was he who persuaded the author to begin his Middle East odyssey

3 The author when he was Chairman of the South Wales Newspaper Proprietors' Association, addressing members

4 The Welsh press that dared, a constant unending initiative. The *South Wales Voice* succeeded in getting £1 a week in pensions for miners. The paper constantly got up stunts like 'We will take 300 unemployed to the circus', or 'Will it be you this weekend?' (a campaign on road accidents), or 'The neglected man – a challenge to the conscience'; and so it went on

5   Lord Mayhew of Wimbledon. He wanted to bring the magazine *Middle East International* completely under his wing. Formerly the head of the clandestine Information Research Department, which at one time had 400 members based in the offices of MI6 at Century House, Westminster, Lord Mayhew was a greatly respected intelligence officer during the war and after. Probably one of the most active pro-Arabs in Britain, he brooked no interference with his views

6   Mrs Elizabeth Collard. She did not want to take the *Middle East International* printing when offered it by John Reddaway. Seen talking with Mr Hijazi and Ghayth Armanazi, now Director of the Arab League, London

7 Examining the disaster after the fire at the *South Wales Voice* press

8 Lord Lyons of Brighton, a life-long friend who acted as a go-between between the author and 10 Downing Street

9 Dr Ali Khushaim who first met the author in 1972 when he was acting Minister of Information for Libya. A lasting friendship began between the two families

10 General Numeiri showing the author 'his dream' of a highway across the desert between Sudan and Libya. Later, the author discussed this dream with Gaddafi

11 The author seen here at a Sudanese Cabinet meeting, the only Englishman ever to be present

12 Ali Shummo examining *Voice* distribution lists in Wales. He was appointed Under Secretary at the Ministry of Information in the Sudan and later in the UAE

13 The author at the *South Wales Voice* with a group of Sudanese visitors, including General Joseph Lagu, Christian leader of the An-yanya Army of South Sudan

14 President Numeiri and Claud Morris

15 The articles by the author in *Al Fajir Al Jadeed* brought Gaddafi and Numeiri closer together in a brief Indian summer

16 Gaddafi in the desert near Sert. He is surrounded by Bedouins who are presenting their problems and airing their views. In the top left-hand corner, the author's arm holding his inevitable notes

17   HM King Faisal of Saudi Arabia shortly before his assassination

18   The author with HH Sheikh Zayed bin Sultan Al Nahyan, President of the United Arab Emirates

19 HE Sheikh Ahmed bin Hamed Al-Qubaisi, former UAE Minister of Information. 'We began as friends, we ended as family,' said the Sheikh

20 In Tunisia. The author is sitting next to HE Abdul Aziz Rowas, Minister of Information for the Sultanate of Oman. The occasion was a meeting of Arab ministers from 21 countries

21 Adnan Omran talking to the author. Omran was then Assistant Under Secretary of the Arab League. He later began the initiative to get the peace talks under way

22 Sa'dun Al Jasim, former Under Secretary at the Ministry of Information, Kuwait – decisive, completely understanding in his desire for better information links world-wide

23 *Centre*: an old friend. Without Sheikh Saud Nasir Al-Sabah, now Minister of Information for Kuwait, the journeys would not have been so successful. He is seen here presenting his credentials when appointed Ambassador to Britain when the author first knew him, with Major-General Fitzalan Howard (*right*) and Mubarak al Muscati (*left*) then Press Attaché at the Kuwait Embassy

24   HM Sultan Qaboos bin Said

25   HH Sayyid Fahad bin Mahmood Al-Said of Oman

26 The author with Abdul Karim Al-Mudaris, today Chief Executive of the Arab British Chamber of Commerce

27 The campaign to save Bhutto's life. 'Mir' Bhutto, his son, taking part in the campaign organised by the author, which attracted world-wide attention and sympathy. It was called the International Convention of Jurists on the Trial of Mr Zulfikar Ali Bhutto and consisted of jurists from all over the world. 'Mir' was assassinated in 1996

28 The author speaking to the international press conference organised by Morris to discuss the Arab image in Western mass media. Beside him is Sir Edward Heath, former British Prime Minister

29 Ibrahim Al-Abed, Director of Overseas Information for the UAE. A friendship which began in 1974 still continues

30 Lord Caradon (Hugh Foot). The author has been a friend of members of the Foot family for 50 years

31 Three-day International Press Seminar in 1984. *Left to right*: the author who arranged the seminar at the Hotel George V, Paris; Isa Ghanim Al-Kawari, then Minister of Information in Qatar, who brought fresh hope for new co-operation between the West and the Arab world; Henri Pigeat, then editor-in-chief of Agence France Presse; Denis Healey (now Lord Healey)

32 The author's son, William, his companion on many of his travels. Pictured here when he was advisor to the Minister of Education, Oman

33 Sir Frank Rogers, Deputy Chairman of the *Daily Telegraph*, an old friend of the author since the days when they both worked on the *Daily Mirror*. Frank and Esme Rogers joined Pat and Claud Morris on a trip to the UAE. Sir Frank later became a Trustee of the Next Century Foundation. *Photograph by Snowdon*

34 Jaweed Al-Ghussein, Chairman of the Palestine National Fund and major industrialist on the Gulf. He is a close friend of the author and was an original member of the Next Century Foundation

35 His Grace the Duke of Devonshire, Trustee of the Next Century Foundation and host of the Chatsworth Seminar. *Photograph Bill Burlington*

36 The author and his wife Pat

'He's got time yet. He has a lot to learn. He always takes decisions without studying them. I tell him to have patience. I told him the other day, if you want to take a decision don't hurry, for God's sake. Study it. Ask the people around. You're a human being!'

It was 5.00 a.m. when I removed my little Sony dictaphone which I had perched on the edge of his desk. We had finished six double-sided tapes. A car and a driver were waiting. We drove first to the President's home in Omdurman where he dropped off with a friendly wave of his hand. The driver returned me to the Sudan Hotel.

– 5 –

Two days later came the 'National Day' celebrations. They took place in the cool – or comparative cool – of the night, in the great square of Omdurman on the outskirts of Khartoum. A semi-circle of chairs had been placed in the centre of the square. In these seats sat a privileged élite of about 150, brought there with all expenses paid. From somewhere behind them came a constant thunder of drums, shaking the night with a tidal wave of sound. Ahead was the dark and ominous shape of an enormous tomb behind which someone was letting off a firework display.

'What's that?' I asked my interpreter, squatting in the sand beside me.

'The Mahdi. The great Mahdi.'

Yes, of course, the tomb of the great and still revered religious leader who led the revolt against the English and killed General Gordon.

'The battle was here?'

He nodded.

It was as though he were there only yesterday. I could feel the ghost of the dead general, killed in the uprising of Sudanese. They were severely punished in the battles that took place when over 10,000 Sudanese with spears died charging the guns of British reinforcements.

In front of the Mahdi's tomb was a podium about 25 feet high. On top was mounted a giant 10-foot by 5-foot picture of President General Jaffar Numeiri. This standard Ministry of Information photograph was obligatory everywhere, but tonight Numeiri's picture had company. By its side was a lesser photograph, modest in comparison, measuring at the most 3-feet by 2-feet. It was of a young, lantern-jawed army Colonel Gaddafi. It seemed that this year on independence day something extra had been added. Muammar Gaddafi, the new socialist ruler who had recently seized power in Sudan's neighbouring Libya, had flown in as a surprise guest. In the shadow of the Mahdi's tomb Numeiri would embrace the young socialist hero of Libya.

As though by a secret sign, a massive battery of kleig lights switched on, transforming the area into blinding daylight. There was a throaty roar. Straight up to the podium drove a black open Mercedes. Standing in the back of the car, his swagger stick waving in his hands like an orchestra leader, smiling broadly, head tossed back, resplendent in a uniform with a chest full of decorations was President Jaffar Numeiri. He strode forward and took a seat at the foot of the podium.

After the roar came a hush of expectation. Then a second Mercedes. The lithe figure in the second car, not content with standing up, had hoisted himself on the back seat. One wondered how he kept his balance. He was waving his hat in the air. It was the young Colonel Muammar Gaddafi. Jaffer Numeiri stood and waved him forward to the podium as the first speaker of the evening. Gaddafi bounded up the steps two at a time.

He began speaking, at first slowly and emphatically, then more excitedly in recognition of the sea of faces in front of him. The interpreter who squatted by my chair kept me up-to-date, paragraph by paragraph.

To my astonishment the speech went on and on. An hour passed. Ninety minutes. We were hearing some vast, quasi-documentary historical survey, it seemed to me. It didn't matter, of course. The speaking head in front of us was being transmitted out through the eye of the television cameras, across North Africa, to Tunisia, Algiers, Cairo and Damascus. Jaffar Numeiri himself, who sat some fifteen feet away, at first shrugged his shoulders. Then he started looking pointedly at his watch.

Muammar Gaddafi's verbal flight had one theme. He was calling out to the Sudanese to unite with the Libyans. He quoted the Mahdi, the Guided One. Remember the Mahdi! Make a common bond. He appealed, he said, over the heads of the Sudanese leadership to the Sudanese masses.

Good Lord, I thought. What a way to put an idea! He had completely by-passed his host. He had ignored the Sudanese government and made his proposition to the Sudanese people as though they were his own Libyans.

After two weary hours of marathon oration, Muammar Gaddafi stepped down. It was past eleven o'clock. He had used up all the prime television transmission time.

Jaffar Numeiri, clearly impatient, now mounted the steps. Just as Numeiri began to speak the heavens opened. Anyone who has experienced tropical rain will know how it belts down. What was left of the great National Day, this once-a-year evening so carefully planned, was a dripping ruin. There was pandemonium. Men, women and children scattered in all directions to escape the merciless opened sky. Cars revved up. Jaffer Numeiri looking around at the shrinking mass audience must have felt some Siberia of the soul.

I went off with my driver, leaving Numeiri's catastrophe behind.

– 6 –

At the Sudan Hotel, next morning, I woke and stared through the window at the Nile. The cypress trees were bent with heat. There was the early buzz of countless insects warming up to conduct their morning expeditions against whatever hapless European or African flesh might be in the offing. After sitting there for the best part of forty-five minutes contemplating my next move, I went into the lobby where the head porter, a genial old retainer from English colonial days was sitting at his desk.

'Where would Colonel Gaddafi be staying during his visit to Khartoum?'

'People's Palace.'

'Where's that?'

'The old Palace up the Nile. Used to be Gordon's Palace.'

'Did General Gordon live there?'

'It was where he died. It's a museum now. President Numeiri has some garden parties in the grounds. Other times it's a guest house for visiting heads of state.'

I walked back to my room and stripped down to my underpants in an effort to keep cool. I switched on the great air cooler in the room, a box-like machine fitted to the window, which thudded away like an aero engine, blasting the maximum air into the hot box in

THE LAST INCH

which I was existing. I took out my Olivetti, placed it on the bed and hammered out a letter:

Dear Colonel Gaddafi,

I was most interested in what you said last night. If I can I would like to help you in your ambition to achieve Arab unity between Sudan and Libya. I would also like to help you in achieving better relationships with my own country and with America.

I attach an advance issue of my new paper *Voice* which concerns the Arab world.

As a journalist and publisher I have lots of good reasons for wanting to see a better and more honest presentation of news about the Arabs. I would like to talk.

Would the journalist's genii who usually stayed with me, help me now?

Taking the letter I walked out to find my driver and accompanying interpreter. Ali Shummo, as the then effective Head of Information, looked after journalists with enormous care. He had given me a faithful driver who stayed with me day and night. He slept in the front seat of the battered Mercedes which Ali had provided for my visit. My interpreter usually arrived in the early morning and stayed all day and sometimes half the night. Sudan, during the Ali Shummo days at the Ministry, was the most efficient country in the Middle East for handling journalists.

'Will you translate this into Arabic?' I asked the interpreter. The job completed I pinned both English and Arabic versions together and handed them to the driver.

'You know where to go?' He nodded.

'Can you deliver this?'

'Insha-Allah.'

I went back to my room and lay down.

At two o'clock in the afternoon I was lying on top of the bed naked when a knock came at the door. I scrambled up and reached for my pants.

An Arab in a smart lounge suit was outside, standing patiently. 'Mr Morris?'

I nodded.

'I'm the Libyan Ambassador to Sudan. The Colonel asks me to say that although he is now at prayers and wants to take a short rest, he has no objection to a meeting.'

The Young Man in Gordon's Palace

My luck was in.

One hour later I arrived at Gordon's Palace and mounted the great stairs to the landing. As I walked up I looked at the pictures on the stairs. All intact as in Gordon's day. I could imagine Gordon standing there at the top of those stairs facing the Mahdi's angry assassins. Then the sudden spear to his heart. Wasn't all this in the film? Who starred in it? Charlton Heston? Incongruous. Life imitating film, once again.

At the top of the stairs was the Libyan Ambassador. He greeted me cordially and I asked his name.

'Yunis Amran,' he said. 'Please come in.'

Yunis Amran took me to a small room. It had seven neatly spaced Victorian gilt chairs. The walls were a delicate blue. There was a fine Persian carpet on the floor. The curtains were tightly drawn to cut the glare. The gilt-edged door – an enormous door through which a giant could walk – was closed immediately behind us to shut out light. The only modern items I could see were a small Philips television in one corner, a fridge and a whirring Westinghouse air conditioner. The cold air rushed into the twilight darkness like the wind off Wuthering Heights.

'Whose room was this?'

'General Gordon's drawing room.'

'Gordon!'

Once again I could almost feel the ghost of the dead General.

An old, white-turbanned Nubian came in. He had red slippers, white robes and impressive grey eyebrows like overhanging cypress trees. He placed a cup of orange tea gently in front of me. I sat waiting.

Suddenly, through a door opposite the one by which I had entered, came a young man of about 21. He might have stepped out of Saks or Simpsons.

I shook his hand mouthing all the Arabic greetings I knew. 'What do you do?' I asked.

'I'm with the Colonel, always.' A comprehensive enough reply.

Before we could exchange another word the door opened again and in came Colonel Gaddafi himself. I had an instant photo-flash impression. Such impressions can be totally wrong, or like a camera eye they can in that half-second be completely revealing. There were the clean-cut features. Handsome. Strong. He had a quiet expression, a pleasant half-smile with even teeth, which he flashed like a character out of a Colgate ad on TV. He was the original 'golden boy'. He wore a very light, yellow cotton 'pyjama' suit open at the neck. His toes peeped comfortably between open sandals. The eyes were clear. There was no tension in the face. It even showed a little suspected irreverence for the clichés of life by the half-smile around the edges of the generous mouth. His hand came out to me.

'Assalamu alaikum,' I said.

'Hello!' He replied in English.

He looked totally different from the speaker who had upstaged his host with all the tact of a bull elephant the night before. Last night's decorated, theatrical individual suddenly appeared shy and anxious to please. He was not for that moment the man of the legend but something far nicer.

Muammar Gaddafi sat on what I had learned was General Gordon's gilt-edged couch. No. He was not what I had expected. No young Cromwell. No Charles de Gaulle. No tough, traditional veneer. The show of ego which had evidenced itself the night before had disappeared.

I opened the interview. 'I'm interested in what you said last night about the unity of Libya, Sudan and Egypt creating a new force in the world.'

'We will – unless the English and Americans prevent it.'

'Oh, that's a very general accusation. Who particularly is to prevent you?'

'The oil companies. They are the difficulty. On the Gulf. In Iran. In North Africa. The English oil men. Your country has caused much trouble.'

'Not the Americans?'

'No. Not as much as you. By no means.'

He started talking quietly about the institutionalised gentlemen of British Petroleum and some of the great Seven Sisters of the oil world. He thought they were an ugly oligarchy.

'You are talking to me as though I'm BP. I'm not even an Englishman. I'm a Celt. We started nationalism. We began revolts long before you fellows.'

He laughed, leaning forward.

'Why don't you revolt now?'

It was my turn to laugh. 'You had a revolution but the Libyans had the Bay of Biscay between you and the English. We only have a river.'

Bending forward and apparently enjoying the turn in the conversation, Gaddafi said, 'You must learn Arabic so we can talk, share.'

I turned the conversation back to what I had in mind.

'Last night in front of the Mahdi's tomb you made many references to religious faith. Do you really feel God's hand is upon you? Do you do God's will?'

He smiled. His face suddenly had the beatific look of a man of total religious conviction. I had seen that look on the face of Billy Graham and even on Frank Buchman converts. He raised his arm. 'Anybody who calls on God's favour will be assisted by God and be successful. God always helps and guides those who turn to him. It is only up to us to turn. If we do so, we have all power.'

'How can I explain your thinking, or that of the Arabs, to the West?' I asked.

He laughed. 'To the Jews? I'm no enemy of the Jewish people. I respect our cousins. I wish we were so united. Well I'm certainly not building any iron curtain about myself or Libya. I only ask that journalists who write from their desks in London come and see us. To me the news media must be a field media, travelling and looking, not sitting, not from desks!'

'What about your own information institutions?' I asked brashly. 'Your Information Ministries have nobody, so far as I know. They are complete bureaucracies. You haven't even got trained journalists. Those you have are exiled or imprisoned. Too much money is spent employing complete incompetents.'

Gaddafi did not try to contest the point. 'Look,' he said, 'I think Libya ought to do more for informing the world, but we are just starting. Sometimes we overlook one front or priority. I suppose information could be a victim.' He shook his head a little wearily. Then he brightened.

'Come often. Talk. Build your bridge. It's our bridge. Make dialogue together. Take the trouble, as you are now, to understand, to exchange views.'

There was an interruption. Another visitor was shown in. Ambassador Amran took me by the arm and whispered, 'This gentleman is the Prime Minister from South Yemen, Aden, to see the Colonel.'

Muammar Gaddafi stood up and embraced his visitor with a kiss on both cheeks. The pocket-size, swarthy Yemeni glanced slightly apprehensively at me, as though he, no doubt a convinced Marxist, was in the presence of a Western interloper of uncertain persuasion. It was a completely unexpected eyeball of hostility after the genial manner of Gaddafi and his Ambassador. As for Gaddafi himself, I was suddenly ignored as though I did not exist. His attention was on the newcomer. The Ambassador waved me to the door. I offered my hand to Gaddafi. He took it, perfunctorily.

I stood on the landing for a few minutes to collect my notes. Suddenly, the young aide came out to join me.

'When you come to Tripoli, call any time. Colonel would like it.' He scribbled an address and telephone number. 'Never bother about ministry or government with us. Just call this number. Where are you staying in Khartoum?'

'Sudan Hotel.'

– 7 –

On Friday at the airport I was in the VIP lounge. I was waiting for the Number Two man of Sudan, Omar Hag Musa. To dignify the occasion, Etherington-Smith now arrived to see Brigadier Hag Musa off. The Ambassador eyed me with surprise.

'Hello. What are you doing here?'

I wondered vaguely what he would make of my flying back with Hag Musa. Word, I thought, would soon get round. To the British Foreign Office I must be looking curiouser and curiouser. It would be harder and harder for them to believe I was just a bloody-minded, independent journalist and publisher looking for work.

As the plane lifted slowly into the hot blue sky, the pilot made a wide swing of the Nile and climbed into the thousand-mile air path to the north. I longed for a cup of piping hot coffee. The stewardess brought it quickly. Through my window I could still see the elephant-like tusks of the Blue Nile and the White Nile and the point at which they joined. Like a break in the road of life, I thought suddenly.

I had made a good and sympathetic contact with President Numeiri. In my brief-case were the Numeiri tapes, enough material for a graphic feature article or a small book.

I had as a bonus met Muammar Gaddafi, an extraordinary meeting which was to open doors to a land I had never visited, seen or contemplated visiting. It was a meeting with its own destiny. Libya, the great 'box of sand', would play its own role in my life and woven into that role was that charismatic young Colonel who would cause such international hullabaloo.

– 8 –

On arrival back in London, I put the eight tapes on Numeiri in the drawer of my office desk in Lowndes Street. I had written up some information from them but hadn't as yet decided quite what to do. To write a Numeiri biography I needed more authentication from the British side and considerable research.

Although I was due to submit my copy to Ali Shummo in Khartoum, I sat on it. I was tired after the long trip and before beginning a complete transcription of the tapes I wanted to stew over what I had seen and heard in Sudan.

Furthermore I had the business of survival. Earning a living for the family was always uppermost in my mind and the problems of rebuilding the family business were laid before me daily.

Several weeks passed before curiosity overcame apprehension. I decided to play back one or two of the tapes and try to get a line on my next move. A quiet weekend stretched in front of me, a good time to collect thoughts and make plans. I looked into the drawer where the eight packages had rested, tabbed Numeiri tape and Numeiri tape, ditto.

It was empty.

– 12 –
WITH G AT BENGHAZI BARRACKS

– 1 –

I was sitting in our London garden eating breakfast and contemplating our problems, depressed at the loss of the Numeiri tapes, depressed at the too slow revival of our publishing business, and worried about the weight of our bank overdraft. I sat drinking coffee and casting around for ideas. One came. We needed a rapid rescue operation – and if someone, somewhere, was still poking a finger into my business and trying to delay my recovery, why not go to a man whom most people in the West would regard as unapproachable, and who enjoyed nothing but worsening relations with the West? It was a challenge. Yes. It was a good idea.

William had walked downstairs and stood quietly staring at me as I shovelled bacon and eggs into my mouth. I pushed my plate aside, took my note pad and scribbled a cable.

'William. Can you send this to Colonel Muammar Gaddafi, Revolution Command Council Headquarters, Tripoli, Libyan Arab Republic? Then give me the times of the Libyan Arab Airline flights from Heathrow for three days ahead.'

My son shook his head and made off, paper in hand. The following Sunday night at eight there was a ring at the door. It was a GPO telegraph messenger, his red bike perched precariously against the gateway. The canary-coloured cablegram read, cryptically enough: 'Refer to your cable to meet Colonel Elgaddafi. Agree discussion as you requested. Cable your arrival. Press Office, President's Sec. for Inf.'

WITH G AT BENGHAZI BARRACKS

– 2 –

The old, cavernous RAF hangar in Tripoli, left behind when the Royal Air Force evacuated, served as a civilian airport building. It was full of chirping birds nesting in the girders above, with masses of people below. The general confusion was multiplied because, as a symbol of revolutionary zeal and Libyan nationalism, Muammar had ordered all signs switched to Arabic. With admirable cheek he had recently asked the sleepy bureaucrats at the United Nations to conduct their affairs in the Arabic language. When this had been refused Muammar abruptly retaliated by banning English from Libya. The language of Montgomery's heroes who had rescued Libya from Rommel, who had turned it over to ex-King Idris, had been obliterated down to the last gents' toilet sign, a very awkward syndrome, as I found, having landed with a need to pee in a hurry. The immigration entry forms were also in Arabic. Confused and alarmed English, American and European visitors suffered delirium.

I was met by a slim PR man of Italian-Libyan background Jelal Gritli. The journey into Tripoli was twenty-three kilometres along a fast arterial road. Dusk was falling. A redness in the sky above the city, like the flame at the back of some great oven, gave me a sense of almost apocalyptic expectations.

After the sudden summons of the Gaddafi cable and the flight from London, came the long wait that faces most people who visit Libya and attempt to see the ruler. My happy instant meeting with the Colonel in Khartoum was not to be repeated. I soon discovered that at home the man was encircled by a thick forest of bureaucrats. I rang the secret number I was given in Khartoum but there was no answer. Patient enquiry every day to Jelal Gritli produced only polite and apologetic evasions. 'The RCC has been informed you are here,' the Ministry of Information Director of Information, Ibrahim Ibjad, kept telling me, with what I felt to be unnecessary emphasis.

'Stay in your room. You will be telephoned.'

Ibrahim Ibjad was clearly the man in charge of my affairs. A good-looking, slender, active man of about 5feet 6inches with a lively face, he wore a grey-brown Italian-made suit and sported a well-laundered white shirt and a check tie. His face was black, his short, clipped hair neatly combed back over the finely boned head. There was something of the Bedouin about him, in contrast to many others whom I met in subsequent visits to government business offices.

'Where are you from?' I asked

'I'm a desert man.'

'Which part?'

'From Sebha. Town in the Sahara.' He took me over to point it out on a map. 'Years ago in Sebha I was in the first student march of Colonel Gaddafi. It was October 1961. We were against Idris Senoussi, the dictator. My life is the revolution,' he went on in his halting English.

The Libyan-Italian interpreter, Jelal Gritli, intervened: 'He was in the Colonel's class at school.' Once when Ibjad was out of the room Gritli opened a drawer and reverently drew out a small photo which showed a young Ibjad with his arm around an even younger-looking Muammar.

– 3 –

It was on the eighth day after my arrival in Tripoli, following a mounting series of protests, that I received a sudden overnight summons to be ready to 'take a plane at dawn'.

The plane landed at Benghazi, a thousand miles down the coast. With me was Jelal Gritli, now attached as my permanent interpreter. The drive from the airport into the town on that early winter morning was interesting enough to make me forget the frustrating sleepiness of his Information Ministry back in Tripoli. We drove past the Mosque of the Two Minarets, a startling sandstone creation whose tall towers rose sharply above the desert road where the soldiers of Italy, Germany and Britain once marched. The mind-boggling sight, however, was the new construction everywhere. Pile-drivers were thumping and cranes hovering. The scene was one of frantic building activity. Money had been harnessed in enormous amounts to rebuild and rehouse. Tens of thousands of Bedouins who had never known anything but a desert tent or galvanised shack as a home had poured into Benghazi to be placed in block upon block of concrete flats and houses. The Bedouin was being urbanised at a startling rate, taken out of the desert where, like a starving hen, he had scratched for a living. He was now being placed in concrete blocks where many had little to do except gab, eat mountains of cous-cous, watch TV, sleep and grumble to the wife. Poverty of body, a critic might argue, had been succeeded by poverty of mind. Nevertheless, the people had been housed. It was Gaddafi's first step for his rehabilitation of the 'masses'.

Our car sped into the Benghazi headquarters of the Libyan Revolutionary Command Council. A blue-beretted soldier at the gate lifted a striped pole. We stopped outside a yellow sandstone barracks. I was shown into a big room. In one corner was a Grundig radiogram. Above it hung an inscription in Arabic: 'Thanks to God Almighty'. There were a few plain sofas.

Again, it was to be a long wait. We arrived at 10.30. At noon we were led off to lunch in a Benghazi hotel. It was just after 3.00 p.m. by my watch when I was, without explanation, led upstairs into a corridor. Off the corridor I noticed ten plain bedrooms, each occupied by a single officer's bed. The only concession to luxury was a good carpet square beneath each bed. At one end of the corridor was an equally plain officers' dining room.

'The Colonel eats there with his officers,' I was told by Jelal Gritli.

At the end of the corridor, through an open door, seated behind a mahogany desk was Colonel Gaddafi. With him was a short energetic man, speaking good English with a slight American twang. The interpreter for the Colonel introduced himself as Saad Mujber.[1] I discovered later he was Director of Libyan Broadcasting as well as being Secretary for Arab affairs in the Arab Socialist Union and interpreter for the Colonel in major press interviews. I was shown in alone. Jelal Gritli waited outside.

The Colonel wore a black polo-necked sweater and a dark, plain suit. His face was full and friendly. Quiet, cool eyes, a quiet voice. A freedom from haste or anxiety unknown in the West gave him a strange calm. There was, odd as it seems, a sense of peace. It was, again, impossible to measure the Gaddafi I found in front of me against the Colonel pictured by the Western media.

'I would like to talk about two things,' I said, after the Colonel invited me to take a little hot lemon tea in a tiny thimble-sized glass. 'One is relations with the West. The other is a problem of my own.'

He smiled. 'You first.'

Briefly I sketched the picture for the Colonel. My publishing business was under considerable pressure in Britain. It was now essential we got extra work, and found funds to finance the work we had already started for the Arab world.

The Colonel replied rapidly in Arabic. Saad Mujber translated: 'We will cable our Foreign Minister. We will ask him to remind his colleagues, the other Arab foreign ministers who are meeting in Kuwait tomorrow, that they should give you publishing work and printing work to support you. We will also cable the Secretary of the Arab League.'

'Thank you, but I don't think a cable to the Arab League will do much good,' I said.

'Why?'

'We first met, do you remember, after I had listened to a speech of yours in Khartoum in which you said that if the Arab world ever wanted an issue forgotten a leader had only to send a cable to the Arab League.'

'You know us!' He laughed. 'If the League and others don't do anything in time, then Libya will take up the whole of your work capacity, and advance resources for the work you are doing. But don't rely on this alone. Other Arab states should work with you, too. You should see them and press them. Try anyone. King Faisal might help you. Sheikh Zayed. Arab unity must be our purpose. Our work with you must be to build a bridge between the Arabs and the West, whatever our individual attitudes. We all, as Arabs, face the same conspiracy.'

'You see it as a conspiracy?'

'I do. For every step the Arabs try to take forward there are those who push us back. This is, after all, your own experience. It is the experience of all of us. It is not the conspiracy of the people. Everywhere we must reach over the heads of governments to the people.'

'Who do you suggest I see in Libya to help me with my problems, now that I have explained them to you?'

'Go and see our Minister of Information, Abu Zaid Durda. He's a good man. Start with him. Tell him all about it. He's in Tripoli and you'll have no difficulty. Tell him what I told you. He'll help.'

– 4 –

I left with Saad Mujber accompanying me on the thousand-mile flight back to Tripoli. Through the plastic Boeing window the coastline below was illuminated in all its great sandy curves by a full moon. I sipped the tepid orange juice served as refreshment and wished somehow, after such a tiring day, that the Colonel had not decreed his country 'dry'.

'You shall see the Minister tomorrow,' said Saad. 'Everything will be OK. We will devote tomorrow to this purpose.'

When the plane landed and he dropped me back at the Libya Palace Hotel, Saad said, 'We'll meet at nine o'clock, to carry all this through.'

Next morning, when I tried to track Saad down to take me to the ministry, he had disappeared. After waiting till noon, I went to the Ministry, then located in a converted block of flats down by the Bourgiiba Mosque to the west of the town. 'Where's the Minister?' I asked. No one knew. I started out that day believing naively that now that I had backing and sanction from the Colonel, something would happen.

'I must really see the new Minister of Information,' I told Ibrahim Ibjad the next day. He had kept me in his office for three hours and then said he was sorry, the Minister was 'unavailable'. It would have to be 'Bukra' – tomorrow.

'Where is Saad Mujber?' I asked.

He shook his head and shrugged his shoulders. Phone calls to the private home and office numbers that Saad had given me only brought the clipped response that he was 'out'. Then 'Bukra', tomorrow, came with the same pattern of delay. From hour to hour I was shuffled from meaningless office to office and told to wait. On the third day I was seen by Ibrahim Ibjad, at 1.00 p.m. after a wait of four hours. He now told me again that it was 'impossible' to see the Minister. The Minister was far too busy. It would probably be best, added Ibjad, if I returned to Britain and waited for a message to come out again.

At this point I exploded. Ibjad was either prepared to ignore completely the request of Gaddafi or he had some motive for delaying matters. Saad Mujber too, who was the only witness to my talk with Colonel Gaddafi, had completely disappeared as though spirited off the face of the planet.

'Do you think I have flown over two thousand miles to Tripoli, waited a week, then flown another thousand miles to Benghazi to see the Colonel, to be told by the Colonel I should return to see the Minister immediately, only to be shuffled back to Britain? I'm going back to see the Colonel and tell him exactly what I think of his bureaucracy! What the devil are you doing here anyway except drinking tea and reading the papers? I'll go back to Benghazi tonight if necessary.'

It seemed to me they were all wandering about in a condition of semi-sleep.

Ibrahim Ibjad allowed his first look of slight concern to cross his face. He unwrapped himself to the extent of shouting across the room to get the help of a deputy who had a better understanding of English. This man said, 'You may not be able to get to Benghazi tonight.'

I immediately thumped the table.

'I tell you I shall speak to Gaddafi tonight even if I am locked in the Libya Palace Hotel in my miserable room!'

Three or four others now began to crowd in. 'Ingelese!' said the interpreter knowingly, as if the word explained everything. Ibjad clutched the desk with both hands. The other Arabs were gesticulating at him. I continued pounding the desk mechanically. 'You cheats!' I roared. 'Liars, caring for nothing, nothing. Saad Mujber's disappeared ... the Minister's disappeared ... Am I in a lunatic asylum? Do you think Colonel Gaddafi will not learn everything of your attitude? I mean you, Ibjad. You are the responsible one.'

The Director of Information underwent a rapid transformation of mind.

'You are our brother,' he said, reaching across in a sudden gesture. 'You are our elder brother. You must not be hard on us. Please, please forgive us.' The stone-walling bureaucrat, who for three days had been playing some game best known to himself, was now suddenly changed as though a light had been switched on. He beckoned to one of the others in the room. 'Imshee! Imshee!' Ibrahim Ibjad rose charmingly and put his arm around me, again breaking out in a fetching smile as though nothing had ever happened and speaking in rapid Arabic.

'Come,' said the interpreter, 'I'm to take you immediately to the Minister. We really don't understand the delay.'

It was a *volte face.*

Ten minutes later my car swept through the green iron gates of the Tripoli People's Palace. This was the old Palace of the now deposed King Idris, its yellow cupolas still glittering in the sun. The white stone-block pillars and green-painted ironwork shielded the palace from the busy Tripoli streets outside. A red, white and black flag of the Republic fluttered from the flagpole. The grounds were immaculately manicured, full of flowery shrubs and pine trees. Up the entrance steps, passing under the golden eagle insignia, I came to a big reception hall. The Socialist Union, the sole political authority in Libya, now used the palace as an HQ. The nearest comparison in Britain would be if you made Buckingham Palace the headquarters of the Labour Party and the TUC.

I sat there in the white-walled waiting room with its high ceiling. Outside was the great terrace where King Idris once strolled. In the room with me were three men also waiting for appointments. They had a look about them of utter defeat, apathy and boredom. One was a young bespectacled student with a Fu Manchu moustache. His head was bent low in seeming despair over some papers. Another wiry man of about 32, with sunken eyes, was picking nervously at his hands. The third, a Lebanese wearing a neat business suit, stared intently at his shoes. Out of the fifteen electric candles in the chandelier, set high in the ceiling, ten were ablaze with unnecessary light. After waiting about ten minutes I was greeted by a meticulously dressed, youthful, angular man with an aquiline face and jutting Roman nose, who had walked in. It was Libya's Minister of Information, Abu Zaid Durda. He was only 28 at the time.

On the way to the People's Palace I had asked my guide what Durda had been doing before he became Minister.

'In jail,' I was told. 'Colonel put him in,' he grinned. Following the revolution, Durda had been governor of a province. During his governorship he once lost his temper and reportedly slapped the face of a member of 'the masses'. The Colonel immediately had Durda arrested. The jail sentence completed, the reformed and apparently repentant Durda had been made Minister of Information. In Libya the Colonel appointed, disposed or resurrected as he pleased the ministers and diplomats over whom he presided like a young master. Later Durda became Foreign Minister and Prime Minister.

'What can I do for you?' Abu Zaid Durda asked politely. I outlined my discussion with Colonel Gaddafi and handed over a note I had prepared on the whole affair. I asked for a grant, an advance, or a loan. He said, 'Leave it to me. I guarantee we will assist you.'

– 5 –

I returned to London full of hope. For once it was not hope too long deferred.

Yusef Az'abi, the thin, slightly tremulous but pleasant Press Attaché at the Libyan Embassy in Prince's Gate, London, telephoned me to come over. It was Friday. I went up the creaky little lift to his top-floor office and he handed me a cheque drawn on the Credit Lyonnaise Bank in Kensington.

'It's an interest-free loan for your work,' he explained.

The episode of the Gaddafi loan might well have ended there, except for a strange happening.

It was a Saturday morning. 'I'll pay in the cheque on Monday,' I told Pat. 'It'll encourage everyone.'

That Saturday I took Dennis Lyons to lunch at the old Isow's Restaurant[2] in Brewer Street, Soho, one of our favourite nosheries with its big green leather armchairs, each labelled with the name of some showbiz patron. I sat in Arthur Askey's chair. I had known Jack Isow since he provided Kosher wartime feasts for wartime journalists like Dennis, James Cameron and myself. The pint-sized, gnarled waiter who had been looking after us both ever since we first started going there came up grinning all over his face, cradling the giant menu. The table began to fill with chopped liver, chopped egg and onion, pumpernickel bread, pickled cucumbers and all the preliminaries to an Isow spread.

'Well, it's bloody good news,' said Dennis. 'I'm delighted. Of course, I wouldn't noise it around.'

'I don't intend to,' I told him munching a gherkin.

'I'm thinking,' said Dennis, 'that if some of those who made all this trouble for you learned about the Gaddafi cheque they might put the wrong interpretation on it. Many would misunderstand. He's hardly the pin-up boy of the British press. I'd keep it quiet.'

'I intend to,' I repeated.

On the following Wednesday, Pat and I had lunch at Vincent Square. She played Chopin, her favourite pieces. She knew about ten of the twenty-four Preludes. All seemed right with the world as I listened to her music. The phone rang. 'It's Manuela,' said the voice. 'I've had a chat with Jelal Keshk. He's here in London from Beirut.'

I hadn't seen Jelal since he'd done the piece on me in *Al Hawadess* which had been instrumental in attracting the *Middle East International* salvation money sent by the Beirut financier, Hasseb Sabbagh. 'He told me the Arab press have been tipped off that you've received a fortune this week from Gaddafi. He made a big thing of it.'

I almost dropped the phone. 'Oh, it's nothing,' I tried to cover up. 'Just to help pay debts, possibly as advance on future work. It has no particular significance,' I claimed.

'Oh, really.'

I could sense disbelief. To Manuela, Jelal Keshk's story must have sounded as if I'd come up on Littlewoods.

'Oh, for God's sake,' I said to Pat, 'if Manuela knows, it means everyone knows. It's the last thing I want breezed around.'

'How did Jelal Keshk know?' asked Pat.

I called Yusef Az'abi, the Libyan Press Attaché.

'It's serious,' he said. 'If this is out, it means there could be a leak in the Embassy.'

I phoned Jelal Keshk at St Ermins Hotel, where he stayed on his occasional trips to London, and asked him around to the house. Handing him a cup of tea, I told him the story. He laughed. 'It's no secret. Arab correspondents have been getting calls.'

'From whom?'

'Other Arabs.' He made a gesture of secrecy, one finger to his lips. 'Tip-offs. The news of what Libya did for you is now in the Beirut papers. The Libyans, too, are very proud of it.'

I was astounded. Hell, Beirut papers!

'There you are,' I told Pat as Jelal left. 'A lot of curious people must know all about it before I even disperse the cheque.' One interpretation remained. Someone had deliberately 'leaked' the information. Someone with access to confidential information had not liked the appearance of the Gaddafi money. But who, and why? It was nothing to do with the Israelis. If it had been, the first thing I would have heard would have been a salvo of Israel's press gunboat on the Thames, the *Jewish Chronicle*. Who then? I could feel a persecution complex taking hold of my journalist's soul. Miles Copeland,[3] former CIA Chief in Cairo, has often said that agencies take a delight in 'punishing' journalists who do not co-operate. Was that it? Or was I just making a mountain out of a molehill?

– 13 –
ENVOYS EXTRAORDINARY

– 1 –

Number 58, Prince's Gate, a large cream-painted building stained by London weather, plaster flaking off the walls, was then Libya's London Embassy. Enormous Victorian windows, ten feet high, were shuttered by grey, foreboding grilles padlocked on the outside. All five floors of the building had grilled windows. On the roof hedgehog-shaped spikes prevented invasion from neighbouring buildings. At first-floor level TV-eye cameras placed on angle brackets surveyed the street. Number 58 stood halfway down Prince's Gate on the left-hand side, opposite the Imperial College of Science and Technology. Visitors turned into Watts Way and mounted the eight marble slab steps leading to a grubby oak door with an entry-phone on the left-hand side.

Once a week, during those early days of the *Voice of the Arab World* and of my Libyan association, I visited the Embassy. Never once did I meet the Ambassador, who was at that time the tall, heavy-set bespectacled Dr Mahmoud Suliman Magrehbi. Oddly, he was Palestinian, not Libyan. All talks at the Embassy so far as I was concerned were conducted through the diminutive, subdued Press Attaché Yusef Az'abi. Occasionally, in response to an imperious squawk down the phone, Mr Az'abi descended in a creaking lift to the Ambassador's room on a lower floor.

Another go-between was the First Secretary, Suliman Gerada, a lean, saturnine Berber who sported dark spectacles to disguise a melancholy mask of a face. He could have been typecast by Alfred Hitchcock for a drama in the Casbah. Mr Gerada appeared to regard the Ambassador with a mixture of icily polite disrespect, fear and kinetic energy. The Ambassador himself was by repute a complex, stubborn-minded person. Before the arrival of Muammar Gaddafi he had led demonstrations of oil workers against Libya's former ruler, King Idris. He was also one of the few men available in Tripoli at the time of the revolution with administrative and political experience.

On taking power, the Colonel had made Dr Magrehbi Prime Minister, thinking that the left-wing orator would be transmogrified into a statesman of sorts. The move ended disastrously when Dr Magrehbi found his actions censored by the Revolutionary Command Council which then led the country under the Colonel's premiership. Using official funding, Magrehbi waged a guerrilla war against the man who had appointed him. He roundly denounced the Colonel. Anti-Gaddafi students and exiles regarded him a supporter. He was to prove a thorn in the flesh of everyone who supported Colonel Gaddafi, and he was in like measure to prove a thorn in the flesh to me.

– 2 –

'How do we get paid?' I had asked Abu Zaid Durda, when we discussed the tasks I would perform following his government's loan to put my firm on its feet again.

'By contract. We'll remit what we owe you to the London Embassy each month. The Ambassador will pay you.'

It seemed easy. What Abu Zaid had left out of his reckoning was that Ambassador Magrehbi was entirely out of sympathy with anyone trying to encourage better relations between Colonel Gaddafi and Britain.

My own work was straightforward. First came a weekly page I was to write for the Colonel's leading morning paper, *Al Fajr Al Jadeed*. Second came the training of Libyan journalists to staff the Libyan papers of the future. Third came the receipt of a daily news bulletin from ARNA, the official Libyan news agency, which we put into English and distributed daily to some 150 British papers. Fourth came a weekly bulletin which carried news of Libyan achievements to hundreds of diplomats, politicians and newsmen.

But Dr Magrehbi had never been consulted and did not agree with any of these activities. He had, of course, omitted to tell anyone that he was already anti-Gaddafi and wanted to see him overthrown.

And there was yet another snag, which I had begun to suspect. For every story I was putting out favourable to Libya there seemed to be a negative tale. It seemed to me that stories were being 'planted' in the press to give the worst possible image of the Libyan regime. We unearthed many yarns put about of Libyan involvement in international affairs that had no basis in fact. Every single enquiry took hours, sometimes days.

One morning we handled a minor story, an account in a London clothing trade paper, *Drapery and Fashion Weekly*. It said that Libyan children were being trained at home in Tripoli as shop-lifters, preparatory to accompanying their parents to Britain on holiday. The children, said the story, were instructed that it was 'a patriotic duty to steal from the British'. On telephoning the editor of *Drapery and Fashion Weekly*, he was embarrassed and would not reveal the name of the writer of the report, except to say that he was a man who had always been 'a most reliable informer'. The story was circulated to a large number of provincial papers before we managed to get it killed.

There were similar stories of varying degrees of seriousness. For example, one national paper published an item stating that a firm in Surrey had received an order for twenty small pilotless target planes from Libya. Some of these robot aircraft, stated the paper, had been handed over by the Libyans to the IRA in Northern Ireland, for use against British troops. I talked to the chairman of the company supplying the target planes. A minute's enquiry was sufficient to establish the fact that the robot aircraft were useless against troops and were merely intended for target practice. None had ever gone to Northern Ireland.

At that time there were also many stories of Libyan actions directed against civilian aircraft. I went to Libya to urge that public denials be made. As a result Major Jalloud, the Libyan Prime Minister, held a press conference where he denied Libyan involvement in any aircraft hijacks or attempts to shoot down civilian airliners, but not one paper in a hundred that had carried reports implicating Libya in so-called 'incidents' bothered to publish his denial. Only occasionally were there admissions that the press was wrong or partly wrong.

William H. Webster, then Director of the FBI, once admitted that reports that a Libyan hit squad had been sent to kill the US President were 'a kind of media hype'. However, only one international paper, which headlined the original charge, printed a single line about the denial by Webster which came a year later.

For a full sixteen hours a day our telephones ran hot. But the one perennial problem was how to get paid. With the Ambassador working actively against us it was an almost impossible equation.

Besides, his Embassy leaked like a sieve. There were plants and counterplants, plots and counterplots. Inspector Clouseau would have had a ball. I could well imagine that every major intelligence agency was well represented on the staff. That the British agencies MI5 and MI6, as well as the CIA and KGB, somehow maintained a 'presence' in the Embassy was a statement of the obvious.

The agencies exercised the usual techniques. Lebanese, Egyptian and Tunisian girls were available for entertainment at Embassy parties. Some of the girls, known as 'Willies', did not even know they were being used as information contacts. Some might have been led to believe they were helping a commercial company or a research organisation, or a business contractor, anxious for Libyan work, an estate agency or even a betting office, casino, or a credit investigation firm.

One rule was never to ask a 'Willie' to do anything her conscience would not permit. According to some circles, the CIA considered the 'destabilisation' of Libyan Embassies of prime concern, as important as the infiltration of Colonel Gaddafi's inner ranks which was proceeding at a rapid clip in the early 1970s, with the apparent aim of 'destabilising' the revolution, or at least surrounding Colonel Gaddafi with American 'agents' with impeccable Libyan or Arab pedigrees.

William Worthy, one-time Professor of Journalism Studies at Boston University, published in November 1981 a CIA document uncovered at the US Embassy in Tehran. This detailed Mossad methods which (i) regarded the Arab confrontation state of Libya as a front-line target; (ii) urged blackmail by encouraging sexual indiscretions as an effective means of influencing Libyans; (iii) described surveillance and entry into Libyan and other diplomatic posts and offices by man-and-woman (paired) surveillance teams. Few intelligence items unearthed by Mossad were not passed to Washington as a matter of co-operation, according to the CIA document. The reverse was also the case.

I myself was about to have my own run-in with what I can only imagine to have been an overture from an intelligence agency. It was a weird experience and in the end undoubtedly served to worsen my problems. Born to be independent, I wouldn't play, not with any of them. Besides, what did the press, the great Fourth Estate, have to do with intelligence services? The two were entirely separate. They had to be. That was what I had been taught at the feet of the Fleet Street

Maestros of my time. That was what I believed. Naive? Yes, I was naive. Blind? Yes, blind to everything except the paramount necessity of keeping the Morris/*Voice* ship sailing.

– 14 –

CIA: MISSION IMPOSSIBLE?

– 1 –

Opposite Gate Three at Rome Airport was the Leonardo da Vinci 'Club Fresca Alitalia Prime Class'. Next door was the cocktail lounge, viciously overcrowded and always overpriced. In the Leonardo da Vinci, however, one was always greeted by a brunette receptionist, seated in one of the comfortably outsize chairs, and promptly brought a glass of champagne.

'Hello. May I sit here?'

A bulky, pleasant-enough-looking man lowered himself into the neighbouring leatherette armchair.

'Where you goin'?'

'Libya.'

'Coincidence. So am I.'

He introduced himself as an attorney-at-law flying in and out of Tripoli to represent some independent oil interests. 'Not big people. Independents.'

'Do I know any of them?'

'Ashland Oil?'

'Yes. I've heard of Ashland.' I had heard of Ashland but didn't know much about it at the time.

Two hours later we were circling the long line of olive groves reaching out like green soldiers from the perimeter of Tripoli airport. I realised that the lawyer had done a job of cautious 'pumping' on the flight. As the Colonel's *Al Fajr Al Jadeed* had sent a driver to meet me, I offered him a lift. He and I both booked into the Libya Palace Hotel. Next morning I asked the desk clerk about the big American.

'That man checked out on the early Alitalia for Rome.'

Puzzled, I soon let the episode pass from my mind and got on with the business of the day.

– 2 –

The ghibli, the sand-filled south wind, blew in from the Sahara and choked the air. I walked onto the verandah of the Libyan Press Corporation building. The Mediterranean, a few hundred yards away, was hidden by sand. My God, I thought, peering out. Obscurity outside, even deeper obscurity within. I felt suffocated. How soon would the ghibli lift? How soon would both the bureaucratic ghibli inside the building as well as the hot gritty Sahara sand ghibli that beat against its wall lift? How soon, if ever, would Muammar beat the bureaucracy suffocating his ideas?

For a week my mind had been preoccupied with money. I had been promised a cheque from the Libyan Press Corporation which ran *Al Fajr Al Jadeed*. The payment would help replace the funds that had been held up by Dr Magrehbi the London Ambassador. That cheque was vital. Only a few minutes before walking on the verandah I had heard the latest. Ten days had actually passed since the cheque to cover my long overdue fees had been signed. It was for an account already six months overdue. 'We will send it to the bank immediately,' I had been assured. 'Your people will get the credit by cable tomorrow, Insha Allah.' My daily call to London to see whether the amount had been credited had drawn a blank. Now, all these days later, the young cashier of the Press Corporation admitted that the precious cheque had rested all the while in his desk drawer.

'Why didn't you take it to the bank after it had been signed?' I asked.

'This is an important cheque. There's a law against my going to the bank with an important cheque unless someone drives me.'

'What law?'

'A law of our corporation.'

After a few minutes of pacing on the verandah to cool my temper my exasperation died. Action was needed. I would get a car and drive the cashier to the bank. Nothing would be left to chance in arranging the deposit of this very special cheque. I walked downstairs and personally ordered a car from the General Manager of the Corporation. There were no cars. At that point none other than the

Secretary of the Arab Socialist Union appeared walking down the street from his own parked car. He hailed me.

'Can I help?'

'I want a car to take the cashier to the bank.'

'Jump in.'

I bundled into his vehicle and sent a messenger up to fetch the young cashier and that precious cheque.

At last we rolled towards the bank in Revolution Square sitting grandly in a large Peugeot with the young cashier clutching the cheque in his hand. The cheque-depositing delegation had now expanded. It included not only the eminent Secretary of the Arab Socialist Union, but also a guard who had joined us, a Schweisser automatic in a black plastic holster swinging loosely from his hip. To complete the party came my own interpreter, Abdullah Nuri. Nuri accompanied me to save any gross misinterpretation of my own wretched language efforts. The hall of the bank when we reached it was filled with a sea of faces. Some sat on the floor in poses of despair. Others were shouting and gesticulating. The entire mass ebbed and flowed, pushing and shoving their way towards the counter rail.

'They're trying to draw out money to go on pilgrimage to Mecca,' Nuri explained.

Behind the counter rail bank clerks in scores lolled around. Some were chatting, rather listlessly. Others were drinking endless Pepsis. Dozens of empty bottles stood like a glossy army around the desks. Some clerks were head-down immersed in *Al Fajir Al Jadeed*, which on that particular morning carried a page article of my own. Others shuffled document slips, studying each document with acute attention. It was like a lagoon of peace, behind the counter rail. Outside, the human tide swayed and seethed.

Suddenly the young cashier from *Al Fajr Al Jadeed*, impatient at the impasse, made my precious cheque plus the accompanying instruction document and deposit slip into a paper dart the shape of a baby Concorde. To my horror, he shot the cheque high into the air. It landed, at the end of its flight, inside the sleepy lagoon of clerks.

My eyes were intent on trying to spot where the cheque had gone. The young cashier disappeared. Absolutely, completely. Where had that bloody cheque got to?

Half an hour later, accompanied by Nuri, I managed to get into the office of a Deputy Manager, a frantic and perspiring Lebanese, to ask him to investigate.

'My cheque disappeared in full flight across your banking hall.'

The Deputy Manager strode off in the direction of his clerking staff, full of evident purpose. In ten minutes he was back. He had discovered the cheque. 'Al hamdulila' (Thanks be to God), he said.

'Will it be cabled to London today?'

'Unfortunately, instructions attached to the cheque don't say that the amount should be transferred by cable. No fee has been allowed for any cable charge. It will be transferred by letter.'

'All right, I'll pay for the cable personally.'

He disappeared again. Twenty minutes passed. I looked out of the window. In the square, twelve enormous palm trees, each at least seventy feet high, swayed in the ghibli. Up the slope stood horse-drawn tourist buggies that now did little or no business and were in fact soon to be abolished. Tourists were not encouraged. I had a feeling it was not going to be a good day. The Deputy Manager returned.

'I'm sorry, the clerks say they can't cable transfer of this money. You are not allowed to pay. It must go by mail. It's not in the instructions that the amount be cabled.'

'I told you I would pay.'

'That's not the point.' He shook his head, pointing through his door. Half a dozen clerks were arguing. 'They're in charge. They say it's their document.'

Nuri drew me aside. 'Being Libyan clerks they won't take orders from a Lebanese. That's the trouble.'

'Can I have the cheque back to take to the Press Corporation so that the instruction is altered?' I asked. 'It's my cheque, after all.'

The Deputy Manager went again to the clerks and returned. 'They say the cheque is bank property now.'

It took yet another two days to get a fresh letter from the Press Corporation instructing the bank to cable the money. I phoned Pat and told her it wouldn't be long now.

'The Libyan students you are training came in today to say they were giving up their lunches to help you until you get paid,' she said. I don't know how they had found out about my troubles, but I sent messages of thanks for their gesture of friendship. It was touching and none of us ever forgot it. Of the many students we taught some have continued to be in touch. Muftah Jewaili is today manager of a printing company in Malta. I still remember the way he held up a plane on the Tripoli airport tarmac so that I could get back to

London on time. Naji Shalgam when last we heard was Libyan Ambassador to Rome. They were fine boys.

– 3 –

At the end of that particular week in Libya an order to clear up yet another 'pending matter' concerning our work in London for the Libyan Ministry of Information was addressed to their Ministry of the Treasury. I took the order along to the Treasury office on the Tripoli Corniche and eventually found an appropriate clerk.

'I can't deal with this until it has attached to it all the correspondence and a copy of the original instructions and contract,' he said weightedly.

'What the devil does he want that for?' I asked Nuri, who had again escorted me.

'It's his rule. He wants to see all the bits of paper concerned with a transaction.'

'But he's already got written authority to ask him to stamp the document.'

'Agreed, but he's looking for a bit of small print to get his nose into. He's justifying his existence.'

'What?'

'I once asked one of these fellows why he didn't act immediately he got documents to pass on. He kept putting them carefully on the bottom of his pile. He kept his desk at least two feet high with papers. He explained that if he had a clean desk people looking into the office might say he had no work to do. His job would not exist. He had to create his job every day by finding this or that extra reason for delay. He re-checks every fact and every previous letter, including any original contract. He has to think of his family, after all.'

In my room at the Libya Palace that night I thought again of the world I had entered. In one of the richest *per capita* socialist countries on earth a journalist hoping to give that country a right to be heard in the world had to spend most of his days chasing overdue payments.

– 4 –

Back in London two weeks later the phone rang. It was the American lawyer I'd met at Rome airport.

'What about dinner?' he asked.

I took him to Isow's and brought Pat along. He wasn't very happy about her coming, but I had an itchy feeling about being alone with him. At dinner he made an unexpected reference to the fact that he was a faithful man of religion. He reeled off a list of prominent US church friends.

'That's interesting,' said Pat. 'I'm a Christian Scientist.'

Funny, I thought. The man had never mentioned religion before. Religion, as a family, is something we discuss continually inside the home but we don't peddle it outside. And yet this American seemed to know a lot that appeared to gel with Pat's own interests, as though he were well informed.

By the time the pudding was in front of us his conversation switched.

'You know, there'll come a time when people's patience might be exhausted with these Arabs. We've had to stand years of squeeze-play. Hell, we're not going to be mucked around for ever by OPEC.' He paused. 'Gaddafi?' His finger jabbed the air. 'He's pushed it too far. I wonder whether anyone could ever take the trouble to get a word to that guy?'

I laughed and said nothing.

'I'm off to Tripoli again tomorrow,' he added as we walked out of the restaurant. 'Could you give me some contacts? I'd like sure as hell to meet some of those guys like the people you know. I had an idea I might one day bring over a New England religious group to meet Colonel Gaddafi.'

I told him it would be best if he wrote a letter which I could hand on for consideration by Abu Zaid Durda, the Minister of Information.

Pat and I dropped the lawyer at the Park Tower Hotel where he was staying. He jumped out and the cab door clicked metallically and finally behind him.

The following week he was on the phone again. I was away. He spoke to Pat. He had once more returned from Tripoli just as I had coincidentally made another trip out.

'I've left a letter for your husband at the Libya Palace Hotel,' he said.

When I eventually got the news from Pat I inquired at the desk of the Libya Palace. There was no letter. What the devil was he up to? What would my new business and publishing contacts in Libya think if they got wind of the fact that the man was chasing me? I wanted nothing to do with all this. The lawyer could, as far as I was concerned, do what he liked, whether he was a courier, an agent or merely a New York attorney-at-law representing Ashland Oil. I was neither his judge nor keeper. But I knew one thing for sure. Any letter left at the desk of the Libya Palace would be read by the local CID within the hour. Maybe he was merely trying to implicate me and upset my legitimate business. In every one of his conversations he had been pushing for contacts or introductions. 'What sort of men were in the press and information field in Libya? Who controlled broadcasting? How near was I to Prime Minister Jalloud?'

He made a final call. It was on a day when Major Jalloud, the Libyan Prime Minister, was making a private visit to London, for a medical check-up.

'Jalloud's in town, I hear.'

'Yes, I heard so.'

'Say, where does that guy hang out, anyway?' the voice persisted. 'I'd love to bump into him.'

'I wouldn't know. If Jalloud or any Arab comes to London for a medical check-up that's his business. I've nothing to do with Libyan politics or their moves. They don't consult me,' I said.

He paused. There was a background noise of voices in the room from where he was speaking, as though he was checking with someone. He suddenly growled down the line, using a slightly hectoring tone. 'He's at a Kensington hotel. I got to meet this guy.'

I looked at my watch. It was 11.00 p.m. I had enough suffocating problems without acting as free tip-off man. 'I'm sorry, I don't understand. I can't help you.'

His voice turned sour. He rang off, clearly annoyed. I was never to hear from him again. It was some years later that I learned that Ashland Oil had been temporarily involved with the CIA.

– 15 –
ROMAN HOLIDAY

– 1 –

The five-storey Hotel Majestic in Rome belies its name, like bogus aristocracy fallen on seedy times. It stands opposite the grimy Ministry of Commerce building on Via Vittorio Veneto. I sometimes made it an overnight stopping place on my way to Tripoli.

'Abdul Qadir?' the receptionist clerk queried. He came back from a quick look at the register, a leering vacancy on his face. 'No.'

Well, I reflected, my Arab friend might have registered under another name, a not unusual custom with some Arabs. I checked in.

Next morning at 10.00 a.m. the phone rang. 'Hullo. This is your friend!' I recognised his voice.

'Where are you?'

'At the Jolly. Could you come here, instead? I'll be in the lounge.'

It was 11.50 on Sunday morning. I walked out, up the street, past the golden swing doors of the Ambasciatori Hotel with its little courtyard entrance, remembering a unique three days Pat and I had spent there in happier times with our three kids. The Via Veneto was glowing in the sunshine. I crossed by the American Embassy, its three black iron-grille gates closed and frowning, the lower-floor windows masked by thick, protective grilles as if ready for a siege. Up past Doney's restaurant with its scores of outside tables with their pink table-cloths beneath the chestnut trees where, in a different era that seemed a lifetime ago, I had liked to sit and watch a caricature of the world pass by. I noticed a few young Libyans sitting there in regulation dark specs, open-neck shirts, Afro hairstyle – some students, some exiles, I guessed. 'You can spot the Libyan mafia. They wear gold-rims,' Abdul Qadir once told me.

At the top of the Via Veneto I turned right through an arch and found myself opposite the Jolly Hotel in the Corso D'Italia. The Jolly is a peculiarly depressing ultra-modern design. The grey girders supporting the hotel, the bone structure as it were, are on the outside rather than being concealed by a decent, fleshy covering. Six flags flapped disconsolately on poles at the front of the hotel.

I dived into the hotel depths, following the red bannister rail down some thirty steps. My eyes swept the lounge. There, in the darkest corner, was Abdul Qadir, round face beaming. He was slumped in his chair, a large tomato juice in front of him, looking far older than his years. 'Bloody Mary,' he grunted to me. 'Have to disguise it. Too many feckin' Arabs about.' He laughed. Abdul always slipped into the odd oath – a habit from his UCLA days in California.

He looked worried. His eyes moved up to eye contact and then down into his Bloody Mary.

'The Americans have been enquiring after you.'

'How d'you know?'

'Their translator in Tripoli has been visiting *Al Fajr Al Jadeed*. The translator works for the paper, but he also helps at the US Mission with Mr Eagleton.[1] Is it Eagleton? He's US Chargé d'Affaires.'

'So what?'

'Thought you should be told.' He played with his gold watch. 'These Americans are close enough to some members of the RCC. There's a chap called Stein about, as well, I'm told.'

I'd never heard of Stein and would know nothing about him until an article by Judith Miller in the *New York Times* revealed that John Henry Stein had been the CIA Station Chief in Libya throughout my Libyan experience. He had been transferred from Phnom Penh, Cambodia, to Tripoli in 1972 and served there until 1974. A US State Department official refused in March 1983 either to confirm or deny to me Stein's role in Libyan affairs during the early 1970s. Stein became Deputy Director of Operations of the CIA in charge of all clandestine operations overseas.

But in Rome at that meeting with Abdul Qadir, Stein was a completely unknown quantity and my only worry was keeping my own ship underway.

'I don't understand,' I said, bewildered at Abdul Qadir's innuendo. 'There's nothing in my articles to complain of.'

Abdul Qadir grunted. He looked at me carefully. 'I had dinner at Andalucia Beach the other night. A few were there with an American called Ed Wilson. You know Mr Wilson?'

I shook my head.

He looked reproachful.

I must have seemed ignorant. It would be many years before Edward P. Wilson, agent extraordinary, was convicted by a court in Houston, Texas, on a charge of selling 40,300 pounds of restricted high explosive to Libya, despite his peculiar protestation that he had been acting on CIA orders.[2]

Abdul Qadir blinked his half-shuttered eyes as he downed another swig of vodka and tomato juice. I left him sitting there, ordered a taxi which tore down the Via Vittorio Veneto as if in the Grand Prix. Picking up my valise at the Majestic, I was quickly out on the motorway, over the flat plain with the green signs all pointing to Fiumicino and the airport.

– 2 –

I arrived in Tripoli and stayed as usual at the Libya Palace. My phone rang. 'Who's there?'

'Alexander Shenkov.'

'Who?'

'From TASS. ARNA the news agency gave me your name. Mr Salah said you'd be helpful to talk to.' Hosni Salah was then the director of ARNA.

Downstairs I was faced with a blond, fortyish, slender, good-looking Russian with a pleasant smile. We sat in a corner.

'I've come over from Cairo on my first visit. It's rather novel. I'm the first Soviet pressman here.' He explained what he knew of the Arab area. North and South Yemen, Egypt and Sudan. He would like to know more about Libya.

Over the table at the little Italian restaurant, Wadi Al Rabia (the Spring River of the Trout), Alexander Shenkov cross-examined me closely about the state of the Libyan economy, my views on OPEC price trends and the attitude of the people towards the Colonel. I free-wheeled through it all, recognising that I was once again being subjected to a friendly de-briefing.

'What do you think of Armand Hammer?' he slipped in, casually, on the stroll back to the hotel. Armand Hammer, the US oil tycoon, was the elderly, hyperactive chairman of Occidental Petroleum (Oxxy to all Libyans). He was one of the greatest friends of the USSR in the

United States and in recent years had become a substantial supporter of Colonel Gaddafi's oil policies in Libya. He was alleged by some to be an American intelligence 'front man' on the same scale as the late Howard Hughes, whose organisation it was also alleged had been used for operational purposes by the CIA. But I held no personal opinion about him other than an irritation that the Americans had apparently pulled the rug from beneath BP and the British Foreign Office. The Americans, I thought, often behaved in a peculiar fashion towards their British allies.

'I'm interested in petroleum. Do many American independents do business here? You ever meet Ashland Oil?' asked my guest.

Ashland Oil? Ah, yes, the American lawyer's firm. I said nothing either about Ashland or the lawyer.

– 3 –

Back in London I had a surprise invitation to lunch from a City firm who specialised in management consultancy in North Africa. The chairman, one of those bucolic Englishmen who can produce a quip a minute, kept up a stream of flattering remarks. He had assembled a varied group. They took it in turns to ask questions. They were trying to assess me. What of school background? Traditions? Politics? Left, right, centre or nowhere? It was all terribly casual. Later came a more pointed question or two.

Back in Libya within the fortnight, I came strolling out of ARNA at lunchtime. Walking down the Corniche I stopped to stand by the harbour where one could easily count the number and names of ships tied up. A gentleman who had been at the City lunch in London was standing there. It was an odd encounter, meeting there on the Corniche and saying hello.

'How are you?' We exchanged pleasantries.

'Just a little visit,' he said, smiling. 'Cheerio old fellow.' He didn't offer an explanation.

Two days later I had a call from the British Embassy and an invitation to a drink. Before the drink I was invited to walk around the Embassy grounds with the First Secretary, Stephen Egerton.

When we had circled the lawn twice he asked me casually whether I knew a particular journalist at ARNA. Yes, a Yugoslavian from Belgrade nicknamed Barney. I knew him. He was an East European journalist who had once worked for Reuters. Reuters had been banned by Gaddafi but their resident correspondent had been hired by the Colonel's official news agency as a translator when the Reuters office shut down. My own office in London was now letting Reuters have the news – something they didn't care for but had to accept.[3]

'Amusing chap, charming wife,' said Stephen Egerton.

A day later at ARNA Hosni Salah asked me at long last to sign the media agreement I had been waiting for to represent the agency in Europe, actually taking over much of the work previously carried out by Reuters. After signing the draft letter, Hosni told me he wanted to have my background recommendations translated into Arabic. He called in a Libyan Arabic translator whom I knew well, and handed him my background notes which were on canary-coloured paper.

'This is confidential,' I stressed.

'Of course.'

I left the office and walked out past the machine-gun post at the door, with its soldier in fatigues curled up half asleep over a sandbag, only to see the translator in conversation in the car park with Barney, the Yugoslavian.

'I'll give you a lift. Just leaving for lunch,' said the translator pleasantly.

I noticed my distinctive-coloured yellow paper memorandum sticking out of his pocket where he had stuffed it.

'I see you've got a little homework there.'

He half smiled but did not reply.

That night the translator called me at the Libya Palace and asked whether I would like to drive around town to see parts of the city I might have missed. When I got into the car the beaming hulk of Barney the Yugoslavian was unexpectedly in the back. We drove for ninety minutes, making small talk all the way. When we returned to the hotel I realised that both fellows had been waiting for me to say something. I had nothing to say.

– 4 –

I was off to Tripoli airport at 4.30 a.m. It was getting light. There was an unusual bunching of secret police at immigration. The immigration man looked at my passport and whipped it behind a screen. One of the Colonel's young officers emerged. I knew him. He gave me a broad, knowing smile of the kind that passes between those who count themselves as some part of a higher élite and handed back the passport.

The Alitalia jet was lifting up into the morning sky, its wing shadow passing over the craggy ruins of ancient Sabratha far below. As the air hostess sloshed my black coffee into the plastic cup, I picked out of my pocket the English version of a letter in Arabic I had left behind for Muammar Gaddafi. It pointed out a vision of the new Libya. It ended with the words: 'Youth should give to the Arab world the only weapon that makes man free – intelligence.' The whole letter was afterwards to be reprinted in *Al Fajr Al Jadeed* as an article. We were at least communicating, the strange maverick Christian and the even stranger Muslim maverick.

Back in London a call from Tripoli informed me that Muammar had gone into the desert, to think and meditate. 'Strong man falls', said the speculative Fleet Street headlines. Next day, as part of the work for which I was now being paid by ARNA, I managed to get a corrective report in the London *Times* and the *New York Times*. Muammar had not fallen and Libya, I thought, could still be the democratic Arab state the young Colonel had once dreamed of.

With the whole of Libya now reading my articles in *Al Fajr Al Jadeed*, I was getting cocky. And I was, of course, reckoning without the curious enquirers and occasional 'contacts' who now appeared to dog my steps.

– 5 –

Some Western diplomats never left me in doubt as to what they thought of my Libyan efforts. I was invited to a dinner party at Huntercombe Manor, Taplow, Berkshire. My host was Graham Thomas, Warden of Huntercombe and an educationist who had spent years in the Sudan. Graham turned to the Irish Ambassador, a fellow guest: 'You know Claud's a friend of Colonel Gaddafi's?'

'My God, then he's no friend of mine!' expostulated the Irishman.

At a Libyan National Day reception I came across Martin Buckmaster, now returned from Beirut. 'Many people talk of being pro-Arab. But, by heaven, now you're making so many North African trips, everybody says you're just beyond!' exclaimed Martin.

I smiled ruefully. Privately, I was beginning to wonder how long it was going to last. Would the struggle for a democratic Libya finally end? Was it mission impossible? Would the eagle or the bear settle in Tripolitania? Would the little nation dubbed a box of sand by Mussolini become an international whipping boy? Would the 'golden boy' play unwittingly into the hands of those who held the whips?

– 16 –
Hard Lines

– 1 –

I have no doubt today that some of the critics or opposition watching us felt they had to stop us by the simplest way. In those days it seemed that Middle East players had a closed club and no one could join unless approved and elected. One way to block unwanted members was to cut the jugular. Cut the money flow. It was not because anyone was specifically hostile to our small company and its publishing or news agency services. They simply wanted us out of the act, possibly with the idea of planting someone more co-operative in our stead. 'Cash crisis' tactics were a method I suspected had been used before, in Wales as in London, in attempts to immobilise my own firm. They had every chance of success.

Our Achilles heel was the remittance of funds from Libya to pay for our work. We now had a substantial staff and expanding offices in Buckingham Gate. Ambassador Magrehbi was a delighted partner, either consciously or unconsciously, in the 'cash crisis' method. He used every possible excuse in withholding payment. I had no idea that Magrehbi was a committed enemy of Gaddafi.

'He says your news releases are not revolutionary or socialist,' reported Press Attaché Yusef Az'abi at a meeting in April 1974. The poor man was an unwilling go-between. 'The Ambassador says you are not putting our revolutionary socialist messages about the Zionist enemy of the Palestinian people. You alter the revolutionary phrases sent by the news agency.'

'What revolutionary phrases?'

'You change words like "The Zionist entity announces", or words like "The American fascist hyena".'

'Don't you think we have to put things in understandable

English for English people?' I countered. 'For years revolutionary rubbish has been sent out that never gets printed. What do you expect us to do? Churn out material to fill Fleet Street waste-paper baskets?'

'There should be exact reproduction of text sent from Tripoli,' Azabi replied patiently.

I gave up. Downstairs I tried to storm the Ambassador's offices. Dr Magrehbi had disappeared. I was starved of funds and tired of battling. I felt that this was the beginning of the end of my commercial story as far as Libya was concerned. It was time for the counsel for the defence to resign and I sent a letter to that effect, addressed personally to Muammar Gaddafi.

A week later there was a conference of Arab Information people in Cairo and I ran into Abu Zaid Durda who had a suite at Sheperd's Hotel. When I told Abu Zaid I had sent a letter of resignation to Muammar a look of horror crossed his face.

He called his Director of Information, the self-same Ibrahim Ibjad. After hearing a few sharp words in Arabic from Abu Zaid, Ibrahim rushed from the room like a scalded cat and was off to Tripoli. I had no doubt why. At all costs, the letter of resignation had to be prevented from falling into Muammar's hands.

Abu Zaid promised to send an investigating committee to London in order to clear up the difficulties between ourselves and the London Embassy.

Two months later Ibrahim Ibjad at last arrived in London with Omar El Hamdi, then editor of *Al Fajr Al Jadeed*. Pat had invited them to tea at Vincent Square. The white climbing roses were out in the garden. We sat drinking tea and munching home-made biscuits. Omar presented Pat with a brass oval tray which she still uses continually. It was a quiet memorable moment away from the pain of Libyan politics. At the end of the visit and after an investigation at the Embassy at Prince's Gate the visiting investigators gave a positive report on our service. There would, they said, be no further trouble from Ambassador Magrehbi. British editors and a group from the BBC and the news agencies met us at a luncheon party I gave at the Waldorf Hotel and confirmed the value of the service being performed.

We were told that we would have a redrafted information and news agency agreement which would by-pass any intervention by Dr Magrehbi. In fact, Abu Zaid authorised Ibjad to sign a new agreement during his visit to London. But Ibjad said that he would prefer me to come to Libya to make a ceremony of signing with Abu Zaid.

Two months later, despite personal trips to Libya, I was still waiting. Visas were becoming more and more difficult to obtain from the Embassy despite direct invitations from the Colonel to 'come'.

In Tripoli meetings with Gaddafi became nearly impossible. 'They say he knows you are here,' was the cautious reply when I phoned the Revolutionary Command Council office. Weeks later I would still be waiting.

By this time we were digging deep into what remained of the Colonel's loan. True, there was some spasmodic payment made direct from Libya for the training of the journalism students and for the newspaper services, but these were not enough to meet our budget. True, also we were now being paid sums from the Arab League for book publishing and printing. True, too, that Kuwait, Saudi Arabia and the United Arab Emirates were beginning to push work our way as our reputation grew. And our old friend Numeiri, as President of Sudan, sponsored a goodwill tour of a team of English soccer stars to play in Khartoum which we arranged. In fact, *Voice* as a publication explaining the Arab viewpoint had by now proved its value and was receiving subscriptions from almost all Arab governments. But we were on a loss-making operation owing to the heavy costs of the Libyan venture.

And yet whatever the difficulties, I found it hard to forget my earlier rapport with the Colonel.

– 2 –

On one of my visits to Tripoli there was an invitation to attend what Muammar's office called 'a picnic'. I found 350 young university students gathered together in the Boy Scout Forest, some 20 kilometres from the city. The forest, an area of about 200 acres, skirted the Mediterranean and was used as a camping centre. In a clearing was an outsize army cooking pot filled with cous-cous. Around the pot were stacked scores of crates of Pepsi. The students had been invited home from their university studies in America, Britain and Europe to meet the Colonel. I found those I met quite bewildered. 'Six thousand miles for a picnic?' one said to me. 'What are they going to tell us that we don't know already?'

Muammar sat in a tent, smiling, confident and acknowledging greetings. Moving around from group to group were various members of his Revolutionary Command Council. I saw the white-faced Major Omar al Mehaishy, who even then must have been plotting his future attempted coup. There, shovelling his cous-cous into his mouth, was the bespectacled Major Abdul Mun'm al Huni, Minister of the Interior, destined soon to become another defector. Mohammed Najm, another of the famous RCC dozen, was planning his own departure. No one could have imagined that the original twelve would shortly have only five members left, Colonel Gaddafi, Major Jalloud, Colonel Abu Bakr Yunis Jaber (the army Commander-in-Chief), Mustafa al Kharrubi and Major al Khuwaildi al Hemaidi.

Colonel Abu Bakr Yunis tried to make a speech but his portable microphone developed gremlins. The attempt was given up. For a while I sat down in the general mêlée beside Muammar. It would be a chance to speak to him. The hot sun was pouring in the open side of the tent. He took a khaki army hat and with a smile gave it to me to fix on my head. A moment later an enthusiastic mother moved forward with a clutch of young children and for the rest of the afternoon he was involved in ritual blessings. There was no chance to talk or even arrange a date. When the admiring mother and children left a jeep screeched up and he was hustled off.

The next sight I had of him was at a Paris seminar hosted by André Fontaine, on behalf of *Le Monde*. It was to deal with Muammar's 'Third Theory' – the theory that capitalism was dead and communism offered no hope. The only path was a third way, a state of the masses where all decisions would (in theory) be in the hands of 'People's Committees'. Because of Muammar's dramatic unpredictability, it was a totally confused occasion. A press conference Muammar had scheduled for the Saturday night of the seminar was cancelled because he was indisposed. To cheer up the despondent gathering of colleagues from the Libyan press and information corps who had to face a hail of criticism about 'unreliability' from the Western media present, I took three Libyan editors and Abdullah Nuri, my translator, to the Crazy Horse Saloon.

Next morning the delayed press conference was scheduled finally for 10.00 a.m. Over 300 people crowded into the lounge of the Plaza Athene Hotel, which would normally accommodate not more than forty. They waited patiently until noon when he finally arrived. Then for fifty minutes Muammar answered questions.

At the close of the conference the Colonel rose to enter the adjoining courtyard, where he intended to say his farewells before leaving. As he walked the few steps between the lounge and the courtyard half a dozen kleig lights, held upright by perspiring, frantic assistants to French television cameramen, bathed the courtyard in an ethereal radiance. The media saint from North Africa, I thought. His slow procession from the lounge to the courtyard was carried out with almost apostolic grace, a fantastic sense of theatre.

He sat down in a pre-arranged chair which was waiting for him. When I went into the courtyard to the 'audience', Muammar rose from his chair at the sight of my proffered hand and embraced me. 'Is everything good with you?' he whispered. I nodded. Perhaps the opposite from the exact truth, but there was little room for dissent in such surroundings. Almost all people become conformist when taking part in a form of court ritual. That was what the morning's 'audience' for the faithful had certainly become. 'When can we talk?' I asked. 'Later,' he said. 'Insha Allah.'

After twenty minutes of 'receiving' French intellectuals, politicians and journalists Muammar retreated upstairs to his suite. Half an hour later he was down again. A cavalcade of fourteen black Citroëns were in line outside the hotel. The street traffic was blocked off. Some 200 gendarmes were lined up by the door, a phalanx of dark blue sentinels. Thirty motor-cycle outriders, engines running, side arms slung conspicuously at the hip, flanked the Citroëns. As soon as Muammar was settled in the leading Citroën there was a whistle blast. The cavalcade swung out. The streets were cleared all the way to Orly airport and the waiting presidential plane.

– 3 –

The fact that Muammar was changing from the man I had originally known was fast becoming evident to others. There was the disorientation of his diplomatic services abroad, now infiltrated on every side. At home, in Libya, by June 1974, there seemed to be a tight encirclement by a clique.

I unburdened myself once again to Omar el Hamdi, still editor of *Al Fajr Al Jadeed*, and one of the few men in North Africa capable of giving a real assessment of world opinion to Muammar. I wrote a 3,000-word statement on the Libyan position in reply to the world-wide press attacks now descending from all quarters. As I told Omar: 'For the sake of Libya's national dignity, let's put this out as a full page in six international papers.' The idea, I discovered later, was blocked before it reached Muammar.

Frustrated, I drafted a new and even more ambitious information plan which I handed in to Ibrahim Ibjad's office for his attention and that of the Colonel. 'It is being studied,' I was told over the next few days. A week passed and I had to leave.

On returning to London I found an Egyptian freelance journalist I knew on board the Libyan-Arab flight. 'I've been asked to go to London to improve Libyan relationships,' he said. 'Can you advise me what to do?'

Not for the first time, I felt I was getting the heebie-jeebies when he pulled a document in a plastic folder out of his pocket. The only difference from the original information plan that had left my London office for Ibrahim Ibjad's office in pristine condition was that the printed heading bearing my company's name had now been snipped off. He had been given the document by the Ministry of Information. I kept a poker face.

In London the Egyptian rang to ask my wife and I to dinner. 'I'm having a great time,' he said. 'Every night I go to a club. They've told me I can bring friends. We get a wonderful meal and drinks.'

'What club?'

'Playboy, sometimes Crockfords.'

I parried his invitation by asking, jokingly, how much he lost every night.

'Oh, £400 some nights, £600 on others.'

The Egyptian freelance had a retinue of Gaddafi stories which he retailed around town in the clubs. He told a story of a writer who had been jailed for printing in *Al Fajr Al Jadeed* a paragraph that an old lady had been mauled by a hyena in the desert. The journalist who wrote the story was locked up on the grounds that the police declared there were no hyenas in that particular part of the desert. They said the story had clearly been invented. The police described it as an attempt to put over an allegorical tale. The hyena was intended to be Colonel Gaddafi. The old lady was the Libyan people. It was a piece of black humour that all these yarns, and many more of the same ilk, were being retailed by an Egyptian who had been sent to London to 'sell' the regime.

Having told the stories and satisfied his companions with endless tales of the new Libya, the Egyptian left London three weeks later, after enjoying twenty-one days of high living. His stay had cost somewhere around £30,000. He may, for all I know, have won adherents to Muammar's 'Third Theory' among the happy rollers at the Playboy and Crockfords.

Pat laughed when I told her the story. 'Working with the Colonel's Ministry of Information is rather like clinging to the back of a Brahma bull. You never know when you'll hit the ground.'

PART THREE

PART THREE

– 17 –
WITH ZAYED AT AL AIN

During this period of hide-and-seek with Muammar I began to visit Abu Dhabi more often. As was customary in those early days of the state, I was immediately taken to Sheikh Zayed. The ruler had not as yet become isolated by security and courtiers as well as an ingenious crowd of opportunists who were even then rapidly targeting themselves on the oil-rich Gulf rulers and whose self-appointed sole purpose was to keep the rest of the world at bay.

Zaki Anwar Nusseibeh, the handsome young Palestinian who had continued to act as Zayed's translator, drove with me in July 1974 to Al Ain in the Buraimi Oasis. It was dark when we swung past a score of neon-bright tubular lights, into the gateway of Zayed's palace. An impassive blockade of Bedouins broke ranks to let Zaki and I out of the car and inside.

Up a few steps, avoiding a carpet where I saw at a glance a hundred or so shoes and sandals piled high which had been left behind by those who had entered previously, we went into a large room. It was the majlis, the democratic meeting place. The oak-panelled room measured about 200 feet square. The walls were faced with inlaid panels of polished pinewood, about 14 feet high. The pine was surmounted by a few feet of white sandstone in which air conditioners were whirring like distant bees. Light was provided by four sets of simple gilt candelabra hanging from the ceiling. A model of an Arab dhow was standing at the entrance door, and far across the room on a table was a white-painted model of a jet which Sheikh Zayed had recently bought for his private travels.

As I walked across the room I saw about fifty people sitting in green leatherette armchairs against the walls on each side. Seated to my left were a couple of dozen Bedouin tribesmen carrying rifles. There were a few soldiers sprinkled among them. Another dozen carried cane sticks held either at their sides, or under the heels of their feet. One tribesman held a stripped-down Hotchkiss automatic machine gun in his lap. And there, coming into focus now, a hundred paces ahead of me, eyeing my progress intently so that he held up conversation with a blue-suited official by his side, was Sheikh Zayed bin Sultan.

'As salam alaikum.' (Peace be upon you.)

'Kaif halek!' (How are you?)

His eyes focused hard and strong into mine, and then held on target so that we were giving each other that penetrating eye-fix, that mark of contact, customary in this desert. He beckoned me to sit while he finished talking avidly to an adviser. The whole room, which had come to its feet as he greeted me, now relaxed again into a distant murmur of conversation.

Suddenly, Zayed beckoned. I walked across to sit beside him. He sat quietly, the heel of his sandal pressed on the small cane stick beneath his right foot. Then he leaned towards me, his jaw strong and protruding, his eyes questioning. 'What do you think of Abu Dhabi?'

Zaki Nusseibeh interpreted and we were to talk for four hours. I came to know a great deal about Zayed, for the purpose behind my visit was to write a quick biography, something I had discussed beforehand with his Minister of Information Sheikh Ahmed bin Hamed. After a long talk when I also told him of my meetings with Numeiri, Faisal and Gaddafi, and my own mission of encouraging not only a 'voice' for the Arabs outside their own country, but understanding within, Zayed said: 'To say the truth is the best service you can give to all of us. We depend on the truth. To tell it without any compromise. You must become the voice of truth. You can help us. And all the Arabs will help you in any way possible. I am determined myself to visit soon some of our friends you have seen, particularly Gaddafi.'

There was a prolonged pause.

'What do you think of Kuwait?' Zayed suddenly asked. 'Do you think we in Abu Dhabi will go in the same way?' He had asked me the same question at our previous meeting.

I answered cautiously. 'I sometimes think from what I see, there is a conscious or unconscious conspiracy by the West to make men lose themselves and lose their roots.'

He listened intently. 'A conspiracy? Yes, of course. Our culture is threatened. We are already under great pressure from Western ways, Western politics, Western politicians.' Zayed's eyes on me were flickerless, motionless, just staring.

I interrupted his thoughts. 'But how do you think the Arab world will go? Reactionary, or liberal? Democratic or dictatorial? Capitalist or socialist? Like the Gulf as capitalist or like, say, Colonel Gaddafi of Libya?'

Zayed's reactions came in a completely un-mechanical and spontaneous way. His hands gesticulated. 'Do these labels matter any more? Do people speak of others as being reactionary, socialist, or this or that? Such words have little meaning. It is easy to take shelter in labels.'

He pushed his head towards me. 'It does not help true friendship. There's an old Arab saying that your real friend is not he who believes what you tell him, but he who tells you what he believes. Yet most people speak according to their label. The truth is that Arabs, like most people, talk in this way, according to the interest they seek. It's rare to find a person who says what is right regardless of his own interest. It is even more rare if he then goes on to live it. This is, as I see it, a great quality in life.'

'How do you find most people when it comes to honesty?' I asked.

'Almost everyone is like a chameleon, taking on the colour of his surroundings,' said the Sheikh.

'This is very human,' I answered.

'It is opportunists who have a label for everything. It all means little. Nothing! Take that word "reactionary". In Islam the word reactionary is "rejir" – meaning someone who leaves Islam and goes back to the past. Yet the Western label "reactionary" is supposed to mean something different. Right-wing. You understand? The Arab world should abandon all its chase after Western labels. There is almost, as you say, a conspiracy against us, to subdue us, to force us to imitate. Instead, the Arabs should see the road to progress as being through Islam.'

'What do you mean?' I asked.

'Being prepared to place our faith first in all our affairs.'

'Islam first in everything?'

'Islam provides guidance. This doesn't mean it quarrels with other religions. In fact, by its own stand, it puts other faiths in high respect. You see, Islam believes we are all servants of God. We're all equal. All of us in Islam have been created by God in his wisdom to serve him and apply his truth to everything.'

'Have you, therefore, a sense of destiny in your work – a sense, if you like, of this guidance of God?'

He thrust himself forward on his chair again, looking at me hard. It was the same question I had asked of Muammar Gaddafi.

'I believe every word I've said. I tell you, this wealth of sand beneath our feet has been walked over by generation after generation. Yet they were unable to use this wealth. The wisdom that enables us to do this comes from God. From no other source.'

I told him I would like to see him again soon. He readily agreed.

'We will talk again,' he said.

'You will remember?'

'Believe me, I shall never forget this night.'

I had taken extensive notes of our talk for a proposed book. We said goodbye. Zayed fixed me in the eye for almost half a minute. We held hands. He spoke rapidly in Arabic while holding my hand. 'We regard you as our Christian brother in the West. We are together. Always.'

As Zaki Nusseibeh and I walked across the room he called out to Zaki. 'He wants your interview translated into Arabic tonight for use in *Al Ittihad* tomorrow,' Zaki told me. For two hours I hammered away on my typewriter, Zaki translating.

When I left Zayed that night, I didn't know that it was one of the last times he would be so accessible, so easy to talk to. He was more than conscious of the looming future. A palace circle was soon to make him far less accessible. The state itself was about to plunge into break-neck expansion, followed by a tangle of federal moves which would nearly strangle it. But neither of us were to know that then.

The next day I was off, returning again to Libya in another pilgrimage to attempt to rescue relationships with the elusive Colonel Gaddafi.

– 18 –
THE DONKEY'S JOURNEY

– 1 –

It was to be several weeks before I could make the familiar journey to Tripoli. This time I flew with that most pleasant, if short-lived, airline, British Caledonian. It was to be swallowed up by British Airways in the not too distant future. Flying with Caledonian was always an efficient flight compared to many other carriers that flew in and out of the 'box of sand'.

In my absence, Omar El Hamdi had been promoted to the Secretary-Generalship of an organisation set up by the Colonel to arrange international meetings all over Europe. Sitting in his office in King Idris's old palace he gave a sympathetic ear to my tale of recent ups and downs. A tough, compact Berber with an engaging smile, the charming and affable Omar had been a lawyer before switching to journalism and international affairs.

'There's a meeting in Sirte this weekend,' he said.

'The Colonel's next big event,' Omar explained to me, 'is a gathering to celebrate the expulsion of the Italians from the area. After that he should be alone. There'll be a chance to see him.'

Piling into a car with a driver-guide provided by Omar, I shot out of Tripoli, past the long beaches on the shimmering Mediterranean, on the road to Benghazi.

'It was here in 1913 that an Italian force was beaten back by the Libyans,' my driver explained. 'The Italians had machine guns. Libya only horses and old rifles. But the Libyans won.'

Sirte had another distinctive claim. It was in this place, in a tent belonging to a tribe of herdsmen called the Gaddafi, that Muammar was born.

On the night of my arrival the site of the historic battle had become an enormous, gaudy centre of celebration. My car weaved its way through hundreds of tents. In some were dozens of sleeping white forms. In others people were eating and drinking. Horses and donkeys were tethered everywhere. In a clearing was a neon-lit ring, illuminated as though for a circus. It was packed with people. In the centre of the ring a man was orating passionately into a microphone. 'He's one of our great poets,' I was told. Every couple of minutes the crowd broke into a frenzy of hand-clapping at the hypnotic cadences. The poet's fine baritone swept out over the desert air, amplified by the microphone. His white, loose shirt hanging over his pantaloon-like trousers shook as he gesticulated and vibrated.

'What's he saying?' I asked.

'He's describing the fighting. How the Libyans assembled in the morning to face the Italians. How they fought through the heat of the afternoon. How at nightfall the Italians fled from the Libyan fury. How the Italians were afraid to return to this part of Libya for seven years after the magnificent defence of Gurdhabia.'

I left the car to join another crowd gathered around a drummer who beat out his rhythms. My driver disappeared to find me somewhere to sleep. The rhythm got hotter. Members of the crowd danced in front of the drummer. At 2.30 a.m. my driver re-appeared. 'Come,' he said, 'your tent's ready at last.'

When we reached my tent I realised why I had had to wait. An Arab family had been unceremoniously turned out to make room for me. My driver laid rugs over the rocky sand. I lay down in a corner. I had no covering and within an hour was icy cold. Before settling down for the night I had been given a tin of pilchards, a tin of sardines and a packet of biscuits, 'in case you want to eat'. Then the driver came with a bottle of pasteurised milk and a can of orange juice. I said no thank you. I was tired. But with a cramp and my shivering I began to think again. Maybe even the sardines would warm me. Eventually I found a way to keep out the bone-searching cold by taking up a corner of the carpet and rolling myself inside it. Anyone entering would have seen an elongated, rather tubby carpet roll lying on the desert floor. Nothing else. My head and feet were inside the carpet. I was grateful to keep my body heat in.

During the night it was all twist and turn, first one way, then another. The carpet was good for warmth, but could not protect me from the pebbly desert. It was about 3.00 a.m. before the nearby poet stopped orating and the drums stopped beating. I dozed off.

Just about daybreak, another ear-piercing voice woke me. It was now the call for prayers. I couldn't return to sleep. There seemed no point.

A water wagon stood outside with a tap to it. I did a blind shave without a mirror watched by a few Bedouin bystanders. For the rest of my toilet I now walked about a quarter of a mile past the red discarded water-melon rinds that littered the outside of the tents, out past the sage bushes to where I could see little sandy hillocks breaking the surface of the endless desert. I had completed my toilet, crouched on my haunches in the dunes, when suddenly I realised I was being watched. About a hundred yards away over the dunes were two soldiers, one of them holding an Armalite at the ready. As I saw them they started to walk towards me. 'Kaif alek. How are you?' I said smiling, hurriedly trying to adjust my pants. 'You have caught me.'

The first one did not smile. 'Documente!' he said in Italian, holding out his hand. 'Documente!'

I had no documents. Who has documents going to relieve himself at 6.00 a.m.? The other soldier nudged his colleague. I was under arrest. We eventually reached a command tent containing a group of officers. My explanation was finally accepted but a soldier still marched me back to my own tent to inspect my 'documents'.

At 10.00 a.m. I was told I was off at last to see the Colonel. My car gunned out into the desert. Dust covered everything like a pea-soup fog. Suddenly, mounting a rise, we came upon two parked Bell helicopters, their huge blue-bottle fibreglass bodies looking enormous in the sun. In tents lined up nearby were the veterans of Gurdhabia, about sixty of them, and not one under 80 years old. In minutes Muammar himself appeared, rising, or so it seemed, out of the dune just beyond the helicopters, making the desert the dramatic ally of his arrival.

He wore a soft white cotton toga. Beneath was an open, white silk shirt. When he dropped his head-dress a brown skull-cap showed. His only ornament was a gold wristwatch. There was the same virtuous frankness about the man's face that I had noted before.

Straight away we went to sit with the veterans. One rose to make a poem to honour Gaddafi. Others clustered around in a circle. Another recited with passion the history of the battle of Gurdhabia. Yet another joined the circle and Muammar lifted his arm with a smile to guide him in. The old man's wizened hands carried a green walking stick. It was Colonel Gaddafi's father. It was the father who now spoke of his son to the circle of veterans, with Muammar laughing at each revelation of his childhood, youth and development into a man.

Another veteran got up to deliver a poem and held Muammar's ear between his thumb and forefinger as he talked. Some veterans were led forward. 'Muammar,' they muttered, 'Muammar.' Some were crying. Some tried to touch his hand. I realised that to these Bedouins he was their deliverer.

Major Jalloud entered the circle, crisp and smiling. Jalloud and Muammar embraced. Jalloud, in blue cotton shirt, jeans and sandals, resembled a young athlete on an afternoon out.

Muammar's own Land Rover appeared next and I noted the two seats in the back, one for him and another for Major Jalloud with a radio telephone perched between the seats on a portable desk. Down the desert I saw a car for Muammar's father, a Peugeot van with a rough bed in the back.

Now came a dramatic moment. Muammar and Jalloud left the old men and walked up a nearby hill of sand. Ahead of them, just before they went, a Fiat water wagon sprayed the path to dampen the sand and keep down the dust. It was a kind of irony, considering what was now to follow, that an Italian vehicle had been used for watering the path of two Libyan leaders.

Muammar walked alone to where a stone had been erected to mark the spot where the Italian forces stood when the battle of Gurdhabia opened. By the side of the stone stood an Italian flag. Muammar inspected it and returned. An army officer now ran up with a fuse wire and ran back. Muammar touched a detonator. There was an enormous explosion and the stone on the hilltop, together with the Italian flag, disappeared in a cloud of smoke a hundred feet high. The veterans cheered and wept. The workers who had gathered nearby went delirious. The crowd at the back of Muammar surged forward like a demented tide. Then Jalloud and Muammar mounted their Land Rover and were driven away.

– 2 –

That night I was invited to stay at a small agricultural research station, a tiny U-shaped building in a desert oasis. I ate my evening meal, a tin plate full of macaroni, with a hunk of mutton, sitting on a grass plot outside the brick building. Muammar sat a few yards away. He spent his time in earnest conversation with an exiled Sudanese political leader, the lanky 6 foot 5 inch Babikar Karrar, a founder of the Islamic Socialist Party, and a former member of the Sudan Planning Ministry until his exile. I knew Babikar and had often spent a pleasant hour with him discussing his version of Sudanese affairs. It was all Arab politics, I guessed. I was neither asked to be included, nor wanted to, although I was beginning to wonder when my own promised session with the Colonel would take place. 'Perhaps later. Perhaps tomorrow. Bukra,' said my driver who sat beside me.

Some members of the Libyan RCC and others went into the rooms of the agricultural research station to sleep. In my room there were five. Major Mohamed Najm, who was two years later to be arrested; three young lieutenants and myself. It was luxury after the rocky desert floor of the night before.

Muammar disappeared to an undisclosed rest place of his own. Sometimes, I was told, he would sleep in a tent with members of his family, using the old mat he slept on as a boy. His father fell asleep on his bed in the back of the Peugeot, parked outside the agricultural station. Nobody made the slightest sign about any future meeting between Muammar and myself.

Breakfast was simple. Hunks of bread, butter and jam. Nothing else. I shared a common bowl with two RCC officers, laughing and chatting together in a mixture of pidgin English and Arabic.

The idea was that this morning I would see the Colonel for our long-delayed talk. The morning wore on, however, with no sign of a meeting and no indication of the whereabouts of Muammar. Eventually at about noon, my driver appeared with a message.

'He says he now has a bad headache. Things are not well with him. It was all too much yesterday.'

'Does this mean a meeting is going to be difficult?'

'I'm afraid so. But he sent a message. He said you would understand. He said, "He's one of us. Mr Claud is our brother." He knows you will understand.' It took a lot of understanding to have travelled a matter of 2,000 miles around the desert and then return empty-handed.

I slept the afternoon away to avoid crossing the desert in the heat and left at 8.00 p.m. on the long haul back to Tripoli. I wondered how long I could keep on 'understanding' while Muammar, who had promised we would build a bridge together, proved so elusive.

On the return journey I was accompanied by a Maltese attached to the Libyan Ministry of Information. He offered sympathy that I had come so far and not talked with Muammar.

'It reminds me of the old Maltese proverb – he came as one donkey and went away as ten.'

I didn't quite feel that. I had come for a purpose. And the purpose had in some strange way been fulfilled by its non-fulfillment. I thought back to my first meeting with Muammar in Khartoum, then to our talk in Benghazi, after which Libya had thrown a rope to help my family drag itself from the terrible hole which had opened up around me as a result of our entry into the Anglo-Arab scene. I would never forget that rope. But I was beginning to realise I could never help the Libyans by continuing to wait on them in Libya or by trying to execute schemes for friendship and understanding which they themselves could not support.

– 3 –

I come now to my final few days in Tripoli and my encounter with the lift at the Libya Palace Hotel, Tripoli.

I got into the lift on the ground floor with five other companions; two Egyptians, two Lebanese, one Canadian. It was an erratic lift at the best of times, with shudders and shakes as it mounted from floor to floor. But on this particular evening it decided to mount a tantrum and shuddered to a halt between the fifth and sixth floor. At first nothing happened as twenty seconds turned into one minute. Then as one minute turned into two, panic among the occupants grew. The air in the lift was suffocating. The passengers began to shake the lift and bang against its sides. I was too preoccupied with fear to do anything. On the fifth minute with a creak and a shudder the lift began slowly to descend. I counted the floors. Fifth, fourth, third, second, first. We passed the ground floor where we might reasonably have expected a release from this horror, but no. It continued to sink.

On the basement floor all concerned breathed a sigh of relief, but only momentarily. There were three sides to the lift, the fourth being left open and having no door. When the lift stopped at the appropriate floor, the lift doors on that floor opened, but they could only be operated by pressing a button on the floor side. At the basement level the lift came to a shuddering halt and the fourth side sprang open, only to reveal an exit which was solidly bricked in. One man began to cry, another to shake, a further to pray. What the other couple did was beyond me. They were probably gripped by fear as I was. A bitter, grinding fear that spelt out that this was the end.

I have once been in an aeroplane where a wing caught fire on take-off, and that was enough of a dosage of terror. The lift at the Libyan Palace, if one could measure terror in decibels, was far in excess of that.

This terror possessed one at least a full minute and when I gave up the hope of rescue the lift shook like an old man with an advanced case of Parkinson's disease and proceeded on its unsteady climb upwards. We all watched transfixed as the second floor gave way to the third, then the third gave way to the fourth. No sign of any door opening. Then, suddenly we were almost at the fifth floor and the lift cage (if that is what you call it) stopped between the fourth and fifth floor. There was about a ten-inch gap between the floors and clearly the fifth floor was open. Without thinking I put my left leg up to widen the gap between the fourth and fifth floor whilst my companions shouted encouragement. Then, suddenly the lift began to move, either as a result of my exertions or on its own erratic account. If it had moved more quickly I would have lost my leg. A fate too horrible to contemplate. And as a final conclusion to this episode we, thank God, drew to a halt on the fifth floor.

There was a curious and excited crowd on the fifth floor, mostly of hotel staff. They stood back, as though savouring at second hand some adventure they had been privileged to watch. The five other occupants of the lift did not hesitate. They disappeared down the stairs. I followed them.

A day later I mentioned the precarious state of the lift to the hotel manager. He shrugged his shoulders. The gist of his reply was that maintenance men were hard to get. Westerners installed such lifts then disappeared and were never to be found again. The nearest repair shop for a lift was 1,500 miles away in Cairo.

I told him I would like my room transferred to the ground floor. He said that there were no double rooms on the ground floor. It would take him a day to arrange the transfer. In the meantime, as I told him, I would prefer to walk up six flights of stairs.

The next day, seated at my typewriter in the room, I heard an unearthly scream. I dashed into the corridor. There was one pathetic man, his head and shoulders trapped outside the lift, the rest of his body presumably dangling inside the lift. Around the lift were a dozen house cleaners and waiters all gesticulating but doing nothing. If one acted, then one might effectively pull the man's head and shoulders out of their sockets. There was nothing much one could do.

The man passed out. Inside the hour I learned he was dead.

That evening I went along to *Al Fajr Al Jadeed*, the morning paper, to see the editor. I protested to him. Surely something should be done. He shrugged his shoulders. 'The hotel is nationalised. The directors are very well up with Colonel Gaddafi. No protest is possible.' I said I would write him a letter or a column – for my weekly articles were well read at that time throughout Libya. He said rather sadly, 'There will be a one-day strike among hotel employees from tomorrow. Besides, the man unfortunately is an Egyptian immigrant worker.'

– 19 –
RETREAT FROM TRIPOLI

– 1 –

Perhaps it had been the icy cold of the Sahara night. Perhaps it was my experience in the Libya Palace Hotel. Perhaps it was the contrasting temperatures and then the race back to London. But when I arrived at Heathrow after my abortive trip in the desert to see the Colonel my legs were aching and I felt an uncomfortable weariness, a kind of influenza below the belt. For the second and third day of my return I struggled on at work.

On the evening of the third day I learned that Sheikh Zayed had now arrived in London. He asked to see me at his ambassador's house in Rutland Gate. Zayed and I spent three hours together. He told me of his own trip to Muammar in an effort to convince him of the need for co-operation instead of confrontation in the Arab world. We discussed the biography I had started at Al Ain. Ali Shurafa was with us as an impeccable interpreter.

In the middle of our talk we were suddenly interrupted by the arrival of the bustling and slightly tense figures of Mahdi Tajr, the UAE Ambassador to Britain, and Nabil Hijazi, his First Secretary. Nabil spoke rapidly in Ali Shurafa's ear. Ali Shurafa bent to whisper to Sheikh Zayed who immediately rose and left the room accompanied by both aides. Something was up. The most logical conclusion from any observer of this scene was that Ambassador Tajr did not approve Sheikh Zayed's conversation with me or of my writing a biography about him. I was left alone at one end of the room. At the other Ambassador Tajr stood at the window, looking out as though avoiding eye contact. I walked over and tried to make conversation, without much success.

'How is Dubai?'

'Very good.'
'I've never been there.'
'You must come sometime.'
'Yes, I would like that.'
'You have only to let me know.'

He avoided any conversation like the plague. I knew him as a man who used his great wealth (the richest man in the Middle East many said) to influence and control the Gulf. He was a man who was not to be put aside.

I realised he had no wish to talk and left him in silence. After a fifteen-minute wait Ali Shurafa returned.

'His Highness has retired,' he announced flatly. I stared rather blankly around. The Ambassador had, unobserved, crept from the room. I did not know what to make of it. For some reason unknown to me the plug had been pulled on our session together.

'Send me anything you write,' Ali Shurafa requested as we said goodnight and I disappeared into the darkness of Rutland Gardens. 'Anything,' he said with emphasis as a parting shot.

The next day I had a heart attack.

– 2 –

The mornings began early at Westminster Hospital. I found myself waking just after 4.00 a.m. Across Horseferry Road I could see the trees in the small park next to the hospital. Usually, at just after four, the night matron would come across to me. 'Cup of tea?'

I was in the hospital intensive care unit. My bed stood on rubber-covered wheels, with a pneumatic jack that lowered it up and down at a touch of a button. Behind the bed on a shelf stood a machine called a cardiorater, measuring about two feet high by a foot wide. Behind the glass window of the machine was a white, bouncing dot of electric light, like a somewhat erratic tennis ball. From the cardiorater wires led down to attach to my chest – one white, one yellow, one red. In another box was a twitching needle with the name 'Heatrator'.

In a corner of the room sat two nurses. In front of the nurses was another monitor screen. Across that screen like lonely green shooting stars, trailing a wake of light behind them, danced the electric impulse of my heart-beat – the sole, simple absurdity to which my life had now been reduced. Occasionally I breathed oxygen through the mask hanging by my side. Each morning another nurse would come in and attach leather straps to my feet. I was like a Roman centurion strapped to the bed while the needle of a cardiograph machine scribbled my story on a graph.

What had happened?

After seeing Sheikh Zayed and staying up with him till 2.00 a.m. I had begun dictating notes on the phone at 9.00 a.m. the following morning to Jenny, my secretary. Jenny had been with me since my John Street days and the Roy Thomson partnership. She was like a member of the family.

I hung up the phone after more than one hour of dictation. There were sudden, intense jabs of pain under my left ribcage. William came into the room at that moment.

'Hold my hand, William.' Those were the last words I had any power to speak. Suddenly my lips moved but my voice wouldn't come. The pain was excruciating.

'Mother, quick!' I heard William shout. I was sinking now as if under chloroform, gasping for air. I pointed to my neck. William loosened my shirt. I felt my ribcage would explode with the unbearable pressure on my chest. A mist came down. There was a split second of swimming nausea. A pattern of tiny dots came to my eyes. I could feel myself floating away. I was moving as though through time and space. There was a distant kind of music, a humming, a kaleidoscope of dream-like images. Then a big wave of clouds like one of those speeded-up action cloud effect films on Cinemascope. It was rather pretty. Quite a relief. Thank God, I remember thinking, it's so peaceful now. It's all over. How good it is now. I began to feel an intense sense of flooding pleasure, a great infusion of happiness.

Suddenly a voice broke into my consciousness crying my name. It was my wife. I opened my eyes and realised they were full of tears. A young man in a Westminster Hospital Ambulance uniform was folding my arms. His companion was making a bosun's chair around my bottom. I was lifted up, wrapped in a red blanket. 'We've got you safe,' said one ambulance man. I remember the ambulance. My family crouched around. Then I remember how, apart from family, Abdusalam Bourgeiba, one of the many Libyan journalism students whom I had been teaching, came into the hospital and waited outside the Intensive Care Unit. 'He is Abu al aila, my father,' he told the nurses.

– 3 –

Gradually, I began to sort things out. I thought of the Arab world I had entered. I began to wonder whether despite all my good intentions to maintain the right of the Arab to be heard, I was now in danger of becoming a bad investment. I had to face the constant necessity of paying bills and meeting the debts arising from my support of Arabs. And when I thought of that, my instinctive reaction was to run a thousand miles from it. To end the day. To fold it up. I could be on the decline, I thought. I could be beginning the shadowy decline which led an honest journalist into the half-lit world of Public Relations. Yet I wanted to deal with the entire truth of my life in the Middle East and outside it, not just the bits and pieces that fitted in with my desperation to keep business rolling and bank repayments made on time after the *Middle East International* disaster.

On my second week in hospital, flowers arrived from Nasser Saif Al Bualy, the Oman Ambassador. More came from Adnan Omran, the Syrian ambassador and from the League of Arab States. There was a bundle of yellow cables six inches high from the Arab world.

William came with a message from the UAE Embassy to say that the Embassy would pay me £9,000 if I stopped work on my biography of Sheikh Zayed. I was much in need of £9,000 but William spoke up for me. He told the Embassy messenger, 'My father's work is not for sale.'

But I was most moved by a clutch of cables from the young Arab journalists whom we had helped to train. These meant most, I suppose, for out of all the mess I and others had made of the past, these young men represented future hope. We had trained twenty-two journalists who were now travelling the world or working as correspondents in places like Addis Ababa, Kampala, Valetta or Rabat. They had been very much part of our struggle against bureaucracy and against the shadowy, shapeless conspiracy that appeared to haunt the Middle East.

After four weeks in Westminster Hospital I was sent home to rest in bed for another month. Christopher Mayhew came to see me. 'You should retire,' he said. 'Time to go back to the country and contemplate the daisies.' I had too many debts to pay, I replied.

'You should go bankrupt,' he said. 'A friend of mine in Bath has. Free with one bound!'

I told Christopher that at any rate it was now appropriate for me to resign my directorship of *Middle East International*. I would make him a present of my forty percent of the shares. It would be a free gift.

John Reddaway sent a letter acknowledging my resignation and enclosing a blank share transfer form. 'We shall always remember all your efforts in starting *Middle East International* and keeping it going,' John commented. 'It is something we shall never forget.'

Whether it was something they would always remember was a matter of conjecture. However, Christopher said he could not afford more than £1 a share for my 40 per cent of the company, i.e. £40. I said again that he could have the shares free.

Two cables arrived from Libya. The first read: 'Our deepest feelings to the sudden heart attack to which you have been subdued. Sincerely hope you quickly recover. Ibrahim Ibjad, General Administration for Information.' Subdued or not, it was still a welcome message of support from the Colonel's Information Under-Secretary.

Not till the second cable arrived six days later did I feel I might seriously be suffering from a brain disorder. It read: 'We would like to inform you that a decision was taken to suspend the contract held with your organisation by the end of October. Meanwhile accept our thanks for your co-operation throughout the previous period – signed: Ibrahim Ibjad, General Administration for Information.' The enemies of accurate information had seen their opportunity. Despite all the sweet talk, I had been fired.

– 4 –

Bill Davidson, my local vicar from St Stephen's, Rochester Row, came around and I told Bill to add his cautionary words to mine in speaking to my family about the future. The Libyan blow had knocked out half our supposed income. I did not know at that moment whether I would recover my health or not. The doctors warned me of permanent invalidism, a lifetime on beta-blockers and drugs, and at the most three or four years to go, even then at a slower tempo. 'You are not to get too emotionally involved with anything or get into intense situations,' I was told.

Our offices had to be dismantled and our lease surrendered. The staff built up for the Libyan press operation had to be laid off. We had quickly to find less expensive ways of conducting what business was left. Whatever the arguments between ourselves and the Libyans,

I knew they would pay no notice period. Indeed, we would be fortunate to receive a penny for the current month. There would be no appeal in law. If we sued the government through the Libyan Embassy it would naturally plead diplomatic immunity. If we sued the government direct, any judgement would be in Tripoli under Islamic law which would be most unlikely to recognise the rights of any Western company.

There remained one possible rescuer, who at least should know of our position – Sheikh Zayed. I drafted a careful letter and William took off for Abu Dhabi. He was greeted with warmth and expressions of concern for his father and it was arranged that after three days he would see Sheikh Zayed. On reaching the Al-Bateen Palace, from which Zayed conducted his administrative business, William was shown at the appointed time of his meeting into the office of the senior official attached to Zayed's court.

William suddenly met a blank wall of refusal. The diplomat's tone implied that Sheikh Zayed would never find time, not even five minutes, for a meeting. To William the response was almost unthinkable. Frustrated and appalled, my son finally returned without a meeting, receiving only a promise which he correctly assumed to be empty that my letter 'would be delivered'.

Before he left, however, the same official again offered him £9,000 (or 50,000 dirhams) to 'stop the book your father has written on Sheikh Zayed.'

'I could not do any deals regarding my father's work,' William repeated. We learned some years later that Mahdi Tajr had lined up someone to do a book on Sheikh Zayed and I had interfered with his plans. The one-time Ambassador was at that time a powerful figure in Abu Dhabi.

My book, *The Desert Falcon*, was eventually published after Sheikh Ahmed intervened and he and Ali Shummo pointed out the services I had done for the state. It was published in English, French and Arabic, and was the only work on Sheikh Zayed. It sold 33,000 copies.

Back home, Pat had to deal almost single-handed with the winding-up of another office now that the Libyan work had gone.

I lay there with plenty of time to think. I remembered that day in the Sahara, when the Maltese spoke to me of the parable of the donkey: 'He came as one donkey and went away as ten.' Maybe this donkey, with all his mistakes, had to shoulder his pack. Insha Allah, the donkey would set out again. As yet he could by no means say he had survived in economic terms. But he was now committed, not so much to the Arabs alone, as to the business of lifting the veil, of pursuing his own right to be heard, of uncovering, if even partially, the truth of what he now believes held the Arabs back.

PART FOUR

PART FOUR

– 20 –
SHAPING THE NEWS

Ali Mohamed Shummo, Under-Secretary of the UAE Ministry of Information, looked from his fourth-floor window in the gloomy ministry building on the airport road. He saw the Jaguar swing in, past the shabby Strand Hotel next door, and draw up. He wondered vaguely why the British Ambassador wanted a special appointment.

Ali Shummo was now an old friend. Years before, at the end of the An-yanya guerrilla war, when I accepted General Numeiri's invitation to fly south with him in his private plane, I had put in a supportive word to the President that he might release Ali to take up a post in Abu Dhabi where he would be a great emissary for Sudan as well as serving Zayed. Ali himself had visited our burnt-out press in Wales and knew our past history. He was a brilliant, highly educated Sudanese who had lectured and served at the United Nations. He had been supportive of the book that I had written about Zayed and had been a sympathetic friend throughout the months of my recuperation.

Some time had passed since my heart attack. The controversial book about Sheikh Zayed had been published by my own company and distributed through Robert Hale in Britain. After the first few hiccups of doubt from palace circles, the fuss about the book died down. Perhaps as a by-product, the UAE asked me to advise them on the setting up of papers and news agencies.

Far from retiring to sniff the daisies, as Mayhew had suggested, I had with Pat's help taken to a regime of positive thought, plus exercise and a few vitamins on the side. Pat now accompanied me on many of my trips to the Gulf and we made a habit of walking in the cooler night air. In Abu Dhabi, Doha, Kuwait or Muscat, we would set off down the local coast road pacing our strides and enjoying the scenes around us. I never swallowed the beta-blockers that had been prescribed. It had been a slow process of recovery, but we were winning through. Like a man saved from the scaffold, I savoured every day. Each one seemed a wonderful bonus. And I had my faith to sustain me.

William, Pat and I, with the constant support of daughters Ann and Margaret, were gathering our second wind. Every morning a newsy 'What the Papers Say' column gave the UAE a view of Britain. Twice a week I sent a signed article on world affairs. The rewards were splendid. The Libyan debts with which my family had been loaded were evaporating. And I had no hesitation in taking on further assignments, in spite of occasional heavy twinges of angina.

However, the mischief-makers did not let me alone.

That morning in Abu Dhabi, the British Ambassador who arrived to visit Ali Shummo was the carrier of a serious complaint. The charge was that I had the malicious and irresponsible intent of damaging US interests in the Middle East.

It was to Ali Shummo that HMG's representatives now unburdened his woes. An 800-word column headed 'Letter from London' had appeared in the English-language daily *Emirates News*. In it, I had pointed out that following the 1973 war in the Lebanon there could have been a conspiracy to divide Lebanon. I reported allegations that the USA, using their Athens and Beirut Embassies as cover, could have been working to 'de-stabilise' the country, an action of pot-stirring which would in the end, I felt, be against world as well as Lebanese interests. I pointed out USA involvement in the area following the brutal murder of three US diplomats, including Richard Welsh, chief of the CIA station in Athens, on the steps of his home. His murder had followed a story in the Athens *Daily News* that Welsh was one of the Middle East's chief CIA operatives.

There was nothing extraordinary about the column. Similar allegations had been made in a number of much more important papers, including the *Christian Science Monitor* of Boston and the *Los Angeles Times*.

Her Majesty's Government, through its representatives, had, in talking to Ali Shummo, made one thing absolutely clear. They would be delighted if all future contributions of mine to *Emirates News* were clobbered by the UAE government.

Ali phoned me in London. 'The insinuation is that the Embassy here might take up the matter with the Minister or possibly with His Highness, Sheikh Zayed,' he explained.

I was flabbergasted. What could be the motive behind such heavyweight moves concerning one article in a paper that would scarcely be read outside the city limits of Abu Dhabi? Why was the British Embassy concerned about an article commenting on the USA?

'What have you told the Ambassador?' I asked.

'Naturally I've consulted Sheikh Ahmed,' said Ali and added that he'd also had a word with the editor of *Emirates News*. It was agreed that the best way to handle the situation was to give the British Embassy the right of reply. If this was suggested it might discourage further moves on the Embassy's part. At least that was what they hoped.

'Of course,' said Ali, 'to have suggestions put about banning you will only do you considerable credit in the eyes of the UAE authorities.'

'Do you think the Embassy will also try the UAE Foreign Ministry?' I asked.

'No doubt,' said Ali. The suggestion they were making was that if the government-owned papers in the Emirates want a 'Letter from London' they would be happy to provide the name or names of features agencies the British government could recommend.

'Was a name mentioned?' For years they'd been pushing the same name.

'I think it was Forum. Yes. Forum Features,' said Ali. 'And I think they've been approached by the *Observer* news service and by Gemini. Several have been named. It's all a bit vague.'

My God, I thought, the same thing's happening in Abu Dhabi as had happened in Oman, where a British envoy had suggested that another British firm, the high-profile Michael Rice, should take over our work. Incredible. Next day Ali rang again. 'The British Ambassador has agreed to write a letter of reply. Let's hope that it stops there.'

It didn't.

A few days later, the editor of *Emirates News* phoned me. He had attended a reception at the Abu Dhabi Sheraton where he ran into a well-informed and voluble American of Arab descent. The official title of the man was Public Affairs Officer at the US Embassy, but everybody, including *Emirates News*, supposed he had wider responsibilities. On the subject of my offending column he showed all the sensitivity of a granite block.

'Neither you nor your paper will obtain co-operation from the US Embassy in getting visas or facilities so long as you use Morris's articles. I'm not reading your rag again, myself.'

HM Ambassador, an old Middle East hand whose earlier posts had included Aden during the 'troubles' there, wrote a long letter of protest to the editor of *Emirates News*, ending with a cheerful warning to the editor about irresponsible journalism and the words: 'You printed it'.

I was now faced with an attack by my own Embassy officials. In the next issue of *Emirates News* in a new piece which further infuriated the Embassy I wrote:

> ... the British Ambassador has misunderstood the reasoning behind my article and attributed to me many statements that I never made. And even if I had said the things that he has 'read into' my 'Letter from London', he appears to be concerning himself about American policy, not the policy of Her Majesty's Government. I am as surprised by his letter as I would be if I had learned that the French Ambassador had taken it upon himself to reply to an article in *Emirates News* raising points about Germany...

It could be a matter of opinion as to whether the article complained of was discreet or not and the British Embassy was perfectly entitled to its own view. So were the Americans. What offended me was pressure on behalf of another power.

Moreover, I was weary of it all. The men in the shadows who never made a direct attack but simply torpedoed their victims out of the water, using unidentified methods, were again trying to cut off a writer's power base.

'I've had enough,' I told Pat. 'First Wales, then London. Then Libya, Oman, Kuwait and God knows where else. Now Abu Dhabi. The rug is always pulled out from under me and no one will admit to anything.'

'Perhaps you're just too independent for them,' she answered. 'Could a UK Cabinet Minister enquire for you?'

I thought of people I knew on the Labour side. Tony Benn. George Wigg.[1] Dick Crossman. Manny Shinwell. Michael Foot. Harry Walston. All stalwarts with a then Labour government.

I remembered one evening when secret services were being discussed over a drink with Dick Crossman, who lived almost next door to me in Vincent Square. Dick had explained how the secret services told nobody, not even himself as a minister of the day, what they were up to. The knowledgeable Dick had quoted the David Maxwell Fyffe Directive of 1952. Paragraph six described the 'well-established convention whereby ministers did not concern themselves with the detailed information which may be obtained by the Security Service in particular cases, but are furnished with such information only as may be necessary for the determination of any issue on which guidance is sought.'

In short, no minister is told anything unless he asks. He is, even then, only told as much or as little as the intelligence services feel necessary.

I sent a protest letter about events in Abu Dhabi to my old journalist colleague, Michael Foot, at that time leader of the House of Commons. Michael seemed by far the best bet among my political options. 'It smells to me of British Embassy pressure, at the whim of the United States, to restrict the freedom of comment of a British writer abroad,' I told him. What was reprehensible was to involve a British Embassy in the 'de-stabilising' of someone who had in no way attacked British interests. Why an unprovoked literary assault on a British subject?

'I'm contacting David Owen,' Michael replied. David Owen was Foreign Minister at the time. I did not know it then but this incident was reputed to lead to the end of the Information and Research Department (IRD), or at least one of the events that led to the end.

I didn't expect any quick response, but a clue to what was happening came when I ran into Martin Buckmaster at a cocktail party at the Inter-Continental Hotel, Hyde Park Corner, two months later. Martin was now elevated to First Secretary at the Foreign Office.

'By the way, Claud, they're taking your protest very seriously indeed at the FO. You've caused quite a stir.'

'Thank God,' I answered. 'Somebody at least is poking into the corners.' I knew too, however, that embarrassment was something the FO intensely disliked.

That summer the editor of *Emirates News* came to London with his wife on vacation. I found them a handy flat just by the Post Office Tower in Bloomsbury. We chatted most days. My column was continuing in his paper. The storm about the offending piece seemed to be abating.

Then at lunch one day, the editor mentioned a casual invitation he had received some time ago to use an organisation called Forum World Features, as well as Reuters. My mind flashed back to Ali Shummo's conversation.

Worried, I began to research the facts. I found out that Forum was headed by a British journalist, Brian Crozier, someone with considerable knowledge of the intelligence field who has denied any connection between Forum and ISC (the Institute for the Study of Conflict). He was also editor of the *Economist Foreign Report*. The record showed that Forum received backing from an American publishing outfit called Kern House Enterprises. Kern was run by John Hay Whitney, an ex-US Ambassador to the UK. Until 1966 Jock Whitney was editor-in-chief of the *New York Herald Tribune*. He had gone on to be special adviser on public affairs to the State Department. Forum seemed to have a library and research staff which it was said co-operated with the London-based Institute for the Study of Conflict.[2] However Crozier denied any link. The institute's main aim was to identify and analyse the threat of Russian expansionism to the West. It was authoritative, well-heeled and appeared exceptionally well run.[3]

There was room for concern about this new competitor. My concern proved well-founded. A telex came from *Al Ittihad* Press and Publishing Corporation, publishers of *Emirates News*. 'Your column is suspended till further notice.' It was signed by the acting managing editor, an expatriate Egyptian I had never heard of. The real editor had gone to the United States for two months.

I was told by an old friend, Abdullah Aman, then Assistant Under-Secretary in the Information Ministry, that the editor-in-chief had been given a first-class Pan-Am ticket to Washington on a sudden 'freebee' as a guest of the US Information Service. At a single stroke, three months after the storm over my article which had roused Anglo-American anger, we had lost our contract.

'So much for all the assurances that it was all cleared up,' I told Pat. 'They've dumped us anyway.'

A further two months passed before I called the editor of *Emirates News*. He had much to tell me.

'There are changes at the British Embassy.' Dispersing personnel had taken their final outings to Al Ain to collect their memorabilia, the Arabic coffee-pots and the silver-coined necklaces. They were off.

Well, I thought, that could be coincidence.

A day later I called the editor again. He had further news. 'The CIA Station Chief in Abu Dhabi, is being transferred. Going to Pakistan I understand.' Well, that could be coincidence, too. He eventually popped up as an editor in Washington.

On the third day I rang a friend at the UAE Foreign Ministry, a former Iraqi diplomat now acting as an Assistant to the Foreign

Minister. He was an assiduous reader of the foreign press. 'I hear that Raymond Close has retired.'

Raymond Close was CIA head in the Middle East, responsible at one stage among others to James Jesus Eagleton, head of CIA counter-intelligence.[4] I was not to know it then but Eagleton had also hit the dust because, in the words of one commentator, he was 'wont to interfere grossly on the flimsiest suspicion in the affairs of other countries.'

It appeared that not only had I been removed from my niche as a commentator in the UAE press, the British and American diplomats who had complained of my work were also out in the cold.

'Put any interpretation on it you like,' I told Pat. 'But perhaps at least we've dented the defences of those who try to shape the news.'

And we had, more than anyone could have imagined at that point.

– 21 –
THE STRANGE CASE OF MARGARET MCKAY

Tom Little called. He always had a sympathetic ear. Tom was both shrewd and loyal and, like many of us journalists, happy-go-lucky and endearingly improvident.

We went around to Locket's for lunch. When the preliminaries were over and I had put Tom in the picture about the loss of our *Al Ittihad* contract, and received his ready sympathy, I asked Tom about the one thing that had now become a burning question in my mind. I had become quite obsessed about intelligence agency interference with the news.

'Tell me about IRD. Do you know about it? What does it do? How does it operate?'

'Well,' said Tom after a full ten seconds of staring into his wine glass, 'it has people all over the place. Even in Hong Kong. It runs the *China News Summary* there.'

'What's that?'

'It takes reports out of Red China and gives them a bit of a twist to keep the rest of the world awake and fighting. Same pattern in other places.'

'Did IRD work closely with intelligence? Is it part of intelligence?' I asked.

Tom went on to tell me that James Swinburn, who headed the MI6 network in Cairo, was employed by Tom as secretary of the Arab News Agency when Tom was head of it.

'What happened to Swinburn?'

'Arrested by Egyptian Intelligence. According to Mohamed Heikal, a British double agent gave him away.'

'And the rest of you?'

'Jailed, then expelled.'

I knew Tom had been jailed by the Egyptian authorities but I had never been told the background. He went into the detail. It seemed that IRD as an information outfit had always been able to call on the Technical Help Department of MI6 known as 'Special Support'. This made it easy to lift bags, use video and audio technicians for eavesdropping on telephone conversations and organise locksmiths. All this was done in the name of supportive collaboration. It had operations going in all trouble spots – Cairo, where Tom was, Cyprus, Aden.

'We were all in it,' said Tom. 'Delmer doubled for us when not working for the *Daily Express*.'

I had known Sefton Delmer when I was on the *Express* as a foreign sub. He was a bear for probing the forest and laying false trails.

'A great guy,' I said. 'In the war, would you believe that when I was on the *Express* I helped plant stories that played up so-called Soviet victories over the Germans? We used to check with Delmer.'

Tom laughed. 'He deserved a bloody K, compared to some copper-bottomed shits who get gongs for minding their P's and Q's. First the Germans. Then the Reds. Then Arabs. God!'

Sefton had run the British black propaganda team at Woburn Abbey during the war. Tom Little's view was that he should have been awarded a knighthood. It was shared by Maurice Oldfield of MI6. Oldfield liked the effervescent Delmer style. A typical example of Sefton's work was described to me by Bill Conner, who had become well-known as promoter of Arab-British University Visits. When Salem Saleh, otherwise known as 'The Dancing Major', was heading up Nasser's public relations drive, his son fell ill with polio. Medical help was offered by the British Embassy which enlisted a Welsh doctor who knew all about polio treatment. Salem was quite moved, especially since he had been slating the Brits. He was amazed, therefore, to read a *Daily Express* story from Sefton headed, 'I don't want your doctor says the Dancing Major'. It was, according to Bill Conner, a classic disinformation story to keep Anglo-Egyptian relationships on the boil, prior to the Suez conflict.

The Locket's waiter filled Tom's glass and brought yet another pot of coffee while we carried on. Tom needed no prompting. He was full of anecdotes and recollections.

'At one point it may have helped to slightly de-stabilise a left-wing MP. I couldn't be sure but it's an informed guess,' said Tom.

'Who?'

'Margaret McKay.'

Everybody knew of Margaret McKay. My name had even been linked erroneously with hers in a Kuwait article. Though we had never met, she had been described to me as a pretty, petite bustling Lancashire MP who had first made her name in the trade union women's movement. Tom now told me his version of the story.

Margaret McKay had become passionately concerned with the Palestinians. She went to Sheikh Zayed after he had just been installed as ruler of the UAE and to everybody's surprise he gave her cash to start a Palestinian PR campaign. When they heard of all that money going to the extrovert McKay, some MPs were concerned.

'It was a minor sensation in pro-Arab circles. The lady started acting like a prima donna at the head of Palestinian processions,' said Tom.

'But why the fuss?' I asked. 'She seemed decent enough, harmless.'

Tom's explanation was lucid. After the fall of Aden and the collapse of Britain's informal empire in the Middle East, the British government came to the long overdue conclusion that it was necessary to have moderate, progressive rulers on the rest of the Gulf. Had they come to this decision sooner, my friend Sultan Ali of Lahej who had had such an influence on my own future might still be at home and the destiny of Britain in Aden might have been different. Who knows?

In Abu Dhabi, Sheikh Zayed was a natural choice. But few wanted heads of state financing a PR campaign run by an MP like Margaret McKay with her suspected far-left leanings. Actually Margaret was never as left as suspected. But at the time Britain was still responsible for Abu Dhabi's foreign affairs and defence and decisions as to who leaned this way or that were left to the Foreign Office in Whitehall.

'Margaret McKay seemed to go a bit wild,' said Tom.

'How? What do you mean?'

'Oh, things like appointments in the friendship society she was about to establish with the Abu Dhabi money. She appointed her daughter, Morag, who's married to a Lebanese airline pilot, the organisation's artistic director. Innocent enough, but you know what politicos are. MPs were a little green-eyed because their own efforts towards Anglo-Arab understanding didn't enjoy similar funding. She upset both the Conservatives and the right wing of the Labour Party.'

'Did she have an office?'

'No. She bought the old Monkey Club in Pont Street. But it was a bit of a cock-up. They wouldn't allow its change of use to an Arab friendship house.'

I knew the old Monkey Club, a five-storey brick building opposite the Cadogan Hotel where debs were once groomed for the season.

Odd to hear of an objection to its transformation into a pro-Arab centre.

Tom paused. 'She was haunted by a lousy press. She was accident-prone. Certainly from what I heard, some people didn't think her the ideal standard-bearer for Anglo-Arab friendship.'

'The poor woman was probably the sole target of the whole anti-Arab lobby,' I said.

'Maybe, but you can bet some Arabists wanted to see her slip on a banana skin. And she did. She made Willie Wilson chairman of her organisation.'

I knew about Willie. Secretary of the German Democratic Government Parliamentary Group. Vice-President of the British-Soviet Friendship Society. Enough to scare the daylights out of any man living with the theory of Reds under every bed.

Tom laughed. 'I need a break,' he said, trotting off to the gents which in Locket's had the word 'Lords' engraved on the door. I followed after him and we returned together to more coffee and the story at hand. When two journalists are together and have a tale to tell they're like two dogs with a bone.

Tom began to outline the possible scenarios if left-wing UK politicians and their friends had won out. Support bodies for the Arabs in the West might supposedly fall under left-wing influence. Left-wingers of the kind likely to be appointed by Mrs McKay could have favoured too many links with republican and socialist blocs in the Arab world, including at that time undesirable Palestinian sections. There could have been Moscow friendship link-ups through her chairman. It was certainly not what was meant to be encouraged with the charity money obtained from Sheikh Zayed.

'According to what you're saying, you don't think much of Mrs McKay,' I said.

'No, that's not true,' said Tom. 'At the time she was the only person willing to carry the can for the Palestinians, so naturally somebody was going to put out a lot of bullshit about her. With all her problems she held up their flag and didn't know or didn't care about the baggage she brought with her and how others would look at it. She seemed politically naive, or so they painted her. A pity. A pity.'

We had been so immersed in our story that it was almost 3.30 p.m. and waiters were hovering. Tom had to be off to the little twelve by twelve office he occupied in Queensway. There was no more time to go into further details, but I knew where to reach Margaret McKay. I knew she had taken refuge in Abu Dhabi, so the next morning I lifted the phone, dialled international and got hold of Zaki Nusseibeh in Abu Dhabi.

'Ah, you're looking for Margaret McKay. She's down opposite the Kanoo Building in a flat just off Sheikh Hamdan Street. Are you coming out to us soon, Claud?'

'Yes, God willing,' I answered with what I hoped was Arab politeness.

I was indeed going out soon on one of the many visits I made to the UAE and when I eventually arrived in Abu Dhabi I decided to call on the controversial Mrs McKay. It was to be the first of many visits.

Margaret had worn well. Neat as a pin, her print frock had a tidy white collar. She was still the vivacious character who had first attracted Sheikh Zayed, with her grasp of what's what. She occupied a third-floor flat in a block known as the Cosmos Building. We sat together in her lounge with a panoramic view of the heart of the city while she generously ad-libbed with a bottle of duty-free Scotch. Her sharp brown eyes twinkled with friendly warmth at the pleasure of a visitor from the UK.

I told her I was writing my experiences on the pro-Arab world and read her my notes of what Tom Little had said. She agreed with the facts and I then asked about her own background.

'I started in a mill in Oswaldtwistle at the age of 12,' said Margaret. 'I first became involved in politics by joining the Communist Party. Later on in my teens I moved over to Labour.'

Taking an interest in trade unions, she became an organiser for the Civil Service Clerical Association and then became Chief Woman's Officer of the Trades Union Congress for ten years.

'Were you ever challenged about your communism?' I asked.

'While I was with the TUC Vincent Tewson, who was General Secretary at the time, once questioned me about my communist connections.'

'Why?'

'I imagine MI5 or someone had been on to him with some rubbish.'

'What did you reply?'

'I told him I was no longer a communist. Indeed, in 1953, before my election to Parliament, I wrote about my conversion from Marxism in a book, *Generation in Revolt*, which Heinemann published. Later I wrote *Victims of Yalta* which had a reference to Stalin's plans of world conquest. It's incredible to brand me a Red.'

I asked her about the funding she got from Abu Dhabi for her PR campaign and she said that the money was made available to pay for such things as an Abu Dhabi–Palestine centre in Piccadilly, trips of MPs to the Middle East, publishing a news-sheet and buying a headquarters in Sloane Street. As for her activities in the House of Commons, her first political lobby group was called the Anglo-Jordanian Alliance and it ended up with a membership of fifty MPs.

'Not bad,' she smiled.

'Did you head it yourself?' I asked.

'I was the prime mover. But I appointed Willie Wilson, at that time MP for Coventry South East, as chairman.' Just as Tom Little had told me.

She said that she was the target of tremendous criticism. The whole Zionist lobby in Britain was of course against her and from what I had heard, the Zionist lobby was not alone. Some pro-Arabs had walked away from the Anglo-Jordanian Alliance.

'Oh, I know,' she admitted when I put the point to her. 'People left. Somebody was putting out all sorts of stories about us. That I was a communist.'

'What about your career as an MP?' I asked.

'Well, in 1970 some people on the parliamentary candidates selection committee of my Clapham constituency were clearly against me,' said Margaret. 'So I calculated I had no chance of renomination and after a lot of hassle withdrew.'

'So you left Parliament?'

'Yes. One of my last memories was a report I was given of a group of MPs in Annie's Bar reassuring each other that it was all right. I wouldn't have my money much longer.'

Christopher Mayhew became the heir to Sheikh Zayed's donation. It was all to go to the ANAF Foundation in Geneva.

That seemed the end of it. Mrs McKay's funding for the Anglo-Jordanian Alliance dried up as prophesied. There was a bit of gossip about the use of Abu Dhabi funds following some mismanagement which she protested was nothing to do with her. Now she lived alone in Abu Dhabi, an exile existing on a pension from Sheikh Zayed – the pro-Arab lobbyist who finally came in from the cold.

Mrs McKay would say no more. She had little enough now, not even a parliamentary pension, a loss which my MP in Westminster,

Conservative Peter Brooke, partly rectified when I brought the matter to his attention. Apart from the continued kindness and support of Sheikh Zayed, she was quite alone in a world which had all but forgotten her for more successful operators.[1]

PART FIVE

– 22 –
THE BHUTTO DISINFORMATION GAME

– 1 –

I coasted down the line-up in the colourless and antiseptic waiting hall. Ahead was immigration. The official took my passport and gave a quick upward flick of his eyes, signalling an army captain just behind him. A soldier, carrying an M6 with the safety off, appeared. I was beckoned to a side room.

Sitting behind a desk was a slender, incisive-looking army major of band-box appearance.

'What's your business in Karachi, *Sir*?' The major had a plum-ripe Oxford accent. He emphasised '*Sir*' in parade-ground manner.

'Visiting newspaper editors.'

He pursed his lips. 'I'm afraid we may be unable to admit you.'

I held back the irritation that wanted to spill into my face. 'What next, then?'

He looked at his watch. 'No return flight tonight. We'll have to put you in a hotel under guard – the Halfway Inn. Then first flight out in the morning.' He rose, holding my passport disdainfully between thumb and second finger, then disappeared through a side door.

I was left alone. It gave me time to think – especially about what had brought me to Pakistan.

I had three aims in visiting Pakistan. The first was to see Zulfikar Ali Bhutto, who was in Kot Lakpat jail, a cement and brick monstrosity of a prison ten miles outside Lahore. He was being held on a charge of 'murdering' a political opponent who had been ambushed in a car and killed. Bhutto was by no means innocent. He had clambered to power over many broken bodies. He was no better and no worse than many of his colleagues in Pakistan politics. Nevertheless, he was being jailed on a faked-up charge.

The second was to pass to Ali Bhutto a little present from friends in London and convey what encouragement could be given. The third was to support newspaper editors under threat of imprisonment because they had sympathised with Bhutto or, more correctly, had stood by their professional principles by still publishing what passed for near-truth in this terrified country.

I was by no means flying entirely solo on this trip. Behind me was the London Committee for a Democratic Government and a Free Press in Pakistan, which I had set up with Jonathan Aitken[1] after a meeting in the House of Commons. At our first meeting we had enlisted David Watkins,[2] Dennis Walters[3] and Frank Rogers,[4] then UK Chairman of the International Press Institute. Some 100 MPs of all parties supported the effort. People as varied as Teddy Kennedy, Ramsey Clark and Conor Cruise O'Brien were already convinced that Bhutto's execution should be avoided and they rallied around. The theme of the committee was a simple one: political opponents should not be murdered.

I had booked a series of half pages in *The Times* and *Guardian* to promote the cause of clemency for Bhutto by trying to appeal to a sense of fair play in General Zia al-Haq, Pakistan's ruler. News releases were going out to countries where the press was already hostile to the new Pakistan regime, not only because of its public floggings for the most minor political 'crimes', but also because of the clamp-down on journalists and the evidence of a possible 'fixed' trial where the slightest evidence in favour of Bhutto had been disallowed.

John Mathew QC, one of our group, had told me that the acting Chief Justice, appointed by Pakistan when his predecessor refused to take the case, must have been prejudiced.

'This man was passed over by Bhutto for Chief Justice when he was a senior judge and when Bhutto himself was in power,' said John. 'This is a man widely believed to be anti-Bhutto. He's reported to have referred to Zulfikar Ali Bhutto as a compulsive liar. How would you like to stand before a court and expect justice while the man who presides and guides the destiny of that court is said to have made such a charge against you prior to your trial and during the course of your trial?'

The QC went on to say that evidence had been destroyed.

'The main charge against Bhutto was one of murder. Therefore a request was made to examine the car in which the murdered man had been travelling. Examination of this car was an important part of Bhutto's defence. The Bhutto side were told that the car had been destroyed.'

– 2 –

Unknown to the public at large, or even to my committee supporters, was one key fact. At the bottom of all the effort, providing the necessary finance, was a single, remarkable Arab ruler, Sheikh Zayed of Abu Dhabi.

Sheikh Zayed had been a friend of Bhutto. He appreciated that there could have been mis-management during the time of the Bhutto regime and that there might have been many internal reasons for a change of government, but the circumstances of the mock trial and the sentencing of Bhutto offended him as it did half the world.

'Zia is wrong in allowing Bhutto to face the death sentence,' he said. 'It's a big mistake. What can be done?'

Sheikh Ahmed bin Hamed, his Minister of Information, and Abdullah Al Nowais, now the Under-Secretary of the UAE Ministry of Information, were present at a court gathering. Ali Shummo had returned to Sudan to take up the post of Minister of Information. At the court gathering Abdullah Nowais suggested my name and I agreed to rally round a group of people who would volunteer their own time and contacts.

A little later five Arab leaders, Sheikh Jaber Al-Ahmed Al-Sabah, the Emir of Kuwait, HM Sultan Qaboos of Oman, Sheikh Khalifa Al-Thani, the Emir of Qatar, Sheikh Zayed and Colonel Muammar Gaddafi, joined in sending appeals to General Zia to spare Bhutto's life. It was Sheikh Zayed who had originally felt in his bones the injustice of the affair. His instinctive reaction was to do something tangible by rousing world opinion.

My committee started work. We did not waste breath questioning the ghastly Bhutto trial which John Mathew had already condemned as a political farce. We confined ourselves to an enquiry into the validity or necessity of any death sentence.

– 3 –

At Karachi Airport that day I held in one hand a brief-case carrying a letter to Begum Bhutto from John Mathew. There were other notes in it that I did not want examined by any inquisitive major. The major had every right to view me with suspicion. I had no doubt a dossier had preceded my arrival. It would be better, I had already decided, to minimise the fuss and retreat gracefully. In my other hand, however, was a duty-free bag. I extracted a box from this and prised the lid with a pen-knife, placing it squarely on the desk.

The major returned.

I lifted the golden lid and the top layer of Romeo Y Julieta Coronas Grandees were revealed in their crisp foil, emanating that special musky smell of Havana cedar wood and fresh tobacco leaf.

I gestured. 'Do you smoke? Please!'

The major took the proffered Romeo, rolled it appreciatively between finger and thumb, then laid it to one side.

'Not now, Sir. Perhaps later.'

I pushed the box forward across the desk.

'I don't think somehow that I shall need these.'

With a thin-lipped smile now threatening to break out beneath his moustache, the major left the room. In five minutes he returned with my passport.

'It's stamped, Sir.'

I bowed and disappeared, not looking behind me at the box of Romeos, a gift originally intended for Ali Bhutto.

– 4 –

My taxi sped me to the Inter-Continental Hotel. There was a twenty-person queue at reception. The clerk, as I was waiting, picked me out and asked me to step forward. It was like some strange exercise in extra-sensory perception. While I was enquiring about a room, the telephone by his side jangled. Handing me the telephone across the desk, the clerk said, 'You are wanted.' The voice on the other end said in a clipped tone, 'Just checking you had arrived.' I asked who it was. 'We are speaking from the airport.' That was all.

Next morning I telephoned the first editor on my list. He asked me to come around. When I arrived at his office, two military men, a colonel and a major, were standing by his desk. The major was my Romeo cigar friend from the airport. He manufactured a smile, then they sat me down and after a few preliminaries continued to talk in Urdu. When they had departed, the editor opened the window to let in the street noises. He leaned over to me to point into the next room. I looked around the open door and saw a clerk taking notes. The editor whispered: 'I think we'd best go outside if we want to chat.'

We took a ride in a taxi. He told me that one of his telex operators had just been arrested on a charge of sending an insulting message. The boy, who was 17, had apparently sent a telex of one of General Zia's speeches to the paper's Lahore office. At the end of the message, he had reportedly tapped out seven words, 'Zia is a son of a bitch.'

'He faces a whipping and imprisonment,' said my editor friend. The editor himself had been asked to quit because of the incident. Some time before as a 'precautionary measure' he had been requested by his proprietor to write out a letter of resignation, leaving the date 'open'.

I asked about Bhutto's case. Why was Bhutto's defence unreported? My editor friend said, 'When Bhutto's defence statement was released I received a call from someone I knew well in the administration who asked what I was going to do with it. I knew the importance of such a call. After considering the matter, I told him we were short of newsprint in any event. We would not be able to carry Bhutto's case next day. No question of censorship, of course!' He laughed.

'It's a tragedy,' I said.

'It's a strange country,' the editor answered. 'It sleeps like a log and wakes up like a fury.'

When I arrived back at my hotel, I received a call from an Under-Secretary of the Ministry of Information. I invited him to come to my room. He was a pleasant young Under-Secretary but when I explained the purpose of my visit, he said, 'I can't really understand why you British want to meddle in the affairs of Pakistan. Surely, you have enough problems and headaches of your own, like Northern Ireland.' As he spoke, the room telephone let out a high-pitched shriek. I jumped. He chuckled. 'Whose bug was that – yours or mine?'

During the night disturbances continued. My telephone jangled seven or eight times. On four occasions when I lifted the receiver there was a buzz of disconnection. Three other times the voice on the other end asked whether I was there and promptly disconnected without further explanation. They were trying to un-nerve an unwelcome visitor.

The next morning I arranged to see another editor, who was also a lawyer. He met me in the lobby of the hotel and took me to an obscure restaurant in a back street of the city. We went in by a side entrance, and up what appeared to be a fire escape. When we got to the restaurant the room was empty of other customers. 'I think we can talk here,' he said. It was all an atmosphere of petty harassment, like a third-rate movie, a nation bent on imitating Harry Lime with every neighbour a third man, a fearful portrait of a Third World future all too evident wherever dictatorial governments raise their heads.

'My main concern is as a lawyer, even more than as an editor,' he said, staring at me morosely. 'The people of Pakistan have witnessed nothing but a political battle in the law courts.'

'I was told it was bad,' I answered.

'You know how the hearings were conducted?' he asked.

'Nothing much.'

'They were taped. But when observations were made favouring Bhutto a hand was placed over the mike so that the evidence was no longer recorded.'

'Didn't anyone say anything?'

'A few mild protests. Then a new mike was installed with an automatic switch. There was a button that could be pressed at the appropriate moment when evidence was wanted to be withheld from the record.'

I shook my head. It was a miserable picture.

'What's the future?'

'Legal disaster. There must be an independent judicial power, independent of all other powers. That's our heritage from Britain, for God's sake. Now the outside world doesn't care.'

– 5 –

I knew Zulfikar Ali Bhutto. I had met him at the Lahore Islamic conference. At the meeting of Gulf rulers he had painted a heady picture of Pakistan providing the manpower to assault the Arab world's enemies. 'You have the money and the resources. We of Pakistan have nothing to give . . .' he had paused dramatically in mid-sentence ' . . . but our blood!'

Bhutto had also promised, much more seriously, an Islamic nuclear bomb. In a theatrical crescendo which to him might have been an inspired bit of kite-flying, but which the Western world would regard with alarm as a terrifying statement of policy, Bhutto had declared that the people of Pakistan would if necessary sacrifice everything for this target. 'They shall eat grass!' he had shouted.

There was no doubt in my mind, even at that point, that the plans for the Islamic nuclear bomb were underway. Indeed that they were probably quite advanced. Bashir Riaz, a former Man Friday of the Bhutto family, working for their party political daily in Karachi, had actually introduced me to the head of the nuclear project.

'The money was coming from Libya,' the nuclear expert had told me. 'Big issues have been at stake. Given the Islamic bomb, Bhutto could have held the power balance in the Arab Gulf and the Indian Ocean – even with regard to Israel.'

'I know,' I admitted. 'But remember Dr Henry Kissinger's reported remark to Ali Bhutto – "If you go ahead we'll make a terrible example of you".'

'Perhaps the terrible example has been made,' said the expert. 'We knew President Bhutto took too many risks, said too much. We believe now that General Zia's officer corps was already infiltrated.'

'There's evidence of that?'

He laughed. 'When is there ever anything but suspicions, conjecture, or informed guesswork?'

There were many others who would see the sacrifice of an over-ambitious Bhutto as avoiding the prospect of Bhutto nuclear domination of the Middle East plus the prevention of any plan by Muammar Gaddafi to enter the game with nuclear marbles.

Even if General Zia had acted independently, the result was still fortuitous from the Western point of view. The Islamic bomb would be halted, at least for the time being. A barrier wall of loyal Pakistani regiments was fronting up to Afghanistan and the Soviet Union. Pakistan was firmly in the Western camp. Massive US aid was en route to the Pakistan people – hundreds of millions of dollars of military hardware free or on the never-never from Fortress America.

It seemed that Zulfikar Ali Bhutto, once he had committed himself to a Libyan partnership and the Islamic bomb, had to go.

All that, however, was not of my concern. I and my friends wanted

Bhutto's life spared. Sheikh Zayed, who stood behind our efforts financially, was determined to see justice. So were all the Americans I talked to – even those most opposed to Bhutto. Judicial murder was not in our book. To remove a President, or welcome his removal was one thing. To chop him after a dubious trial during which he was not allowed to present all the evidence in his own defence was quite another.

– 6 –

I stayed in Karachi two weeks. All my requests to travel north to see Bhutto were rebuffed. I knew that unless I could get through the Karachi bureaucracy I would never get to Pindi and Kot Lakpat jail. I tried daily to see Mme Bhutto, who was under house arrest, but it was impossible and I left Pakistan, stone-walled in my efforts, and returned to London.

The authorities, in a conciliatory gesture, released a couple of newspaper editors from jail. General Zia al Haq appeared to be changing tune. Perhaps, it seemed to the optimists on my committee, he was reacting to world opinion.

Zia, in a smart manoeuvre, next appointed to his London embassy a new Director of Information, Qutabuddin Aziz, a quick-witted diplomat. A former head of the United Press of Pakistan, he had once or twice contributed to my paper. I took Qutabuddin to lunch a couple of times, receiving as I thought guarded assurances that, once the trial was over, Bhutto might possibly be allowed to retire, under house arrest, to his country estate.

As if to implement the idea of clemency in the air, Zia now cranked up his own campaign with Qutabuddin innocently following instructions and activating the British press from his Lowndes Square Embassy HQ. Several Middle East leaders were assured quite emphatically that Ali Bhutto would not in the end be executed. Sheikh Zayed and Sultan Qaboos of Oman and the Emir of Kuwait were so informed. Clemency would be exercised.

The feeling now expressed by Pakistan's diplomats throughout the world was that they regarded any campaign for clemency for Bhutto as completely unnecessary. A campaign conducted on a wide scale might merely prove an embarrassment and, indeed, make it more difficult for Zia to show clemency to Bhutto when the moment arrived to do so.

It was all in the long run to be revealed as a clever tactic by Zia in a campaign intended to placate Arab as well as Western public opinion. The important thing from General Zia's immediate viewpoint was that it worked.

As a result, support for the campaign of the London Committee slackened. Sincere friends of Bhutto's, in Arabia as well as world-wide, came and asked me to hold up our fight. To add to the supposed 'improved climate', reports of the lifting of 'punishments' against journalists arrived from Pakistan. General Zia told Ramsey Clark, former US Attorney General, in Islamabad, that 'there had not been a whipping for three months'. He promised another caller, Yassar Arafat, that the climate was improving. Arafat, too, got the impression Bhutto's life would now be spared.

I decided to make another trip to Pakistan, this time planning first to see General Zia. We exchanged letters and a date was proposed. The only points made by his aides at the time was that Zia wouldn't wish to enter into a detailed discussion of the Bhutto case. Despite the assurance of 'clemency' I felt that I must travel to Rawalpindi myself in a final effort to visit both General Zia and Ali Bhutto. It seemed to me quite possible that Bhutto might agree to remove himself from politics and retire from the scene. Any assurances he could give to quieten the fears of the 'hang Bhutto' lobby would be welcome.

I contacted the office of Abdullah Al Nowais at the UAE Ministry of Information to inform them of my plans. The reply came back by phone after a long silence. 'You should drop your campaign. It's not necessary for you to visit General Zia. We are assured Bhutto will live.' After that message I went on my knees and prayed. If God spoke to me at that moment it was to tell me to board the first Karachi flight from London and ignore Al Nowais's instructions. I did not.

– 7 –

It was a moment in my life I shall always regret. With the help of Sheikh Zayed we had raised £60,000, all of which had been spent on a conference, advertisements and my trips to Pakistan. The committee had no funds for further air travel. We had already overspent on the campaign. I was told that Zayed had actually provided half a million pounds but the rest was not available. I had already had to ask Bhutto's son Murtaza (Mir), a willing ally, for money to pay for our last big parliamentary lunch.

At that time there was no way I could personally afford the Karachi trip and the fortnight it might entail in a hotel waiting to see General Zia and possibly, in the end, Ali Bhutto himself.

Mir Bhutto, then in London, suggested as an alternative that I send a letter via his cousin who was shortly to visit the jail. I wrote to Bhutto that Pakistan needed inspired thought as never before. It needed reconciliation and leadership more than martyrs. I wrote that I felt the world needed men of Third World experience who could look beyond immediate difficulties and see what lay ahead. I closed by saying that I retained confidence in the final, positive triumph of good. With the letter I sent Bhutto a book, *Abandonment to Divine Providence* by Father Caussade. Both book and letter were carried by Bhutto's cousin and handed to him personally in jail. It was the last letter he was to receive.

A few days later, back in London, I found I could not sleep. I woke in the early hours with a sudden, complete sense of shock, a feeling that something had happened. I sat up, waking Pat. It was 3.30 a.m.

Dreaming, I had seen, as though flashed on a screen in front of my eyes, the face of Ali Bhutto – a face etched clearly in every detail. Then, as suddenly, it vanished.

Had I been dreaming? I tried to dismiss the apparition and went down to make a cup of tea. Half an hour later I was asleep again.

It was 8.30a.m. when the phone jangled.

'Hullo?'

'News desk. *Evening Standard*.'

'What's up?'

'Ali Bhutto was hanged in Rawalpindi central jail this morning.'

'What time?'

There was a pause at the other end. 'Five hours ago. Can we have a comment?'

Bhutto had been dragged, protesting they said, from his cell. We learned later that he had been chained to a steel bed twenty-three and a half hours a day in a cell ten by seven feet which swarmed with mosquitos. He had been strung up like a run-of-the-mill murderer without ceremony, dignity, compassion or time to compose himself.

Those of us who helped in the campaign received silver medals from the Bhutto family with an inscription reading 'Martyr Bhutto. Distinction for freedom, courage and dignity.'

I am haunted still by the knowledge of how General Zia subdued world opinion during my visit to Pakistan by assurances he never kept. This is the epitome of the disinformation game, breeding cynicism, despair, the defeat of honesty in media and democracy in government. It was my first big lesson of cheating in the big league. It was not to be my last.

A few years later General Zia was blown up in an aircraft. The 'ifs' were still there, however. If I had gone to see him, if he had kept Ali Bhutto in prison or house-arrest this story could have ended on an optimistic note.

Some years later I was asked to meet Benazir Bhutto at a House of Commons lunch. I did not go. I have never met her. How could I explain the deep shame I felt that when my conscience said I should 'go', I had stayed put?

– 23 –
'WE'RE ALL PALESTINIANS NOW'

– 1 –

I was constantly reminded that many Arab writers and journalists had paid a price for the right to be heard, a price far greater than anything ever extracted from Westerners like myself.

A call came from Jelal Keshk, the Egyptian columnist who now worked on *Al Hawadess*, the Lebanese magazine. 'Come to dinner. I've invited Salem Al-Lowzy, my boss. He'd like your views on our magazine.'

I turned up with Pat at Jelal's flat in World's End, Chelsea. Salem arrived. Aged around fifty, a rotund figure of fatigue in a pin-striped suit, the well-groomed Levantine press boss exuded the tired charm of a smartish operator who knew too much for his own good. His intuitive brown eyes surveyed everything in sight. Salem was one of the irrepressible journalists of the Levant, and was famed for his indiscretions and his keen sense of acquisition rather than his diplomacy. He had made a reputed fortune and many enemies out of his own brand of political commentary. Once when Salem visited Sheikh Rashid, ruler of Dubai, Ambassador Mahdi Tajr was present.

The Ambassador said, 'I think you only visit us because of our money.'

'Do you think I come for your wisdom?' replied Salem.

Salem asked me to read his leading article. This I did, aloud to the dinner party. It was outspoken. It promised to interpret the Arabs without fear or favour. I congratulated Salem.

'We're supported by all Arabs,' he said. 'Our policy is independent. Telling it the way it is.'

After that night our paths parted and it was a considerable time later when I again heard news of Salem.

'We're All Palestinians Now'

He had gone to Beirut to attend the funeral of his mother. Afterwards, he had left for the airport driving along the stretch of road from the city lined with maple, cypress, fig trees and lovely terraced vineyards. He had dismissed the idea of any guard. He carried no weapon. His car was stopped at a road block. He was taken out for questioning.

His captors took the writing hand which had written the editorial I had read and praised so flatteringly at the World's End dinner party. They dipped it in a pail of acid. Finally, and mercifully, they took Salem Al-Lowzy outside, propped him against a cypress tree and shot him.

The Arab press had been warned. Someone had got their own back.

I heard the story while I was having tea at Grosvenor House in London with two Arab friends. 'Those that did it had tried and failed before. They were offered two and a half million dollars for the job,' I was told.

I shrugged my shoulders in despair. Al-Lowzy was only one of many. I remembered Yusef Al-Sib'aee, a former Minister of Culture in Cairo, who gave university lectures on the subject of 'Al Haq' – truth. His truth, his passionate belief in his own right to be heard, brought its own consequences when he was shot down in Cyprus.

More names flashed before my eyes like a cinema film of a great people intent in contradicting its principals, on rending itself. There was Saif Ghobash, in Abu Dhabi, a friend who had played the interpreter role in one of my first talks with Zayed. A boy from Ras-al-Khaima, he once worked as a London dish-washer. Then the Russians recognised him as a potential high-flier. He was awarded a scholarship to Moscow University where he wed his lovely Ludmilla. He returned to the Gulf to become Minister of State in the UAE Foreign Ministry.

One day Saif was on the tarmac of Abu Dhabi airport, playing his part in saying farewell to a delegation from Damascus. On the airport roof a gunman from a Palestinian group based in Baghdad took aim. He missed his target, a Syrian minister. The bullet caught Saif, one of the best and most emphatic friends the Palestinian people had in Abu Dhabi.

Then there was the evening in London when the voice on the telephone had been that of Christopher Mayhew.

'I hate to bother you. Could you do something for Said

Hamami? I told him you were the one person who might put him right.'

I promised I'd look into it. Although at the time I saw little of Christopher, we still had a common commitment to better Arab-British understanding.

Said Hamami was an articulate communicator. As head of the PLO Office in Green Street, Mayfair, the black-haired, clean-looking, always-smiling Palestinian had wooed the press, dispelling the bad-boy image of the PLO. He did not make the mistake of some who preceded him in the past, and others who followed; the mistake of associating too closely with the Marxist-Trotskyist groups who once tried to make the Palestinian cause their own. *The Times, Telegraph, Guardian* and other 'heavies' were carrying more stories sympathetic to Palestinians than they had for years.

Said phoned to ask for a meeting.

'What's the problem?'

'At the moment the PLO have offices with the Arab League in Green Street. They're not good.'

The League rented 52 Green Street. At this select address, in an elegant Georgian brick building, the PLO possessed what could only be described as a handkerchief of unacceptable floor space in an unkempt basement.

'I've no money in the kitty, but have received a promise of funds from an Arab ambassador to get a new office. More secure. An independent place. At the moment anyone can walk right in on me.'

'What's the difficulty?'

'I need someone to fix up the whole thing. Handle it discreetly. Nobody should know.'

I sympathised.

The PLO had the same right to be heard as the next group. Said confided that he had been having talks with Israeli moderates in Paris. 'We're moving from conflict to co-existence. From that to reconciliation. I met General Pilud (the Israeli "dove") and others.'

'Said,' I said, 'I hope you're not under threat.'

He laughed. 'What, in Mayfair?'

Three weeks went by, and arrangements progressed. My secretary Jenny had helped locate and approve three rooms at 92 Bond Street, W1. Said was on the phone. 'I'm giving a party. Can you come?'

In his top-floor flat in Bryanston Square were about sixty Arabs of various nationalities, but principally Palestinians with a sprinkle of predictable sympathisers from such organisations as Amnesty International, CAABU, as well as the obscurer Hampstead trendies, and a tiny Vanessa Redgrave contingent from the fringe of Earls Court. Halfway through the evening, Said stopped the chatter and in the middle of a cluster of people proclaimed, 'Here's to Claud Morris who's getting me a safe, new office.' I wondered why he bothered to make the announcement. The last thing I wanted was to be identified in any public way for a private gesture. Whenever I wanted to help I did so secretly and privately from what resources I had.

Afterwards, thinking over the evening, I walked towards the nearby Churchill Hotel and into the lounge for a stiffening cup of black coffee. Hamami, I felt, had blown it.

My alarm was multiplied next day when Said rang me.

'I have the payment of the rent confirmed. The Libyan Embassy are underwriting it.'

'You've been talking to them?'

'Only this morning.'

My heart sank. I knew that the Libyan Embassy was packed to the roof with informers. It was the most unfortunate of confidants.

Two days later my solicitor David Harrel, was on the phone.

'Everything was going through in relation to that lease. Gasters, Hamami's solicitors, were happy. But this morning I received a call. The lease in W1 has been suddenly withdrawn.'

'No explanation?'

'Nothing. Gasters say Hamami very reluctantly accepts the position. He's resigned to it. Won't apparently need your guarantee or further action.'

I was at home one afternoon when two officers of Special Branch that I knew came to the door.

'Hamami's been shot by a gunman who got into Green Street.'

The assassin had walked in from the street, accompanied by other students. Said's patch was open to all-comers. One just went down a flight of steps to the basement. There had been Said, no doubt smiling and cordial as usual. He had returned from lunch, having been told to expect a call from a student. It was obvious that he knew the assassin. He was smoking his usual after-lunch cigar. The student came in. A few words passed. The assassin pulled the trigger, escaping up the basement steps as effortlessly as he had entered.

– 2 –

Memories invaded my mind. I remembered a scene during my first visit to Amman. I could see myself, again, in my hotel room. A Palestinian editor had planned to meet me that morning. When my breakfast tray arrived I had found a note under the toast. 'Hotel surrounded. Can't get in to talk.'

After reading the note I had walked out onto my second-floor balcony. Below was a swimming pool, emptied, a dirty smudge of water resting on the bottom. On the house-top just beyond I had suddenly seen a figure in khaki stroll on to the roof, placing himself almost directly beneath my window. The soldier fondled a submachine gun and stared fixedly in my direction. He moved away. We were surrounded all right.

At 10.00 a.m. that morning Peter Sallah of the Ministry of Information arrived at the hotel. 'Come along. I've fixed an appointment with the Prime Minister,' Peter announced.

Half an hour later I was shaking hands with the dark, handsome and charismatic Wasfi Al-Tal, then Prime Minister of Jordan. 'Palestinians? Your hotel surrounded! My dear friend, I'm myself a Palestinian,' Wasfi assured me. 'True you see tanks in the streets. But are these to keep you from the Fedayin?' He laughed. 'Did you know I wanted the King to turn the whole of Jordan into a Fedayin state?'

He waved his hands apologetically. 'Instead of them accepting that, Fedayin apparently want to argue with us.'

He put his arms around me as we parted. 'We're all Palestinians now,' he said.

Shortly afterwards Wasfi was shot down by Fedayin in the entrance of the Cairo Sheraton Hotel. The Aulul Al-Aswad, otherwise known as Black September, did the job. His body would lie there, next to the poster saying 'The Sheraton Welcomes You', next to the flower shop and the plate glass doors, while one of the Fedayin licked his blood.

I didn't suspect that later still I would open the *Egyptian Gazette* to learn that the gunmen were completely freed by a Cairo court or that I was to read the headline celebrating their release to freedom – 'Triumph for Egyptian Justice'.

– 3 –

Fifteen thousand people crowded the streets of the Palestinian and Muslim suburb of Beirut called Tarik al-Jadeed at Said Hamami's funeral. The voiceless ones.

Perhaps, I thought, he'll meet Wasfi Tal in the hereafter. And Salem Al-Lowzy, and Saif Ghobash and Yusef Al Sib'aee and all the others who tried and died. I like to think so.

On the day of Said's funeral I turned to a poem of Dag Hammarskjold:[1]

> What have I to fear
> If their arrows hit,
> If their arrows kill,
> What is there in that
> To cry about?
>
> Others have gone before
> Others will follow.

As I read the verse I thought: How long will it take, how much useless waste will there be in pursuit of the Arab right to be heard if Arabs continue to work against Arabs?

– 24 –
UNEXPECTED GREMLINS AND MOLES

– 1 –

One of the greatest solo public relations performances in Paris is to be seen daily at Les Princes restaurant in the Hotel George V. The youthful *sommelier*, a handsome young man, bursting balloon-like out of his trousers, gold chain draped around his neck, has a fascinating twitch of the eye. As he brings the chosen bottle forward, cradled in the whitest of napkins, he looks at his guest as though entering some affair of the heart. His left eyelid drops in a conspiratorial wink. He handles the corkscrew lovingly with a slow and delicate twist of the wrist. He then waits appreciatively for his guest's approval, lifting his eye questioningly.

'C'est bon.'

The guest flicks his head. A smile swiftly crosses the *sommelier's* face as he fills the glasses, places the bottle back in its ice bucket or basket, as the case may be, and walks grandly away.

André Fontaine, editor of *Le Monde*, viewed the act as appreciatively as I. We were lunching together, discussing not only the known prejudices of the West against the Arab, but the appalling way some Arab governments handled their press relations.

'An Israeli minister said the other day that the Israelis were fortunate because some Arabs did their work for them,' I said. André agreed. The Arabs suffered from lousy presentation. It was like serving a good wine with bad manners.

The reason for my trip to Paris was to arrange a European distribution network for a new weekly we were about to launch. It was now as near as dammit to realisation, but as usual in any project aimed at helping understanding in the Middle East, there were gremlins and moles everywhere.

Unexpected Gremlins and Moles

I had just flown back from Abu Dhabi after a meeting with Crown Prince Sheikh Khalifa bin Zayed, Zayed's eldest son, who in the years I had known his family had developed into a good-hearted and sympathetic man. He is now Deputy Supreme Commander of the UAE Armed Forces. Sheikh Khalifa had approved a UAE investment in the new weekly. Sheikh Ahmed bin Hamed, Abdullah Al Nowais, Ibrahim Al Abed, director of the news agency, and presidential adviser Zaki Anwar Nusseibeh had all been in attendance.

Sheikh Khalifa and I had by now been friends for over a decade. Because I had always felt him to be the best bet for the peaceful future and eventual democratisation of his country, I had defended his right to succeed his father when this was attacked in the London press.

Sheikh Ahmed's family and mine had become close friends. As Ahmed more than once reminded me, 'We began as friends, we ended as family.'

Abdullah I first knew as a perceptive ex-Cairo University student, attached to the PR department of the Ministry. Zaki came from one of the oldest of Palestinian governing families and had brought his considerable diplomatic skills to serve the UAE. Ibrahim, another Palestinian, was a friend of long standing. I regarded them all with the affection of an elder brother, or 'father', as they liked to call me.

'I'll leave the details in the hands of the Minister of Information and ask him to carry it through,' said Khalifa. It was a royal seal of approval.

The night after the meeting with Sheikh Khalifa I went to see Sheikh Ahmed at his villa to discuss how he would deal with the matter. Ahmed sat me on a couch while he, Abdulla and Ibrahim all said their prayers. I watched the three arched backs, heads touching the carpet, and thought how at long last we could be grateful that with Khalifa's ready generosity a project was to be founded which would provide a lasting bridge to Arab-British understanding. It would justify the long-term efforts of us all.

'Before we implement Sheikh Khalifa's wishes, I think you should bring along written commitments from the other Arab shareholders,' said Ahmed. These were Sheikh Saud Al-Sabah,[1] an old and a good friend of mine and Kuwait Ambassador to the US, Faisal Marzook Al Marzook of *Al Anba* newspaper, Mohamed Al-Khalifi and Yusef Darwish representing Qatar's press interests.

It was an unanticipated delay but I had no option and agreed to get letters of agreement from the other shareholders involved. I had no idea that there were persistent gremlins and moles dogging my footsteps.

– 2 –

Omar Al Hassan, head of the Arab League, telephoned me. 'I would like to have your new paper proposals to show to the Arab ambassadors in London at their monthly meeting. In confidence, of course,' he said. 'They may be getting queries from other sources outside the UAE. I know that Saudi Arabia could be interested in nominating a Saudi paper to join you.'

'It will be absolutely confidential?' I queried.

'Of course.'

I thought the idea was probably a useful one.

It was two days after the ambassadors' meeting that Frank Rogers phoned. Frank, now Chairman of East Midlands Allied Press, the biggest independent group of magazines outside London, was to be a British director of the new publication. With Jim Coltart, Chairman of the Thomson Foundation, Tom Hopkinson, Lord Marsh of the British Newspaper Publishers Association and Lord Caradon as an Arabist, I felt we would have a good, sound board. I hoped too that eventually that able ex-editor of the *Spectator*, Sir Ian Gilmour[2] would join us along with Jonathan Aitken in an unbeatable combination.

'I just had a call from the *Jewish Chronicle*,' said Frank. 'They have every detail of the new paper – costings, circulation plans, financing, names of directors.'

I was floored. Astounded.

'What did they say?'

'They asked how I could allow myself to be associated with a pro-Arab paper considering my responsibilities to other shareholders in my own public company. They suggested it might be an embarrassment if raised at a public meeting of EMAP.'

'What did you reply?'

'I told them we printed all kinds of papers. We didn't ban a paper because of Arab connections. But where the devil did they get the documents?'

The *Guardian* ran a report – 'Mole at Arab Embassy' – and asked plaintively: 'How did the *Jewish Chronicle* get the top secret story of plans for launching a new paper, the *Arab Chronicle*?'

Almost everyone connected was now approached.

The freelance author and journalist Marion Woolfson offered a clue when she said that the 'leak' had been sprung through a press department employee of one of the embassies. Someone had apparently leaked the document to the Israeli Press Office and it duly reached Geoffrey Paul, editor of the *Jewish Chronicle*.

I knew from past experience what would follow. All the British investors in the project would be 'nobbled'. Their names would be published in the *Jewish Chronicle*. Papers like the *Financial Times* and the *Guardian* would reprint the names with comments. Furthermore, I had problems on the Arab Gulf. There had been a sensible request for a round-table meeting of all the potential shareholders, but whenever I fixed a date convenient to one, another cried off.

– 3 –

The hazards of pro-Arab publishing are known only to those who practise it. The embarrassing 'leak' to the *Jewish Chronicle* coincided with a collapse of the Kuwait stock market. This removed from the scene one or two investors from other Arab countries apart from the UAE. Sheikh Ahmed's condition that agreements with the shareholders outside the UAE should be signed before the UAE contributed could not now be fulfilled. There was, at this point, too much against the project both economically and socially.

There comes a time in the Middle East when you have to give in or go mad. I was trying to do what the Arab Gulf Co-operation Council could not themselves achieve – get the Arabs together. It was either stop or have another heart attack.

'I can cope with newspaper competition. I can cope with most problems. Even bad economics. What I can't cope with is the collapse of the Kuwait stock market and divisions within the Arab camp,' I told William.

So I cleared matters up and eventually sent back any deposits on shares. Reluctantly I surrendered our promising association with Faisal al-Marzook of *Al Anba*, Kuwait. He had generously sent his ten per cent deposit at an early date, and would have been a grand ally under different circumstances.

– 4 –

The de-railing of the *Arab Chronicle* was no isolated instance of the accident-prone state of Arab–Western press relations. The Secretary General of the League of Arab States, Chadli Klibi, had heard at this point of the seminars I arranged from time to time to bring Arab editors together with editors from the West. The aim was to build what I called a 'Fourth Track' in international relations. 'Track One' was normal diplomatic relations between governments, including military pressures. 'Track Two' was the powerful force of the law. 'Track Three' was religion and the churches. 'Track Four' was the press.

I felt that editors getting together could increase Arab–Western understanding. They were an elite group of opinion-formers. The eventual aim was to promote world peace and understanding through the media.

Chadli Klibi appeared anxious for involvement. 'I would like to meet some of your editor friends when next in London,' he told me.

Again I contacted Frank Rogers, who more than most men lived out the practical idea of building understanding through media relationships enthroned in the Charter of the International Press Institute. Frank rounded up friends. I phoned others. Where an editor could not attend he promised to send a leader-writer, diplomatic or Middle East correspondent. I booked a suite at the Dorchester for a private dinner for the Secretary General. He was travelling from Tunis to join us.

Came the day I was in the West Country and took the afternoon train up, only to be greeted by a surprised wife and a shattered secretary, waiting desperately at the end of Platform 4 at Paddington.

In the afternoon some unnamed girl from the Secretary General's office had placed a clumsy telephone call to my office to ask for the guest list. My secretary had provided half a dozen names of some guests she knew to be coming, a representative bunch from Fleet Street plus BBC World Service radio chiefs and others from television. It was by no means a complete list, for at least three editors said they might send substitutes, so were named by paper rather than individual.

Jenny had no idea that all conventional norms of etiquette were now to be shattered.

To everyone's amazement, at three o'clock that afternoon the same girl from the Secretary General's office rang each intended dinner guest direct and promptly told him the dinner was 'off'. The Secretary General would not be coming. No explanation. No apology.

The next morning, egg still on my face after an evening of apologies to men who had kept the date open for weeks, I happened to call on Mohamed Heikal, ex-editor of *Al Ahram*, who was staying at Claridges on his annual visit to London. I told Mohamed the story of the Secretary General's dinner defection.

'Good God!' he said. 'The Secretary General, Klibi, rang me up and asked could he come along to Claridges to sit for the evening as he had unexpectedly found a dinner date cancelled – or so he was told by his aides. He said nothing of your dinner. I'd have been glad to have attended myself. I'd certainly have told him not to miss it.'

I was finally offered one reluctant explanation. The aides around the Secretary General had felt that some awkward questions might be asked by such a varied group of editors. Therefore it was best to withdraw. They were not going to expose their man. The extraordinary thing was that the great man himself was never, I gathered, consulted. No one considered the impropriety of ringing the guests direct at only a few hours' notice without even informing the host.

While he held office Secretary General Klibi still continued to complain about the image of the Arab promoted by an unco-operative British press.

– 25 –
DARKNESS BEFORE DAWN?

– 1 –

The dusty brown exterior of the Hotel George V rose five storeys above the Avenue George V. The flags of France, West Germany, Austria, USA, UK and the Gulf States flapped in the Paris breeze. Crossed palm leaves decorated the entrance lobby as the crowd of over 200 editors, writers and diplomats moved toward the banqueting hall.

Seated at the top table were three leading Europeans – ex-Chancellor Helmut Schmidt of Germany, ex-Chancellor Bruno Kreisky of Austria and Denis Healey,[1] Shadow Foreign Secretary in the British Parliament. In the chair was André Fontaine. A hundred editors from British and European papers were present. It was a seminar sponsored by Qatar, that pear-shaped peninsula on the Arab Gulf, and organised on their behalf by our company.

Our first seminar following the Bhutto London seminar had been on the Arab Image in Western Mass Media and was sponsored by Sheikh Zayed. It had gone well. Jonathan Aitken had rallied around with others like Dick Marsh, then Chairman of the British Newspaper Publishers Association, and Edward Heath, who gave the keynote speech.

Some of us believed that much of the improved perception of the Arabs at that time was due to lasting links created on that occasion.

This next seminar five years later had such Arab editors-in-chief as Nabil Khoury of *Al Mustaqbal*, Mahmoud Al-Sherif of *Ad Dastour*, Youssef Alayan of *Kuwait Times*, Khalid Al-Maeena of *Arab News*, Ghassan Tueni of *Al Nahar*, all working in groups to present problems to be answered by people like Henri Pigeat, head of Agence France Presse, André Fontaine, Martin Woollacott, foreign editor of the

Guardian, Roger Matthews, Middle East editor of the *Financial Times* and Joe Fitchett of the *International Herald Tribune*.

As the International Press Institute was to write later: 'It was the most distinguished gathering of everybody of importance in European media.' The *UK Press Gazette* was to describe the proceedings as 'essential background for every foreign editor or Middle East correspondent.' Russell Twisk, then editor of the *Listener*, was to write: 'What I heard and saw will change the way the *Listener* looks at the Arabs in future.' The Arabs were at last gaining acceptance in the media. Years of work was paying off. We were now, at last, beginning to drive the nail the last inch. That was the message.

Even a paper normally expected to be hostile, the *Jewish Chronicle*, called it 'a brilliant exercise in sophisticated public relations'. A Jewish journalist, Chaim Bermant, remarked after talking to a group of Arab editors: 'To my astonishment we talked as friends. They don't hate me.' The decision to invite him had been taken after much heart-searching by both the sponsors and myself. 'La charité sauvera le monde' (Charity will save the world), said my French colleague, Eric Rouleau of *Le Monde*.

Nuri Birgi, the Turk who had proclaimed, 'Never speak of our opponents as enemies, but always as "our friends who do not understand us"' was there, and Dr Bruno Kreisky told the editors gathered at that seminar, 'Go and talk to those most opposed to you. It's surprising what you will learn.'

The seminar had only one theme – establishing understanding through media. Diplomats and politicians often failed. Why not editors of all viewpoints to create a new way? This had been the theme of our work for years.

Among the observers were members of the French Assembly, including a future Foreign Minister, representatives of Franco/Arab institutions and representatives from the EEC and AGCC.

Every Paris radio station and two TV channels sent delegates. There were 10 editors and 19 commentators from France, 6 from Germany and Austria, 3 from Italy, 4 from the US. We arranged to broadcast daily three-minute TV packages to 27 stations.

We had however, reckoned without the negative spirit that walks the streets ...

– 2 –

The first sign of trouble came shortly before the seminar's gala dinner. There had been a call from the Arab Gulf sponsors, way back in the Emiri Palace in Doha, Qatar. 'Arab intelligence has told us a terrorist group is on the way.'

The Quai d'Orsay rang. 'Will you take all precautions?' They had independent information. I looked through the list of likely targets and called the secretary of Crown Prince Hassan of Jordan, billed as one of the gala dinner's leading speakers. 'We, too, have received independent information,' came the confirming voice. 'His Highness has already decided to pull out.'

At the dinner ten bodyguards were scattered across the room. One sat with Bruno Kreisky, two with Helmut Schmidt; three stood behind the TV cameras near Yassar Dura of World Television News; two were at the exits. We had twelve more private detectives watching entrances, stairways, lifts and bedrooms. The whole thing had turned into an elaborate nerve test.

'See if you can close the dinner before 11.30,' the Sureté warned. The speeches over-ran. Denis Healey was rounding off: 'Our thanks are due to Claud Morris who has screwed the nuts and bolts together. I hope he keeps on screwing for a long time!' His audience roared. I was looking at my watch. At that precise moment I wasn't too sure about screwing anything – or being screwed.

Two anxious figures from France's domestic intelligence services, Direction de la Surveillance du Térritoire, and another who had casually identified himself as an assistant to the legendary Bernard Gerard, the head of France's counter-intelligence, were semaphoring from side tables. Time was running out. They suspected that the 'terrorist' group were to hit us, regardless, before midnight. But who were they? Who?

Most of all I wanted to get Bruno Kreisky out. I had been told he had been in the middle of controversial negotiations with Israel over Arab prisoners and was, in the view of the Sureté, a number-one target. At 11.30 approximately I closed the dinner before the magnificent dessert had been served, much to the alarm of the head chef. We hustled Bruno into a convenient back-stairs lift.

The Sureté, with commendable efficiency, took two protesting guests out of the lobby and bundled them into a waiting *voiture de police*. They were deported, proclaiming their innocence all the way to Charles de Gaulle. According to *Le Monde* a Frenchman, a *barbouze* or false beard, with extremist links and scant sympathy with any moderate Arab States, had been to the Bekaa Valley in Lebanon and given the tip-off details to an Arab hit squad. The Frenchman was a leading pro-Arab. The extremists were, as always, working towards the destruction of any moderate approach.

– 3 –

The second upset which followed was not to be so immediately disposed of, for there now began one of the great blood sports of the envious, 'the killing of a success story'. Vitriolic criticism started, not from any anti-Arab source as might be expected, but in an article in a well-known Arab daily, *Al Anba* of Kuwait. The article was by a Palestinian author, Nasser Nasashabi, who was a former Cairo editor. Through an oversight, he had not been invited to the seminar and was determined to put his feelings on record.

In spite of his condemnation, the conference was recognised as the best public relations exercise for the Arabs ever seen in continental Europe. And indeed, eventually the 'years that the locusts had eaten' were restored to Morris International. True friendships never die in the Arab world no matter how the world tries to undermine them.

– 4 –

In a final flash of curiosity I decided to see the author of the article that had tried to torpedo the seminar. I rang Nasser Nasashabi at his Geneva home. 'I'm in my London flat tomorrow,' he said. 'Come around.'

A soft-footed pretty West Indian maid with Rastafarian dreadlocks came to the door and showed me into a reception room and study, dominated by a magnificent oil of Jerusalem by Lawson Booth that almost filled a wall. The bookcase next to the desk at which the author sat was full of framed personal photos. Seeing me glancing at these he said: 'You'll find me here with leaders like Reagan, Nixon, Fahd of Saudi Arabia and Hussein of Jordan.'

Nasashabi, bespectacled, wore a blue blazer with a pink hanky flapping out of the breast pocket. I commented on his library. 'I've written twenty-five books,' he told me. 'You know I speak fluent Hebrew and French as well as English and Arabic.' He traced his line back to an ancestor who arrived in Palestine from Egypt in AD 900.

I tackled him on the subject of the seminar.

'I didn't attend the seminar myself, although I was in Paris at the time and heard from many sources how terrible it was,' he said.

'How was it terrible?'

'The invited speakers were terrible. It was terrible – terrible – to invite well known personalities like Schmidt and Kreisky to curse and criticise us without any objectives.'

I was amazed. Did he include Healey?

'Yes. The lot.'

I could remember that Denis Healey had criticised Syria at one point. Helmut Schmidt, a pioneer of Ostpolitik and dialogue with Russia, had preached a non-aligned Gulf. Bruno Kreisky had pleaded for an understanding of the Arab cause by other Jewish 'doves' like himself and co-operation between the Jew and Arab to permit a Palestinian homeland. What was wrong with all that?

The author looked at me pointedly. 'I refuse to discuss hostile points about the Arabs.'

'Hostile?' I was amazed.

'These people take it as a hobby to come and attack the Arabs. All they come for is to hunt for scandal. To have statesmen turning into philosophers and telling us what to do in an arrogant way is something I don't accept.'

He summed up neatly: 'The seminar also invited some Jews. Why? Look at the behaviour of the Murdoch press.'

'Actually,' I said, 'only one Jew was invited, Chaim Bermant, a noted dove much criticised for his writings in the Jewish press.'

The author then poured out a list of a tribe of papers. 'The *New York Times*, the *Miami Herald*, the *Los Angeles Times*. All run by Jews.'

I mentioned Andrew Neil, editor of the *Sunday Times*, who had spoken at the seminar on Arab mistakes in informing the West.

'Exactly my point,' said the author. 'The Arabs who paid the seminar bill were ignorant that such names were to be invited. They don't have the experience to know. But it was terrible to invite such names.'

I asked whether he had been influenced by anyone.

'I wrote my article from my own feelings, of course.'

What did his article or articles intend to do?

'My Number One target in all writings is the Arab leaders and what they should do. I don't address the public in the West. That's a waste of time.'

Why?

He was emphatic. 'Events. Events and events only are able to convince the world. One day events will convince the world about the Arabs. The West will only be convinced through events.'

There was something in what he said. He was a suave, brilliant Palestinian. But I couldn't agree with his point of view any more than he could agree with mine.

I said my goodbyes. If such a seminar was not broken up by pump-action shotguns of Arab patriots, it could well have been obliterated by the pen of such an Arab writer. That was certainly what he wanted. He was a man who did not then believe in dialogue of any kind.

Well, I thought, as I went down Lowndes Street, the man represented that group of Arabs who really prefer permanent adversary status. They have their opposite numbers in the West and certainly in Israel. Further talk was useless. He would probably have his wish, too. A seminar on such a scale might never be repeated. Someone must be laughing, somewhere.

Then again, I thought, perhaps it was the darkness before dawn. The story was not over, not by any means. I was still pursuing my objective, in Solzhenitsyn's words, to fulfil the law of the 'last inch'.

– 26 –
THE BOX OF TRICKS

– 1 –

Approximately nine months after my protest to Michael Foot about the role the US Embassy and the British Embassy in Abu Dhabi had played in getting my regular column banned from *Emirates News*, Dr David Owen, then Foreign Secretary, closed down IRD – the Information Research Department. The Foreign Office moves slowly. The closure followed the warnings to me in September 1976 of Martin Buckmaster of the Foreign Office and of Lord Paul Gore-Booth, a former head of the Diplomatic Service. – the warnings that I had upset someone's Whitehall applecart.

When David Owen had considered all the evidence, for and against, he had swung to the conclusion that closure of IRD was the best course.

Only three years before, the predecessor to Owen as Foreign Secretary had been an old friend of mine, Anthony Crosland. Tony had fought the next seat to mine in Bristol when we both stood for Parliament. He had already pruned the IRD employment list of journalists whom he had assessed in his characteristic style as 'too erratic and too bloody reactionary'. A later review by Sir Colin Crowe had proposed further cuts.

At the time of its final demise there were only about 100 employees, a dramatic drop from its earlier operational strength. The final staff, according to my information, was a collection of veterans, some of Fleet Street origin, some emigrés from behind the Iron Curtain and a few cordial enthusiasts whose 'Reds under the bed' beliefs had often, it was claimed, been justified. In addition to the London staff there were around 100 others under what was called 'light cover' playing solitaire in embassies abroad.

The Box of Tricks

The closure created no ripples, for IRD was on the secret list, paid for from secret funds, but it did appear in the unclassified Foreign Office directory. The reason for its final closure was later told to me by Norman Reddaway (no relation to John Reddaway). Norman, a gentleman of abnormal discretion with an impenetrable polite charm, had been introduced to me as long ago as 1972. A member of a wartime private intelligence army called 'Phantom', Norman had entered the Foreign Office and became IRD's civil service inspirer. He had become generally recognised as one of the most knowledgeable 'black' or 'grey' propaganda experts available in Britain. Later before retirement, he was our ambassador to Poland during a tricky period of the Cold War and later still a trustee of the Thomson Foundation.

When we ran into each other at a luncheon I asked Norman for his version of why IRD had been shut. He told me he suspected the closure had been due to a threatened 'leak' concerning missing papers. There had been a loss of files from the London office of the Institute for the Study of Conflict. That quite distinguished Institute reportedly connected with Forum World Features, the news agency whose virtues had once been preached by those in Abu Dhabi who didn't altogether care for my own brand of news agency activity. Both the Institute and Forum had been headed by Brian Crozier.

According to American sources the US publishing outfit Kern House Enterprises, run by Jock Whitney, supplied the funds for the Forum World Features project. Brian Crozier has himself denied all personal knowledge of the links between Forum World Features, Kern House Enterprises, the Institute for the Study of Conflict and the CIA. However, the loss of the ISC files had been widely publicised.

Crozier, while emphatically refuting any CIA links known to him, claimed the loss of the ISC files to have been engineered by the KGB. The few in the know in government circles were paralysed by the thought that these files might be leaked by the KGB to embarrass Harold Wilson's Labour government of the day.

There was, reportedly, pressure from the American side to carry on and 'ignore this or any other incident'. Richard Helms, as a one-time head of the CIA, himself interested in the Arab Gulf through such things as his advisory role with Ashland Oil, had given his testimonial. Forum, said Dick Helms, 'had become a respected feature service well on the way to a position of prestige in the journalism world'. He had added, in another inter-departmental memo in Washington, that

Forum World Features 'had provided the United States with a significant means to counter propaganda'. In a footnote, Helms said that Forum functioned 'with the knowledge and co-operation of British Intelligence'. He failed to add that the CIA was indirectly Forum's paymaster.[1]

– 2 –

Although much of IRD's work might be shown as effective in the paper war against Communism, nobody wanted investigative reporters digging too deep into any IRD dirty linen basket. Too much 'grey' propaganda had been put out which, although it might not contain direct lies, did include factual material to which 'twist' or 'spin' had been cleverly added. Dr Owen, as British Foreign Secretary, had had enough.

Writer on intelligence Chapman Pincher observed that the department he described as 'modestly effective' was closed by Owen and by Jim Callaghan (then Prime Minister) because the Labour government desperately needed to 'pacify its far left'.

The decision to close had on the whole been welcome in Whitehall. Sir Maurice Oldfield, responsible for collaborating with IRD in some Persian Gulf affairs, had agreed with Owen's verdict.[2] People in the normal Foreign Office Information Department, a tame enough show by comparison, detested the existence of a clandestine department.

Ray Whitney, retiring head of IRD received an OBE and went on to head for a while an alternative but more moderate service called the Overseas Information Department (OID). By 1981 OID had disappeared into the Foreign Office Information Department.

Mr Whitney, a most able if aggressive man who had the bad luck to be the last head of a department which was regarded as politically unpopular, soon found himself at the top of a list of candidates for the safe Conservative seat of Wycombe, from which base he pursued a career in Parliament, rising to become a Foreign Office junior minister at an early date.

One diplomat who rejoiced as the last nail was driven into the coffin of the whole venture was Hilary King, at one time Ambassador in Conakry in the Republic of Guinea. He drew attention in a letter to *The Times* to the possible dangers of the IRD operation as a whole. Welcoming Dr Owen's decision to dismantle IRD, Mr King explained that he had come across examples of unsubstantiated, misleading or clearly erroneous reports being incorporated as firm intelligence by IRD in highly classified reports prepared for the guidance of ministers and senior officials. One example of this was an ostensibly somewhat hair-raising report about the country in which he was ambassador but which appeared to conflict with the information available to him locally. When he asked the IRD for the source of their report, he was told simply that they had access to secret reports which he had not seen. As it happened, Mr King had seen the secret reports relating to the country where he was serving. Many contained little more than trivial bazaar gossip. None confirmed the accuracy of the report which IRD had submitted to ministers. Returning to the charge, Mr King was eventually able, with some difficulty, to establish that IRD's only source for their rather alarming report was a clipping from a south German local newspaper. Asked why they had submitted their report to ministers without first checking with the embassy on the spot, or even with the FO's own (bona fide) Research Department in London, the man in IRD replied, without apology, that the German newspaper clipping seemed to bear the stamp of truth.

I was certain as I read Mr King's words, and afterwards discussed his observations with him, that I had been tried and sentenced in the early days because I wouldn't play the game.

Gerald Long, at the time general manager of Reuters News Agency, in spite of the fact that he discovered the agency was being paid £28,000 a year as a subsidy by IRD, had already begun negotiations to bring an end to the relationship. It took him six years to unravel the ties.[3]

– 3 –

I had decided that it might also make sense to see both Ray Whitney and Dr Owen, his boss when IRD closed.

Ray Whitney was waiting for me in Room 25 on the second floor of the Norman Shaw building, an annex to the House of Commons which stands between what was once Scotland Yard and the Thames embankment. He was a stylish military-type man of about 50, of sharpish appearance, white shirt, pinstripe suited, with a fashionably knotted tie.

'I'm writing about my own experiences,' I explained. 'I've spent a long time in the Middle East and it's a personal story, partly concerned as I see it with disinformation.'

'How do you define disinformation?' he asked warily. 'What do you mean by the word?'

'Disinformation – or what one thinks is disinformation – depends on one's point of view.' I was struggling to explain, not too successfully as it soon became obvious. 'Governments might not release the whole of the news. That could be disinformation, the disclosure of only part of a story.'

'Why are you here? What are you after?' he asked in a rather snapdragon fashion.

'You were head of IRD in its last years. I thought you'd tell me something about IRD and answer a few questions.'

He looked at me as though I was slightly unhinged.

'Look,' he emphasised, 'IRD was engaged in a very simple exercise of providing some press releases and articles distributed through embassies abroad and by various other means. I think you've got a touch of the John Le Carré's!'

'But not a word was known about IRD for years,' I said. 'It was a hush-hush operation up to the day David Owen closed it and even after.'

'I'm not telling you anything,' he said, maintaining a splendidly straight trajectory. 'I signed the Official Secrets Act when I joined the Foreign Office and I'm keeping to it.'

He made a move across the room waving his arms. 'Look, I'm not telling you. I'm not writing for you! I might do a book of my own one day, but I'm certainly not writing yours.'

'I wasn't expecting you to.'

'You're unable yourself to tell me what disinformation is,' he parried with a smile.

'I define disinformation as the sort of thing Sefton Delmer of the *Daily Express* was brilliant at after the war – all the stories planted in Egypt in Nasser's day and indeed in Aden by disinformation experts. I . . .'

He broke in. 'Delmer? Long before my time. Come on now, you've got to do better than that!'

I stood up and made for the door. It was time, I thought, to leave the canny patriot. 'Goodbye to you. You're very aggressive.'

'Nonsense. My friends call me the most reasonable of people. Anyone will tell you that. You come here to talk about disinformation but you're hedging all the time. Incapable of giving a straight answer. You're afraid to debate. Why don't you come back and sit down?'

Rather hesitantly, I sat down once again. He straddled the chair in front of me, inquisitorial fashion. I said nothing.

Maybe he was giving me up as a lost cause. 'I call it lying,' he suddenly volunteered. 'Lying!'

'All governments lie,' I said.

'But how do you define disinformation?' he asked. The man was determinedly inquisitorial.

I fingered the relevant chapters of my book I had in my hand. 'I'll read you some examples.' It was, I thought, the best way. I intended quoting one by one the cases, as I saw it, of disinformation.

He interrupted. 'Are you telling me you can't define what disinformation is without turning to your papers? I'm not having that! Come on!' He obviously knew all about interrogation.

I put the book chapters away and raised my arms in the gesture of hopeless surrender.

In a harshly effective way I suppose he considered me defeated. Maybe he was right. Maybe, I reflected, we were all defeated by semantics.

I tramped up Whitehall, branching off at Admiralty Arch towards 10, St James Square. Chatham House is the HQ of the Royal Institute of International Affairs. Professor Fred Halliday from London University was to give a lecture on Islam.

Over a drink before his talk I asked Halliday, 'How would you define disinformation?'

'Disinformation is something your enemies do.'

I might not always agree with Fred, but I wished I'd thought of that answer, though I doubt if Ray Whitney would have accepted it.

– 4 –

Following the negative meeting with Whitney I had tried my luck with David Owen, suggesting we meet. In a friendly personal note Owen wrote back: 'I'm sorry but I still feel bound by the Official Secrets Act in this whole area, and so I cannot give you an interview on this issue.'

There it was. The lid might have been taken off the British government's box of tricks at Riverwalk House by the release of some official documentation at the Public Records Office, but, or so it seemed, the two men who had been responsible for IRD felt the box should be shut and remain shut.

There was, however, one person who had no such inhibitions. I went along for a visit with Michael Foot, and afterwards sent him my chapter on 'Shaping the News'. When I called Michael for his observations he said, 'It's all there. It's OK by me. How soon do you publish?'

A more impartial observer than either Michael or I was Sir Richard Beaumont, our former Ambassador in Egypt, now chairman of the Arab British Chamber of Commerce and one of the more prudent British envoys during a stormy period of Anglo-Arab relations. Sir Richard said to me during a talk in his office overlooking a leafy Belgrave Square that, 'The closure of IRD brought to an end an inglorious chapter in the history of the Foreign Office.'

– 27 –
DARKNESS IN MY EYES

– 1 –

Wrongs accidentally perpetrated in the course of intelligence or information work can, of course, be righted. IRD had been a long time going, but following its close-down and the open revelation of the scope of IRD activities, life in the early 1980s had taken a turn for the better so far as my own family was concerned.

The bank, which had initially frozen my company's accounts and given our deeds of buildings to a second creditor without consultation, had taken the unexpected step of looking with favour on a small settlement for the total cancellation of the amount still owed by my South Wales publishing companies. It had returned my guarantees. It had handed back insurance policies and other securities. The action could of course have been a complete coincidence, but our solicitor, David Harrel, was delighted. As he saw it, 'Somebody up there has a conscience.'

I had felt like some character in a bad play who had been on a long trial for something which he didn't understand and who is suddenly hauled in out of the cold for reasons he still didn't understand.

Diplomatically and politically, our publishing house suddenly gained new friends. Harassments ceased. There were invitations to embassies whose doors had once been shut. Michael Adams wrote in *Middle East International*'s anniversary issue: 'Claud Morris, a co-founder of the magazine took on, courageously and at considerable cost to himself, the responsibility for publishing what we all knew would be an unpopular – as it proved, a dangerously unpopular – publication.'

– 2 –

Years later, after the trauma of the Paris seminar and all else had died away, I decided to put it all down, warts and all, and complete my book.

I rang Christopher Mayhew and took him to lunch at Locket's, the scene of so many meetings over the years. I wanted to check out more background information and get his views on what had been an extraordinary piece of my life. Christopher was in good form. He said, 'One of the advantages of getting old is that you can say and do as you like.' I heartily concurred.

He stuck very much to a story given me earlier by Ian Gilmour. It was that his ANAF Foundation, which had more or less taken over the work pioneered by Margaret McKay and others, was completely divorced from Foreign Office influence. I asked him about the unusual story of Mrs McKay and he was frank: 'I'd nothing against her. In fact, she was a particularly courageous lady. But in the view of most people she didn't show a lot of discretion in handling the money.' Margaret's own protestations were that she had nothing to do with financial management.

'Did the Foreign Office get involved?' I asked.

'No. Not at all. It was the early days of CAABU and we were terribly short of funds. So Harold Beeley and myself, as I remember it, went along to see some Abu Dhabi people. It had simply been suggested that it was pretty ridiculous handing out Zayed's money in an ad hoc fashion. If money was available, why not funnel it through an independent foundation with proper trustees?'

'So you set up ANAF – Arabische Nicht Arabische Freundschaft?'

'Yes.' He laughed. 'That German name! From memory we got an agreed annual sum for the first seven years. But it's been a long time now.'

'Wouldn't it have been better had you been more public about it? Why the Swiss address, for example? Did you or the Arabs fix that?'

'We arranged it. The Arabs had nothing to do with it so far as I remember. We simply, as I recollect, invited one of them to attend our meetings as an observer. As for being public about things, in those days we didn't want to have the Zionists on our tail. There's less concern about that now.'

I asked Mayhew about IRD saying that it had been much criticised and adding that he himself had readily defended it when questions had been raised.

'Of course I did. It was a bloody good job. I'm proud of what it did. Of course, IRD wasn't so concerned about the Middle East as about the Russians.'

I broke in: 'But it had its links in Cairo. Tom Little, for example, and others, like Sefton Delmer, who was involved in intelligence.'

Mayhew interrupted: 'Who paid Delmer?'

'The *Daily Express*, I guess.'

'But he was really MI6?' Mayhew asked. He made his statement into a question in the Arab manner, thereby not making it a confirmation.

'As lots of others seemed to be,' I added. 'After all, IRD was mixed up in Aden. What about the way in which IRD planted British morale-boosting stories in the Aden press so that reporters could quote these tales and send news back home – although things were often faked?'

Mayhew smiled. 'Did we do that?' He paused and then gave me both barrels. 'Oh, I suppose we did. Well, a good job too.' You could only admire his resilience, and indeed his elegant mandarin tone.

'Do you remember the publisher?' I asked after lunch as we strolled back to the House of Lords. 'Do you remember I had a chance to buy a publishing business, Elizabeth Collard's *Middle East Economic Digest*, and you put me off by telling me you couldn't be linked to them?'

'Did I? What a pity. I did you out of something there.'

'What about John Reddaway?' I asked. 'They say he appointed a parliamentary group chap who worked from Paris, who was ex-IRD, ex-MI6. The records show that.'

'Yes he did. But I don't think it was because of any IRD or MI6 connection. The intelligence stuff was a long time ago.'

'John Reddaway was intelligence Chief in Cyprus?' I queried.

'Yes. Well, obviously I should think. He was in charge after all. But it was nothing to do with any wider scene later on.'

I challenged him: 'You know that when you removed the *Middle East International* printing from my printing works you put a nail in the coffin of the works.'

He said, 'No, did I?' And then as an afterthought added:

'Well, as one gets older one forgets some things.'

– 3 –

The government papers concerning IRD had already revealed to me the name of the brilliant Foreign Office high-flier, the fervent anti-Communist who had established a reputation within the Labour Party for weeding out Labour MPs who might have owed their allegiance to Moscow and revolution rather than to Westminster and parliamentary democracy. Apparently he thought some MPs were actually reporting to Soviet intelligence officers in London. It was he who had originally founded IRD.

The name was Christopher Mayhew.

When I finally heard his name in this to me surprising context, I reflected how different things might have been had I known of his role as founding father of the clandestine information brigade.

Would I have asked Mayhew to become an associate in as volatile an arena as the Middle East had I possessed some magical Long Tom, some high-powered lens that photographed the hidden bits of the IRD past? As Ben Bradlee, editor of the *Washington Post* was to tell me later, 'Calculated lies and the wilful deception of the public for political ends still continues apace. What an awful price we have to pay for any such lies under any name.'

Mayhew, of course, could take refuge in apologia such as his patriotic duty to do a bit of early dive-bombing at the opening of the Cold War, to counter Communist propaganda. It was he who had ghost-written some of the most thoughtful speeches of Ernest Bevin, which had helped the setting up of the Marshall Plan as a barrier against the spread of Stalinism. He had, indeed, set the agenda as adviser and pointer of the way, not only to the IRD in Britain but to its imitators in the CIA and even unknowingly to the KGB. Propaganda had thrived before, but it was Mayhew who had fair claim to have initiated the post-war pattern.

In his autobiography[1] Mayhew described his experiences in the war as an intelligence agent with the Strategic Operations Executive (SOE) and the path of self-discovery that had led him to become a committed Cold War warrior. He continued, briefly, to relate how in peace time he sold the Prime Minister the idea of creating the IRD as a weapon to 'carry the propaganda war into the enemy's camp'. This had to be organised secretly, undisclosed to Parliament or people, 'since anti-Communist propaganda would be anathema to much of the Labour Party'. He added that it could 'probably claim a modest share of the credit for stemming and turning back the Soviet ideological offensive'.

Mayhew emerges in his biography as a talented and complicated man who had in early life been a leftist public schoolboy and university graduate. In his own words, he had his 'cards marked by MI5 for going to Moscow in "bad company"' (e.g. the unforgivable Soviet spy Anthony Blunt). He once spoke at the Oxford Union in favour of the motion that 'this house prefers the Red Flag to the Union Jack'. All this made his conversion to the certainties of anti-communism the more spectacular.

Had the left in the Labour Party known one tenth of what Christopher Mayhew had secretly been up to they would have had apoplexy.

I wondered whether he knew anything of the tricks that IRD got up to in regard to people like myself. Did he realise what happened to individual hacks who got in IRD's way? Or did he share the conclusion of Neal Ascherson of the *Observer* who, in a column referring to similar situations where intelligence services became entangled with approaches to newsmen remarked, 'A mere hack is dispensable.'

Had he any idea of the campaigns conducted by sincere but perhaps over-suspicious officers of Her Majesty's Secret Services? Did he realise that, long after his own departure from IRD and from government, there were some coves in that gentlemen's intelligence club who might be capable of using the knuckle-duster as well as ruining journalistic reputations?

Apparently he did not. As he said later: 'We should have been complimented about what we did. Should you not give us some credit for telling the truth, in a good cause, at some political risk to ourselves?' And, again: 'IRD was highly secret and a grade more respectable than just dealing in black propaganda. We were dealing in the truth.'

Nothing in Mayhew's autobiography indicated that the man who initiated IRD and whose ideas about occasionally cooking the news or 'putting a spin on it' in order to enlighten the world about Soviet misdeeds were soon religiously copied by a grateful CIA. Nothing in his autobiography indicated that he ever knew what his merry men got up to either in his absence or after he had quit the clandestine information field. Christopher, now Lord Mayhew, could not have known the bruising inflicted on some subjects by IRD's attention. Otherwise he could scarcely have stood by.

– 28 –
WAS MY JOURNEY REALLY NECESSARY?

– 1 –

The air was warm and the heat gentle. The blue Indian Ocean lapped the sandy bay, its calm surface smoothed as if flattened by an iron. In the middle of the bay an Omani gun-boat swung lazily at anchor. To the left and right the buff-coloured pock-marked Omani mountains rose out of the sea to invade the land.

Pat and I had come to Oman at the invitation of Prince Fahad, Deputy Prime Minister for Ministerial Affairs.[1] It seemed right that the book which would give my version of how the Arabs and their Western friends had been victims of disinformation campaigns throughout some of the most crucial years in Middle East history should be cobbled together under Arab skies. So Pat and I took a plane to Muscat.

It had been twenty years since I first met Fahad. I knew him when he was Foreign Minister, then Minister of Information, and now as Deputy Prime Minister for Ministerial Affairs. 'Come with your wife. Come and enjoy a holiday,' he had urged. It was an irresistible invitation, a moment for a check on life's interim balance sheet.

Fahad had arranged for us to stay at the magnificent Al Bustan Palace Hotel on the shore of the Indian Ocean. Then, at Fahad's suggestion we boarded a plane for Salala, spending a week there. Pat investigated as many events in the lives of the ladies of the area as were open to her. I sat writing on the balcony of our room, watching the sand and sea stretch out limitlessly towards distant Aden.

Every day from dawn till 10.00 a.m. I wrote and re-wrote, looking back for the first time over the experiences that all those years ago in South Wales had determined me to throw some weight behind the modern Arab cause. The decision to do so had changed my family's life. Was the self-induced death of my Welsh newspaper which still haunted me worthwhile? Had it been rubbished by events? What had been my own subsequent role – if it was worth anything?

I certainly had not courted popularity. A writer on the London *Financial Times*, reporting my activities, had once rung up to ask whether I would mind being described as an 'Arab Lobbyist'. I minded.

I had been described in blunter terms. It was at a cocktail party given at Brooks's Club in St James Street by Naim Atallah, the Palestinian publisher. I had been gossiping to one of Naim's young publishing assistants when across the room swayed a Middle East commentator. He was a pleasant man. I had known him for years. But that night he moved up like a sniper emerging from the cover of that classy crowd and said loudly, 'Come outside and put up your fists, you bloody Arab whore! The boys say we ought to beat you up one night.'

Apparently I had written a piece in *Voice* on the destabilisation of the Middle East. It had upset this commentator. As I went home that night I had wondered who 'the boys' were.

I told Jonathan Aitken of the incident and my piece in *Voice*. 'You'll never hear from him again,' said Jonathan, who knew more about these mysteries than I. He was right. I never did.

– 2 –

The tall stories from the most unexpected of sources were continuous. HE Abdul Aziz Rowas, Oman's Information Minister, hoisted a warning flag when I talked to him.

'Distortion of news is happening to us every day. The destabilisation stuff, the stirring up and emphasising of local differences. But it's not only Western media that does it. The USSR is in it. We're unimpressed by either side. The attitude of the Russians to the Arabs or the attitude of the Americans to the Arabs represents two sides of the same coin.' He laughed. 'Vodka-Cola! They expect us to mix the two and drink it. They come and spend two nights in Muscat, go away with a notebook full of distorted facts collected from a few expatriates. They feed these half-truths and fictions into the news machine and overnight become experts on the Arabs!'

Thinking things over in the quiet atmosphere of Oman, I began to strike a balance. At least, I thought, I had helped to make a few characters who had made the name Arab sound like a terminal illness more appreciative of the Arab right to be heard.

To me the work had been straightforward. It was that of a journalist and publisher seeking a right for every man to be heard, to have his words published and printed without threat or harassment.

But as I re-examined my own notes and diaries I began to appreciate more and more the underlying reality that the Western governments do not welcome maverick operators near the centres of power in the Middle East. That was the long and the short of it. It was nothing personal to me. It was a hard fact of life.

I had no quarrel with the right of intelligence agencies to their own views, operating, one hoped, in their national interest. My great concern was the growing certainty that these agencies were often given half-truths which they embellished in order to discredit individuals who for one reason or another they wanted thrown into the rubbish bin. It was misuse of power, misuse of the press, misuse of their brief.

How much could I tell of all this, I asked myself as I sat scribbling in the Muscat sun? How much, without betraying confidences? I remembered the words of Sheikh Zayed when an Englishman once came before him to discuss publication matters. 'What have you done with your diaries?' asked the Sheikh. 'In the bank,' said the Englishman. 'That's where they should stay,' remarked Zayed with a chuckle.

Well, I thought, some of my own diaries will have to stay in the bank, but I'll follow the Sheikh's first words of advice to me. 'Tell the truth. This is the best way to help us.'

– 3 –

Towards the end of our memorable visit to Oman, Prince Fahad and his wife invited us to dinner. It was a perfect evening with the stars hanging like lanterns over their garden.

Our visit was drawing to a close and we were talking in a reflective mood at dinner. After a delicious meal Fahad and I walked through his maturing gardens. The air was soft and there was a cool breeze.

'I wonder at the failure to give Arabs an effective Western voice,' I said. 'Sometimes I feel like a chap I knew in the war, a journalist who specialised in public affairs inside Whitehall, and afterwards wrote a book called *Was My Journey Really Necessary?*'

'You've had many struggles,' prompted Fahad, a smiling, slender virtuoso of Arab affairs, handsome and easy-mannered. I had always found him as rock-like beneath the surface as his memorable country.

'Many failures,' I added.

I talked of Wales, the starting point of my story, and the slaughter of the *South Wales Voice*. Then of my meeting with Sultan Ali whose appearance on the scene with tales of British disinformation tricks had launched our entire family on our adventures. Well, it was over – at least so it seemed. Pat and I would soon be home in the reality of London.

– 4 –

There was smog as we landed at Heathrow. We arrived at Vincent Square and after a short cat-nap I walked to my office.

My direct route lay down a narrow thoroughfare called Kinnerton Street. As I walked I was thinking back to the old *South Wales Voice* in the valley, whose files, running back a century, still stand in my son's office. I liked to think that when that old lady folded she was actually knocked out for the right reasons. I liked to feel above all that her spirit continues to rise high over her green Welsh valley and that, whatever we have done in a wider field, we have not entirely let her down.

At No. 37 Kinnerton Street is a rather eccentric but lovable establishment which makes a business of collecting antique newspapers. There is a wall display of radical papers published in nineteenth-century Britain, ranging from William Cobbett's *Register* to the rascally Horatio Bottomley's *John Bull*. This rare collection of fading, crinkly old papers, fragile with age, contains many a long-buried title that reminds me of our *South Wales Voice* aspirations in the paper's hey-day.

I picked up a paper there called the *Black Dwarf* dated 29th December 1819, edited and published by a press pioneer called T.J. Wooler, at 76, Fleet Street.

Well, I thought, Britain as it was in 1819 might be comparable to the Arab Gulf as it exists for the journalist of the late 1980s. Britain was at that time a nation emerging from a deep past into the traumas of the nineteenth-century industrial revolution, just as the Arab Gulf is emerging from its past into the traumas of cold modern technology.

I browsed over an extract from the *Black Dwarf*'s editorial, realising

The Last Inch

as I read that journalism and political power had never enjoyed each other's company. They never would. The editorial read:

> Hated by all who hate the people and slandered,
> By all who slander the people, I am identified,
> With the country whose battles I have fought,
> And whose causes I have defended as my own.
>
> But I am not taking leave of the public,
> Nor will I take leave of them,
> Until the public cause shall triumph,
> Or until I am numbered with the dead.
>
> Unless arbitrary power shall tear me from the light,
> Or barefaced despotism arrest my pen.

I bought the old newspaper and took it home. As an editor, as a publisher, or as anything you like to call me, including a damn fool who had fallen foul of some bizarre situations, I could neither add to nor improve on those words. They said it all.

EPILOGUE

– 29 –
THE TWO COUSINS APPROACH

In the spring of 1989 a weary and worried man invited me to his home in Bishop's Avenue, north London. I had known Jaweed Al-Ghussein for over fifteen years. A handsome man, sharply and fashionably dressed, he was one of the select group of Arabs who had made a fortune out of building hospitals, bridges and pipelines for Abu Dhabi. Equally at home in Savile Row or in the Hafeet mountain range, we had often met in London, on the Gulf or in the Levant. A trusted man of great kindness, he could trace his family back for a thousand years.

This Arab friend had invested funds in land, in flats, in real estate of all descriptions. His investments made during the boom years of the 1980s, flourished. He was now deeply concerned.

Would peace ever come to the Middle East? The long Iran–Iraq war, the decimation of the Lebanon, and the seemingly endless tragedy of Palestine haunted both of us.

Moderate Arabs and moderate Jews were being pushed aside. The Intifada was seen to have failed. There seemed no way out except war on a greater scale than ever before, and Jaweed abhorred the thought.

Every attempt to bring together Palestinians and Israelis who believed in compromise had failed. One attempt by Said Hamami, PLO Chief in Britain, had ended with a bullet in the stomach from his own side. Another attempt by Issam Sartawi, a courageous but foolhardy leader, ended with Sartawi's slaughter at a public conference in Portugal. Naji al Ali, the famous and independently minded cartoonist was butchered on a Kensington pavement. There were numerous others, mostly led by Palestinian factions pursuing each other to an early grave.

But there had been attempts at progressive actions on the Jewish side too. One by Lord Goodman led to official condemnation from the Israeli Government. Another attempt by Uri Aveneri, the Israeli writer, had not got off the ground.

Jaweed and I agreed that a fresh approach should be made. We resolved that a fresh attempt should be made to work with those in Israel and the Arab countries who were receptive to moderating thought. We felt that private diplomacy would get further than public diplomacy; that one could get more done out of the public eye than in it. Indeed, secrecy was vital. A quiet approach might begin the process of healing the divisions between the family of Arabs and Jews. We placed great store on winning individuals' confidence and friendship before any policy issues were tackled.

Why should not these two cousins settle down to an harmonious future as the end of the twentieth century approached?

The object as we saw it was to improve understanding and foster, in particular, mutual interests so that trade and commerce could flourish. As we walked and talked in his garden, Jaweed wondered how much it would cost to mount such a campaign? He explained that there was not too much money about to spend on such a purpose since most felt that to encourage something of this kind would be a total waste of money. In the cut-throat world of Arab politics, one had to be careful.

He knew that I had mounted successful public affairs campaigns on behalf of the Gulf Co-operation States. Over two decades I had tried to change the perceptions with which the outside world perceived the Arab. We walked and talked for over an hour and a half as I outlined a plan.

What we were now discussing would not be a campaign in which political parties took part, but rather an approach to the élite, to the opinion-makers, to individual members of the Jewish and Arab community. We would organise a keyhole plan to allow the key to turn in the lock. We needed to approach people who, as Beaverbrook used to say, 'could alter the price of cheese'. People who were thinkers and who could move others.

How much would it cost, my friend asked again. I told him about £30,000 to see whether the scheme was viable – a small enough amount. Probably far too small, but knowing that there was no government budget standing behind us, I felt that it was all that could be afforded.

In due course the £30,000, and another £10,000 for extra expenses, turned up, which Jaweed had collected.

The Two Cousins Approach

'Now you've got money where are we going to start?' my friend asked.

My immediate reply was 'Israel'.

I boarded an El Al plane with my son William, bound for Tel Aviv. We had no back-up, just the names of two or three journalist friends and academics and my connections through the International Press Institute which I had alerted to my trip. William was by now an old Middle East hand.

Having obtained a comfortable room at the King David Hotel, we set out on our adventures to bring peace to the Middle East.

William had been to Jerusalem before on a pilgrimage with an Irish priest. I was a Christian with a small 'c', but I had never been to Israel before. None the less we felt well armed.

The first person we met was Lucy the wife of Sari Nusseibeh and we made the plan plain to her. Sari Nusseibeh, a leading but moderate campaigner for Palestine, had left for New York on a lecture tour that morning.

My idea was to select 100 people out of the population of the West Bank who could be a self-governing body. I would publish their names and details privately. Lucy said she could get together six people to do the work who were largely trusted relatives. It was estimated that the work would take up to six weeks.

We had an adventurous month ahead as we also had to find profiles of 100 Israelis in order to bring a sensible attitude to bear on the situation.

Simultaneously, with Lucy's trusted relatives' work, I organised a canvas of Israelis who felt that inspiration was imperative. There numbered some 70 persons both in the Knesset and outside. Some of these names came from June Jacobs, soon to become the enterprising head of the International European Council for Jewish Women. Among the names submitted was Uri Savir, yet to be appointed Director General of the Foreign Ministry, and Yossi Beilin, the bright young Labour MP who could claim to be a driving force behind the idea that Gaza first was the single-minded target.

Among those ready to listen with confidence was a former Minster of Justice, Haim Zadok; also the President of the Israeli Council for Foreign Relations, David Kimche.

Last but not least was the lively and plucky editor of *Davar* newspaper, Hannah Semer, whom I determined to take to England as an ambassadress for the best and most reasonable of Israelis. We also contacted six national newspaper editors, including Ari Rath, the former editor of the *Jerusalem Post*, and eventually one military man whose name carried obvious weight, General Haim Barlev.

At one stage we were attacked by three Palestinian boys who chucked a huge stone through the rear window of our car, almost killing William and Saida Al-Ghussein, Sari's sister, a spirited woman who knew Jerusalem like the back of her hand and whose father had once been the Jordanian Ambassador to London.

In the end, ninety-four Arab interviews were completed. From this list it was seen that the people concerned were often middle-class intellectuals, lawyers and administrators, who had been accustomed to democracy and familiar with its workings.

There were brilliant women like Hannah Ashrawi. They included the traditional families. Some of them, like the Nusseibehs and Dakkas, had been in Jerusalem for a millennium. Others, like Faisal Husseini and the Nasashabis, have equivalent local roots. They could provide the government ministers and civil servants of tomorrow. The new Palestine had to have the potential to be a democracy that would find a place in the world. The list showed that there was, quite apart from Palestinians overseas, an authentic local leadership who were ready and waiting.

It was the first time that such lists of Palestinians and Israelis had been put together.

William and I returned to Britain and immediately began to run out of funds. The work was more costly than I had envisaged. There was no more money to carry on the campaign. It was suggested that we should try the wealthy Palestinians in London for individual donations. Yet only one responded, so slight did they think our chances were. They wrung their hands with concern, but none would produce a penny. They had all been bled white.

One Palestinian supporter we enlisted was Zein Mayassi, a generous man who lived in Chelsea. A second was Tewfik Al-Ghussein, Jaweed's son.

I went on one hopeless trip to Geneva to appeal to a Central Fund, run by Dr George Abed. In despair I was recommended to visit Ambassador Nadim Dimeshkie of the Lebanon, who had a suite at the Grosvenor; an elegant man whom I had known for a dozen years. He listened carefully and then said, 'I recommend you see Christopher Mayhew, before going any further.'

Christopher Mayhew invited me to lunch at the House of Lords

The Two Cousins Approach

but was certainly not encouraging. He said wryly, 'It seems to me like a Mossad plot.' It was true that one of our supporters in Israel was David Kimche, who had been the head of Mossad in Africa, but David had resigned from Mossad when he disagreed with the actions of the Israeli government over the invasion of Lebanon. He became president of the non-party Israel Council for Foreign Relations.

There were brighter spots on the horizon, however. The Foreign Office under Douglas Hurd, prompted by the alert David Gore-Booth, gave us real support for initial travelling expenses to fly Israelis to London, and continued to support us. But facing the fact that we still had not enough, I decided to make a fast trip down the Gulf and had a much more encouraging result.

In Oman HM Sultan Qaboos, well-known for his generosity, granted us a founding gift of £40,000. In Dubai the generous Sheikh Mohamed bin Rashid Al Maktoum had our case presented to him by Dr Sheikh Khalifa Mohamed Suliman. He donated £20,000. In Qatar the Crown Prince and Heir Apparent[1] gave us £15,000. Their generosity in a crisis was not to be forgotten and indeed, I must personally thank Sayyid (Prince) Fahad for his great help to me and the Foundation.

I next went back to London to introduce my plan to the Jewish community. Four of the community came forward – most insisting on anonymity. They contributed between £1,000 and £10,000, and my home team contributed time and resources freely.

By now a Foundation had been formed and had achieved charity status. We called it the Next Century Foundation because we knew we had a long row to hoe – a long way to go before any real peace could be seen.

Barney Hayhoe, now Lord Hayhoe, a strong defender of causes and former War Minister and Minister of Health, became a trustee along with Frank, now Sir Frank Rogers, our family friend of so many years. In time, Barney resigned and was replaced by a stalwart supporter, the Duke of Devonshire.

As more interest was engendered others joined us. Russell Twisk, now Editor-in-Chief of the *Reader's Digest*, became a founder member of our Advisory Board, along with old friends such as Sir Richard Luce and Lord Christopher Tughendat, June Jacobs, Sir David Alliance, Lord Beloff, Peter Shore, Dr Garret FitzGerald, Andrew Stone, Lord Merlyn Rees and Lord Finsberg.[2]

The Next Century Foundation was formed through long-standing friendships. There were hardly more than a dozen of us in all.

The Foundation insisted that the atmosphere had to change first. A new spirit was needed to create new thinking. Only with a new spirit were new approaches possible. It was for each side to listen to each other. Two cousins might quarrel, but inevitably the forces of history would bring them together again. As Lord Weinstock put it succinctly to Douglas Hurd: 'The sole object [of the Foundation] was to contribute to the creation of a situation where life could be more tranquil in the Middle East and to reduce the danger of an explosion affecting the rest of the world.'

Our meetings are without publicity, in total confidence, in a spirit of candour and absolute frankness. Our activities have been variously called 'alternative diplomacy' or 'track two' diplomacy, a phrase by Joseph Montville, or 'complementary diplomacy', a phrase preferred by Eric Rouleau, former French Ambassador to Tunis and now a roving ambassador for France. As a diplomat he preferred this supportive phrase.

From Tel Aviv MPs, editors and former ministers of government have been invited to attend. Slowly, with patient listening, the work has expanded both at home and abroad. Friends were found among the doves at the Israeli Foreign Office. A shift of values was taking place in a key section of professional people concerned with foreign affairs. The Israeli and Egyptian Ambassadors proved formidable allies.

The Duke of Devonshire with typical generosity, offered us his magnificent home, 'Chatsworth', as the setting for our first conference which was attended by Palestinians, Israelis and representatives from Jordan, Saudi Arabia, Egypt and Syria. Little did the Duke know that his hospitality to us would entail the presence of 100 policemen wandering around the grounds of Chatsworth acting as security throughout the conference.

Chatsworth, it seemed, was the watershed. The Madrid Peace Conference began within days of its conclusion and it is interesting to note that three of our members from the Arab side and four of our members from the Israeli side were selected as peace negotiators both there and subsequently in Washington.

Today a change of attitude has begun to take place. It may take decades. It may not be perfect, but it is a beginning. The clock cannot be turned back. There is, however precarious, a level of understanding between Arab and Jew. People can start building relationships. That was unthinkable a few years ago.

David Gore-Booth (now High Commissioner for India) said: 'The work of the Foundation during the years is certainly impressive. It is something you and I have worked for all our lives.'

Sir Richard Luce, one of our founding members, wrote: 'A new opportunity is emerging for the Western world and for the international community to work with the moderate forces of the Middle East. The Foundation is a lubricant behind the scenes.'

When two sides begin to meet under the Foundation's umbrella, they are able to speak frankly and confidentially about the problems they face and the challenges they receive. Policies, politics, justice and injustice are debated. Positive bridges are proposed and often implemented. Questions are put forward as to how to encourage friendship between diplomats; how to encourage links between editors and writers; how to encourage political understanding and conciliation between politicians and businessmen of far differing views.

This may seem very little, but by holding to the aim of understanding, the Foundation has touched the lives of many and produced changes in situations of which even we are not yet aware.

But moderating thought is always attacked by ignorance and fear, both of which are manifested in violence and extremism of all kinds. The road to harmony is a long, hard one.

We have reached a point where man must either solve his problems in the Middle East or be destroyed by them. We must go forward. We must support the moderating forces of the world, for to give way to extremism is to give way to the forces of darkness everywhere.

As Afif Safieh, the erudite Palestine National Council Head of Mission in London, said at a Foundation meeting, 'If we continue to follow a policy of an eye for an eye, we will all end up blind.'

We have come a long way, but the last inch may be the hardest.

– 30 –
MORE HASTE LESS SPEED

I was staying at the Al Bustan Hotel, Muscat, as a guest of Prince Fahad, now the Deputy Prime Minister for Council Affairs of Oman. I had flown out from Heathrow and two days later was still aching with that deep weariness that enters the very marrow of the system after years of air travel.

My son, William, who by now had taken up a post as adviser to the Vice Chancellor at Sultan Qaboos University, was already busy erecting a University Press, and training native Omanis. His wife, the slender, petite Veronica was by his side together with Joseph, Loveday and Samuel, who were then aged ten, eight and five. We were a delightful picture of happy families as we sat in the luxurious lounge attached to the bedroom suite. The children and Veronica went off to play by the pool.

This was my third trip to Oman in an effort to hold further talks about a small conference to be given under the shelter of the Deputy Prime Minister and HE Yahya bin Mahfoudh the Minister of Education. Arrangements were now in the final phase. Invitations had gone out. The Omanis, who had already provided funds to help launch the Foundation, had now offered to host a superb event. Sultan Qaboos was a courageous man. It was an action which took the greatest courage. Here was a man who has suffered criticism and misinterpretation all his life, but carried on.

At my hotel I was finalising the plans of the seminar, when I suddenly received word that authorities in Oman felt that the whole scheme should be put off until the following year with the Ministry of Foreign Affairs playing a major part. It was undoubtedly a sensible idea but I was completely taken by surprise. We were only a few weeks away from take-off. Perhaps we were going too fast, but the cancellation took all of us by surprise.

The Ministry of Education had offered to pay all expenses of the Foundation up to date but that was not the issue. The issue was the importance of the conference for the better understanding of Middle East relationships.

I had planned to go to Tel Aviv immediately after the Oman trip as I had been invited to lecture at the university there. I decided to keep the plan.

Two weeks later I arrived in Tel Aviv with Pat, my wife, who was calm and patient. The seminar at the university was a gathering of graduates numbering some 300. I spoke on hopeful future co-operation between Israel, Oman and the Gulf states, future relationships between 'the two cousins'.

After the first five minutes on the podium I found my voice dying away. I did not know it then, but my 'span of attention' had run out, a warning. I ignored any weakness, any sense of confusion and dizziness, and kept on striving. Pat looked at me with alarm.

I looked around at the students and realised that Dr Asher Susser, the Head of the Moshe Dayan Centre for Middle East and African Studies, was looking curiously at me. I conquered my dizziness and returned to my speech.

Two days later I was in London. It was a hot sunny June day. At 2.30 in the afternoon I decided to walk part of the way back from my office to my house. I was tired and wanted to go home. Without a hat to cool my over-heated head, I started off.

Arriving home I went out to the garden room where we often work, rest or just sit. Pat gave me a hot cup of tea.

Suddenly as I raised the tea to my lips it spilled over my shirt. It was burning hot and I leaped up like a scalded cat, then stumbled and fell against a chair. It was like being pole-axed.

I heard Pat shout something, although I could not tell what. Afterwards I was told she had cried out to Joseph, my eldest grandchild, who was home from Oman for the summer holidays. He was within reach of a telephone. Pat dictated to him the number of the ambulance service. 'What shall I say?' shouted Joseph. 'Tell them it's a stroke,' Pat shouted back.

The next I knew was coming out of a coma perhaps thirty or forty hours later – unable to move, touch, talk or communicate, surrounded by three nurses at the Westminster Hospital. I was paralysed. The body felt like a balloon after the air had been expelled.

Later (how could I tell the time, I had been unconscious or semiconcious for all those hours) I could feel Pat's presence by me. Then coming into focus was my daughter Ann, my son-in-law, Danny, and my assistant, Christine. The first conscious thought was of my work, who would carry it on?

I remember seeing my little group depart, except for Pat who stayed holding my hand. I felt tears in my eyes. There seemed to me to be a complete loss of my faculties, a loss of control, and then there was the frustration.

Two days later a doctor took the trouble to explain to me what had happened. Unlike a heart attack or a thrombosis, a stroke was solely concerned with the brain. A part of the brain had been 'knocked out'. One couldn't say exactly what part or how much had been affected. Cells had been destroyed and it was the work of the patient with the help of therapists and family to re-train the healthy parts of the brain to take over the job of the lost cells. The time for recovery was estimated at anything from six months to five years. This would depend on the patient.

My speech began to return slowly, first words, then sentences. A speech therapist, Amanda Mosely, came along and I learned I had lost the ability to spell. 'Don't try to do numbers,' she said. 'Be careful handling money.' I could hardly tell the time. It was impossible to read words. I couldn't remember names quickly and sometimes when searching for words felt terribly angry. An insidious list of things grew and grew and grew. Lengthy rest periods became part of my day. Depression, guilt, irritability. A tendency to burst into despair. It was, so Pat told me, a lesson in overcoming.

Pat stayed by me and gradually her positive Christian philosophy struck root. (She is a practising Christian Scientist.) She read to me although I could barely listen. How I love her. What tenderness she gives and support in all the reckless things I do. Do I deserve this? On balance probably not. I feel that I have let so many people down in my life.

Professor Lant, the neurologist, came around and pronounced me something of a miracle. I was already speaking, though with considerable difficulty and some incoherency. And I was walking around the ward, slowly – but walking. He ordered a brain scan and then expressed himself rather surprised. They were searching for a cause. My stroke was apparently still a mystery. I was sent for special investigations to the National Heart Hospital. No evidence of a blood clot could be found. Eventually he pronounced me fit enough to move.

He said it was the most rapid recovery in the recent annals of the Westminster Hospital for a man of my years. Probably because I had some real purpose in staying alive.

I had to be careful. But I could move. I could write rather clumsily holding a pen in my right hand. I could not drive a car, as my distance judgement had gone, but I could walk across the street with some help.

Today the brain goes at a fast pace when called upon but I still become stultified when speaking sometimes. I cannot speak at any meetings that I arrange for the Foundation. Pat says it puts a blanket on my ego not to speak. My 'attention span' is getting longer – sometimes as much as four hours before what seems like cotton wool descends over my brain. Then, a rest for 40 minutes or so and up it comes again.

In moments of reflection, I look back to the days at the *South Wales Voice* and the fire in the valley that started it all, the brick-by-brick building of the Next Century Foundation; the many friends I have made.

William is still in Oman building up the new University Press. He was instrumental in the seminars and meetings that have played a part in the Next Century Foundation. Pat is a very full partner in a news agency which we run on behalf of certain Gulf countries. Ann, my eldest daughter, edits *Voice* with a skill that makes her old man blush with pleasure, as well as taking over our public affairs work. Margaret, my youngest daughter, who became a highly praised soloist in an American contemporary dance company, is now artistic director of a leading British contemporary dance company. We all rely on her special spiritual qualities and insight. It is very much a close family and an even closer family business.

And as for me? I have worked all my life like a steam engine, and now God had given me a new direction. My work with the Foundation cannot stop, cannot be halted. Soon the new century will be upon us and we must be ready.

As Solzhenitsyn said, '. . . the aim is not to finish the job quickly but to reach perfection.'

ABBREVIATIONS

ANAF	Arabische Nicht Arabische Freundschaft
AGCC	Arab Gulf Corporation Council
ARNA	Libyan News Agency
CAABU	Council for the Advancement of Arab-British Understanding
CIA	Central Intelligence Agency
CID	Criminal Investigation Department
EMAP	East Midlands Allied Press
EEC	European Economic Community
FBI	Federal Bureau of Investigation
FO	Foreign and Commonwealth Office
GPO	General Post Office
HMG	Her Majesty's Government
IRD	Information Research Department
ISC	Institute for the Study of Conflict
KGB	Soviet Union Intelligence Service
NGA	National Graphic Association
OBE	Order of the British Empire
OID	Overseas Information Department
OPEC	Organisation of Petroleum Exporting Countries
PA	Personal Assistant
PLO	Palestinian Liberation Organisation
PR	Public Relations
RAF	Royal Air Force
RCC	Revolutionary Command Council
SOE	Special Operations Europe
TASS	Telegraph Agency of the Soviet Union
TUC	Trades Union Congress
UAE	United Arab Emirates
UCLA	University of California at Los Angeles

NOTES

Epigraph
1 Alexander Solzhenitsyn, *The First Circle*, The Harvill Press, 1968, translators: Max Hayward, Manya Harari, Michael Glenny.

1 The right to be heard
1 Lord Lyons of Brighton, one of Harold Wilson's so-called 'Kitchen Cabinet' and in his day one of the best innovative PR men in the UK. Ex-*South Wales Voice* political writer, 1953–4. Later co-founder, Traverse, Healey and Lyons, London and Managing Director, Interpublic, New York and London.
2 Lord Goodman of Goodman, Derrick & Co. Solicitors.
3 Sir Anthony Berry was killed in the IRA bomb explosion at the Brighton Conservative Party Conference, 1984.
4 Lord Mayhew, currently Liberal Democrat Party spokesman on defence, House of Lords.
5 Lord Caradon, later British representative at the UN and author of the famous resolution 242.

2 Fire in the valley
1 Rabbi Meir Kahane was a controversial member of the Israeli Knesset and a leading figure in the Gaza uprising of settlers in 1988. He died in 1990.

4 Death of a newspaper
1 Sigmund Warburg, head of Warburgs the merchant bankers, had already contacted me through a mutual friend.

6 Unforgettable friends
1 The Martin Buckmaster I had known in Beirut became Viscount Buckmaster of Chiddingfold, First Secretary, Foreign Office.

2   Hasseb Sabbagh. Reputed at the time to be one of the PLO's main bankers.

7   The hornets' nest

1   Michael Rice and Company were at the time Public Relations Consultants to the State of Bahrain, as well as the League of Arab States. Later, they became consultants to the Sultanate of Oman, the State of Qatar, the Kingdom of Saudi Arabia (antiquities and cultural matters). The Michael Rice Company from time to time employed former British diplomats, and was constantly and flatteringly recommended by the British Foreign Office to Arab countries interested in British PR representation.
2   Nasser Seif Al Bualy, later Omani ambassador to Britain.
3   James was to be eventually replaced in the Gulf region by Anthony Ashworth, one-time knowledgeable field operator of the Information Research Department (IRD), who organised Oman's information set-up on crisp lines.

8   Abandoned

1   Lockets is now under new ownership and is named Shepherds.

9   The crash

1   Ladislas Rice was then Chairman. Dick Stokes was Chairman of *Burton Contact* editorial board, the paper we printed and published for the Group. Clifford Jupp, ex-British Embassy, Cairo diplomat, was at the time Burton public relations manager.
2   Sir Monty Finniston, then Chairman of British Steel.

10   The great King of Arabia

1   Majlis – reception or meeting room.
2   Sir Alan K. Rothnie, later British Ambassador to Switzerland. Now retired.

12   With G at Benghazi barracks

1   Saad Mujber later became Director General of the Libyan News Agency (ARNA) and Libya's Ambassador to Iran.
2   Jack Isow closed in 1976.
3   Miles Copeland, former CIA agent in the Middle East, reported on various devices used by the CIA including astrology, in order to plant agents as members of the 'inner circle' around various world leaders (*The Times*, 21 May 1988).

NOTES

15 Roman holiday

1. See note 4, ch. 20.
2. Ed P. Wilson is now serving a 52-year jail sentence in the full knowledge and co-operation of the CIA and FBI. Source article on CIA cover organisation called 'Consultants International' by Peter Maas, *New York Times*, 13 April 1986.
3. Within two months Reuters had set up a monitoring service on Malta for Libyan news and cancelled service arrangements whereby my company in London was feeding them with news from Libya. The next I heard of the East European correspondent was when Amnesty International approached me in London to ask for my help. He had been arrested in Tripoli as a spy. Thanks to Amnesty's efforts, he was subsequently freed. He then worked in Eastern Europe as a stringer for Fleet Street papers.

20 Shaping the news

1. George Wigg (Baron Wigg of Dudley) was appointed Harold Wilson's 'sniffer dog' on security matters when Wilson was becoming alarmed at the power he felt was being exercised by MI5. George kept in close touch with such disparate personalities as Tom Driberg and Sir Maurice Oldfield and appeared to have almost unlimited access to every politician and civil servant of note.
2. Those most connected with Forum or the Institute for the Study of Conflict at the time denied any personal knowledge of CIA involvement. The US custom is often to fund internal US commercial companies as 'agents of influence'. The overseas contacts of such companies may know nothing of any intelligence connection. The Institute, under the Chairmanship of Michael Goodwin, has achieved worldwide recognition for academic objectivity.
3. Brian Crozier denies any personal knowledge of CIA involvement with Forum or the Institute for the Study of Conflict.
4. James Jesus Eagleton was sacked in 1974 principally for organising 'Operation Chaos', a vast illegal mail-opening, phone-tapping and surveillance operation in the US. See 'Subversions' by R.W. Johnson, *London Review of Books*, 4th June 1987.

21 The strange case of Margaret McKay

1. Margaret McKay died in Abu Dhabi in 1996.

22 The Bhutto disinformation game

1. The Rt. Hon. Jonathan Aitken MP, merchant banking entrepreneurial nephew of the late Lord Beaverbrook. Aitken is a courageous defender of Freedom of Information rights in Parliament.

THE LAST INCH

2   David Watkins MP, then chairman of the Labour Middle East Council, later Director of CAABU.
3   Sir Dennis Walters, Former Chairman of Conservative Middle East Council.
4   Sir Frank Rogers, Former Chairman of East Midlands Allied Press (EMAP) and later Deputy Chairman, the *Daily Telegraph*.

23   'We're all Palestinians now'

1   Dag Hammarskjold, former UN Secretary-General (April 1953–Sept. 1961), killed in a plane crash while on a peace mission.

24   Unexpected gremlins and moles

1   HE Sheikh Saud Al-Sabah, former Kuwaiti Ambassador to Washington; now Minister of Information.
2   Now the Rt. Hon. Lord Gilmour of Craigmillar.

25   Darkness before dawn

1   Now The Rt. Hon. Lord Denis Healey CH.

26   The box of tricks

1&3   See *British Intelligence and Covert Action* by Jonathan Block and Patrick Fitzgerald.
2   Confirmed by Sir Maurice Oldfield's biography. See also Peter Wright's *Spycatcher*, Heinemann, 1987.

27   Darkness in my eyes

1   Christopher Mayhew, *Time to Explain*, Century-Hutchinson, 1987.

28   Was my journey really necessary?

1   HH Sayyid Fahad bin Mahmoud Al Said, now Deputy Prime Minister for Council Affairs (Prince Fahad).

29   The two cousins approach

1   Now the Emir of Qatar, HH Sheikh Hamad bin Khalifa Al-Thani.
2   A strong supporter of the Foundation until his sudden death in the autumn of 1996.

REFERENCES AND SOURCES

Amnesty International papers.
Barron, John, former US naval intelligence officer, *KGB Today*, Hodder & Stoughton, 1984.
Bloch, Jonathon and Fitzgerald, Patrick, *British Intelligence and Covert Action*, Brandon Books, Dingle, Co. Derry, 1983.
Boyle, Andrew, *The Climate of Treason*, Hutchinson, 1979.
Bradlee, Ben, editor, *Washington Post*, and others. Also, Cameron Memorial Lecture, April 1987.
Harper, Stephen, *The Last Sunset*, Collins, 1978.
Hudson, Richard and Ingrassia, Paul, *Wall Street Journal*, New York.
Johnson, R.W., Fellow of Magdalen College, Oxford, *London Review of Books*, 4 June 1987.
Legum, Colin, *Observer*, 24 January 1982.
Leigh, David and Lahmar, Paul, *Observer*, 14 December 1986.
Mayhew, Christopher, *Time to Explain*, Century-Hutchinson, 1987.
Penrose, Barrie and Freeman, Simon, *Conspiracy of Silence*, Grafton Books, 1986.
Pilger, John, *Heroes*, Jonathan Cape, 1986.
Pincher, Chapman, *Too Secret Too Long*, Sidgwick & Jackson, 1984.
Pincher, Chapman, *The Secret Offensive*, Sidgwick & Jackson, 1985.
Raviv, Dan and Melman, Yossi, *Every Spy A Prince*, Houghton Mifflin, 1991.
Rees-Mogg, Sir William, former editor London *The Times*, writing in the *Independent*, 28 July 1987.

The Last Inch

Rockefeller, William partner, Sherman and Sterling, New York. Chairman of the Metropolitan Opera Company.

The Agony of Pakistan, The Trial of Zulfikar Ali Bhutto, published by London Committee for Press Freedom and Democratic Government in Pakistan.

INDEX

Abdullah, Rashid, 63
Abed, Dr George, 220
Adams, Michael, 78, 205
Aitken, The Rt Hon. Jonathan MP, 170, 188, 192, 211
Akl, Basl, 50, 51
Al-Abed, Ibrahim, 187
al Ali, Naji Salim, 217
Al Bualy, Nasser Saif, 46, 146
Al-Ghussein, Jaweed, xiv, 217
Al-Ghussein, Saida, 220
Al-Ghussein, Tewfik, 220
al Haq, General Zia, 170, 171, 173, 175–9
al Hassan, Omar, 187
al Hemaidi, Major al Khuwaildi, 124
al Huni, Major Abdul Mun'im, 124
Al Jasim, Sa'dun, 45
Al-Kawari, HE Dr Issa Ghanem, xiii
al-Kharrubi, Mustafa, 124
Al Khalifi, Mohamed, 187
Al Khuraigi, Mansour, 69–74
Al-Lowzy, Salem, 180, 181, 185
Al-Maktoum, HH Sheikh Mohamed bin Rashid, xiv, 221
Al-Marzook, Faisal Marzook, 187, 189
Al-Maeena, Khalid, 192
al-Mehaishy, Major Omar, 124
Al-Mudaris, Abdul Karim Abdul Kadir, 33
Al-Nahyan, HH Sheikh Khalifa bin Zayed, 187
Al-Nahyan, HH Sheikh Zayed bin Sultan, President of the UAE, 9, 10, 21, 22, 38, 39, 40, 41, 131, 134, 143, 148, 153, 154, 162, 163, 165, 166, 171, 176, 177, 178, 192, 212
Al-Nowais, Abdullah, 171, 187
Al-Qubaisi, HE Sheikh Ahmed bin Hamed, xiii, 38, 41, 62, 132, 148, 155, 171, 187, 189
Al-Sabah, HH Sheikh Jaber Al-Ahmed, Emir of Kuwait, xiii, 171, 176
Al-Sabah, HE Sheikh Saud, 187
Al-Said, HH Sayyid Fahad bin Mahmood (Prince Fahad), xiii, 210, 212, 213, 221, 224
Al-Saud, HM King Faisal bin Abdulaziz, 69–73, 77
Al-Sherif, Mahmoud, 192
Al-Sib'aee, Yusef, 181, 185
Al-Sudairi, Sheikh Fahd, 75
Al-Tal, Wasfi Moustafa, 184, 185
Al-Thani, HH Sheikh Hamad bin Khalifa, Emir of Qatar, xiv, 221
Al-Thani, HH Sheikh Khalifa, former Emir of Qatar, 171
Alayan, Youssef, 192
Algosaibi, HE Dr Ghazi, xiv
Alliance, Sir David CBE, xiv, 221
Almanquor GCVO, HE Sheikh Nasser, xiv
Amran, Yunis, 87
Aman, HE Abdullah, 158
Anis, Ahmed, 33, 35, 43, 58
Amran, Yunis, 87, 89
Appiah, Joe, 7
Arafat, Yasser, 6, 177
Ascherson, Neal, 209
Ashrawi, Hannah, 220
Assam, Salem, 67
Assem, Ali, 4
Atallah, Naim, 211
Aveneri, Uri, 218
Az'abi, Yusef, 99, 101, 102, 121, 223

INDEX

Aziz, Qutabuddin, 176

Barlev, General Haim, 220
Beaverbrook, The Lord, 8
Beaumont, Sir Richard KCMG, 204
Beeley, Sir Harold KCMG, 10, 370
Beilin, Yossi, 219
Belgrave, James, 46
Beloff of Wolvercote, The Rt Hon Lord Max Kt, 221
Benn MP, The Rt Hon Tony, 156
Bermant, Chaim, 193, 196
Berry, The Hon Anthony, 8, 32, 57
Bevan MP, The Rt Hon Aneurin, 23
Bhutto, Zulfikar Ali, 169–79
Bhutto, Murtaza ('Mir'), 178
Birgi, Nuri, 193
Bloch, Leonard, 26, 27
Bourgeiba, Abdulsalam, 145
Bowden, Geoffrey, 27
Bradlee, Ben, 208
Brooke MP, The Rt Hon Peter CH, 166
Buckmaster of Cheddington, Lord Martin OBE, 41, 119, 157, 198
Burgess, Guy, 10

Callaghan of Cardiff, Lord James, 200
Caradon, The Rt Hon Lord Hugh, 11, 12, 188
Caradon, Lady Sylvia, 12
Clark, Ramsey, 170, 177
Close, Raymond, 159
Collard, Elizabeth, 12, 32, 43, 45, 51, 52, 207
Coltart, James, 8, 188
Conner, William, xiv, 3, 5, 161
Copeland, Miles, 101
Crosland MP, The Rt Hon Anthony, 198
Crossman MP, The Rt Hon Richard, 156
Crowe, Sir Colin, 198
Crozier, Brian, 157, 158, 199

Darwish, Yusef, 187
Davidson, The Reverend William, 147
Dawdry, Vanda, 6
Delmer, Sefton, 161, 202, 207
Devonshire, Andrew 11th Duke of, xiv, 221, 222
Dimeshkie, Nadim GCVO (Hon.), 30, 220
Dunlop, Kay, 14
Dura, Yassar, 194

Durda, Abu Zaid, 36, 96, 99, 103, 112, 122, 123

Eagleton, James Jesus, 115, 159
Eakes, Louis, 20
Egerton, Sir Stephen KCMG, 117, 118
Elgindi, Thelma, 6, 18, 19
El Hamdi, Omar, 122, 125, 126, 135
Etherington-Smith CMG, Sir Gordon (Guy), 79, 80, 90
Evans MP, Gwynfor, 4, 7

Fernandes, Christine, xiv, 226
Finsberg, The Rt Hon Lord Geoffrey MBE, KCVO, 221
Fitchett, Joe, 193
FitzGerald, Dr Garret, 221
Foley, Charles, 10
Fontaine, André, 124, 186, 192, 198
Foot, The Rt Hon Michael, 157, 204
Fyffe, David Maxwell, 156

Gaddafi, Colonel Muammar, 36, 82, 84–91, 93–101, 103, 108, 110, 117, 118, 121–6, 132–5, 137–40, 142, 143, 146, 171, 175, 181
Gerada, Suliman, 102
Gillon, Dan, 25, 27
Gilmour, The Rt Hon Lord Gilmour of Craigmillar, 188, 206
Ghobash, Saif, 39, 181, 185
Goodman, Lord Arnold CH, xiv, 8, 217
Gore-Booth, HE The Hon David CMG, 220, 222
Gore-Booth, The Lord Paul GCMG, KCVO, 198
Gritli, Jelal, 93, 94, 95
Gulliford, Jacqueline, xiv

Halliday, Professor Fred, 203
Hamami, Said, 181, 182, 183, 185, 217
Hammarskjold, Dag, 352
Hammer, Arnold, 116
Harrel, David, 61, 62, 183, 205
Hassan, Colonel Kamel, 79
Hayhoe, The Rt Hon Lord Barney KCVO, 221
Healey, The Rt Hon Lord Denis, 192, 194, 196
Heath, The Rt Hon Sir Edward, 192
Heikal, Mohamed, 160, 191
Helms, Richard, 199

INDEX

Heymann, Louis, 14, 15, 57
Hijazi, Nabil, 143
Hitchens, Alan, 18
Hogan, John, 27
Hopkins, Peter, xiv
Hopkinson, Sir Thomas, 188
Hurd, The Rt Hon Sir Douglas, 221
Husseini, Faisal, 220

Ibjad, Ibrahim, 93, 97, 98, 122, 123, 126, 147

Jaber, Colonel Abu Bakr Yunis, 124
Jackson, Colin, 47, 48
Jacobs, June, 219, 221
Jalloud, Major Abdussalam, 104, 113, 124, 138
Jenkins, Doreen, 18, 29, 30
Jeralah, Ahmed, 45
Jewaili, Mufta, 110
Jones, Jennifer, xiv, 145, 182
Joseph, Leopold, 15, 57

Kahane, Rabbi Meir, 19
Karim, HH Sir Sultan Ali Abdul, 3, 4, 48, 162, 213
Karrar, Babikar, 139
Kemsley, The Lord Gomer, 8, 17
Keshk, Jelal, 41, 42, 100, 101, 180
Khoury, Nabil, 192
Khushaim, Dr Ali Fahmi, xiv, 36
Kimche, Dr David, 25, 26, 219
Kimche, Jon, 25, 27, 29
King, Hilary, 200, 201
Kissinger, Dr Henry, 175
Klibi, Chadli, 190, 191
Kreisky, Bruno, 192, 193, 194, 196

Little, Tom, 13, 19, 20, 48, 78, 160, 207
Loeman, Don, xiv
Low, David, 8
Lloyd, Bryn, 27
Lloyd, Sylvia, xiv, 27
Long, Gerald, 201
Luce, The Rt Hon Sir Richard, 221, 222
Lyons, The Lord Dennis, 6, 7, 10, 22, 26, 27, 28, 100

McKay, Margaret, 45, 162–6
McNeil, Hector, 10
Magrehbi, Dr Mahmoud Suliman, 102, 103, 108, 121, 122

Mahfoudh, HE Yahya bin, 224
Mahmoud, Kamil Hassan, 79
Marsh, The Lord Richard, 188, 192
Mathew QC, John, 170
Matthews, Roger, 193
Mayassi, Zein, xiv, 220
Maybee, Timothy, 30
Mayhew, The Lord Christopher, 9–13, 17, 19, 21–4, 26, 30, 31, 34, 44, 45, 47–9, 51, 52, 55, 146, 147, 165, 181, 182, 206–8, 220
Miller, Judith, 115
Miller, Maralyn, 27
Mintoff, Dom, 7
Mohamed, HE Hassen Said, xiii
Montville, Joseph, 222
Mujber, Saad, 95–8
Musa, Omar Hag, 90

Naim, Major Mohammed, 251
Najm, Mohammed, 124, 139
Nasashabi, Nasser, 195–7
Nasr, Bahi, 47
Neil, Andrew, 196
Numeiri, General Jaffar, 79–85, 90–2, 123, 153
Nuri, Abdullah, 109, 124
Nusseibeh, Lucy, 219
Nusseibeh, Sari, 219
Nusseibeh, Zaki Anwar, 72, 131, 132, 134, 164
Nutting, Sir Anthony, 13, 19, 49–52

O'Brien, Conor Cruise, 170
Oldfield, Sir Maurice, 9, 161
Omran, Adnan, 146
Osman, Dr Khalil, 79
Owen, Bob, 20
Owen, The Rt Hon Lord David, 157, 198, 200, 202

Paul, Geoffrey, 26, 189
Pincher, Chapman, 200
Pigeat, Henri, 192
Pritt, D.W. MP, QC, 12

Rath, Ari, 220
Reddaway OBE, John, 11–13, 19, 23, 34, 43, 47, 50–3, 78, 147, 207
Reddaway, Norman, 199
Rees, Ebenezer, 17
Rees, The Rt Hon Lord Merlyn, 221

INDEX

Riad, Mohamed, 47, 50
Riaz, Bashir, 175
Rice, Michael, xiv, 43, 44
Rogers, Sir Frank, 170, 187, 190
Rothnie, Sir Alan, 76
Rouleau, Eric, 193, 222
Rowas, HE Abdul Aziz, xiii, 211
Rowland, R.W. 'Tiny', 79, 82

Sabbagh, Hasseb, 42, 49, 50, 51, 100
Safieh, Afif, 223
Said, HM Sultan Qaboos bin, xiv, 171, 176, 221
Salah, Hosni, 116, 118
Saleh, Salem, 161
Sallah, Peter, 184
Sartawi, Issam, 217
Savir, Uri, 219
Schmidt, Helmut, 192, 194, 196
Semer, Hannah, 219
Shalgam, Naji, 111
Shenkov, Alexander, 116
Shore, The Rt Hon Peter MP, 221
Shummo, Ali Mohamed, 79, 86, 91, 148, 153, 154, 155, 157, 171
Shurafa, Ali, 143, 144
Sindi, Abbas, 67, 68, 75
Shinwell, The Lord Emanuel, 9, 156
Stein, John Henry, 115
Stoddart, Dorothy, xiv
Stone, Andrew, xiv, 221
Suliman, Dr Khalifa Mohamed, 221
Susser, Dr Asher, 225
Swinburn, James, 160
Sykes, Manuela, 5, 6, 12, 56, 100, 101

Tajr, Mahdi, 143, 148, 180

Talal, HRH Crown Prince Hassan bin, 194
Tems, Mick, 29, 30
Thomas, Graham, 119
Thomas, Vernon Morley, 8, 9, 16, 18, 26, 27, 61
Thomson, The Lord Roy, 8, 11
Trevaskis, Sir Kennedy, 4
Tueni, Ghassan, 192
Tugendhat, The Lord Christopher, 221
Twisk, Russell, xiv, 193, 221

Wahbi, Ahmed Abdul, 69, 71, 72, 73
Wallace, Edgard, 12
Walters, Sir Dennis, 170
Warburg, Sir Sigmund, 23, 26, 29
Watkins, David, 170
Weber, Dr Rene, 22
Webster, William H., 104
Weinstock, The Lord Arnold, 222
Wells, John, 50, 51
Welsh, Richard, 274
Whitney, John Hay (Jock), 158, 199
Whitney MP, Raymond, 200, 201–3
Wigg, Sir George MP, 156
Williams, H. George, 54, 55
Williams, Margaret, 54, 55
Wilson, Edward P., 115
Wilson, The Lord Harold of Rievaulx OBE, 6, 9
Wilson MP, William, 163, 165
Wingate, Roger, xiv
Winniberg, Michael, xiv
Woolfson, Marion, 189
Woollacott, Martin, 192
Worthy, William, 105

Zadok, Haim, 219

UNIVERSITY LIBRARY

this book as soon as you have
in order to avoid a fine it m